New Eucharistic Prayers

AN ECUMENICAL STUDY OF THEIR DEVELOPMENT AND STRUCTURE

Edited by
FRANK C. SENN

Paulist Press • New York • Mahwah

Book design by Nighthawk Design.

Excerpts from the English translation of the eucharistic prayers from *The Roman Missal* © 1973, International Committee on English in the Liturgy, Inc. (ICEL); excerpts from the English translation of *Eucharistic Prayers for Masses of Reconciliation* © 1975, ICEL; excerpts from the English translation of *Eucharistic Prayers for Masses with Children* © 1975, ICEL. All rights reserved.

Library of Congress Cataloging-in-Publication Data

New Eucharistic prayers.

    Includes bibliographies.
    1. Eucharistic prayers.   I. Senn, Frank C.
BV825.5.N48   1987   264'.36   87-15579
ISBN 0-8091-2912-4 (pbk.)

Published by Paulist Press
997 Macarthur Boulevard
Mahwah, New Jersey 07430

Printed and bound in the United States of America

Contents

Essayists

Msgr. Alan F. Detscher, Director of Liturgy, Roman Catholic Diocese of Bridgeport, Ct.

Arlo D. Duba, Dean and Professor of Worship, University of Dubuque Theological Seminary, Dubuque, Ia.

Gordon W. Lathrop, Professor of Liturgy, Lutheran Theological Seminary at Philadelphia

John H. McKenna, C.M., Professor of Theology, St. John's University, Jamaica, N.Y.

H. Boone Porter, Editor, *The Living Church,* Milwaukee, WI.

David N. Power, O.M.I., Professor of Systematic Theology, Department of Theology, Catholic University of America, Washington, D.C.

John Barry Ryan, Associate Professor of Religion, Manhattan College, Bronx, N.Y.

Gail Ramshaw-Schmidt, President of The Liturgical Conference, Philadelphia, Pa.

R. Kevin Seasoltz, O.S.B., Ordinary Professor, The Catholic University of America, Washington, D.C.

Frank C. Senn, Pastor, The Lutheran Church of the Holy Spirit, Lincolnshire, IL.

James F. White, Professor of Liturgy, University of Notre Dame, Notre Dame, In.

FRANK C. SENN

Introduction

One of the most remarkable aspects of recent liturgical revision has been the proliferation of eucharistic prayers. Christians in Western Churches may have become so accustomed to having a selection of eucharistic prayers from which the presiding minister chooses one for a particular celebration that it may have all but passed out of memory that this was not always the case. To be sure, eucharistic prayers abounded in the ancient church. Anton Hänggi and Irmgard Pahl collected nearly a hundred prayers, parts of prayers, or fragments of prayers in their anthology, *Prex Eucharistica*.[1] But for nearly a thousand years, from the early Middle Ages until the sixteenth century, there was only one eucharistic prayer used in the Western Church: the Roman Canon. It was called "Canon" because it was the rule. Joseph Jungmann has documented the existence of hundreds of textual and rubrical variations in the Latin Mass during the Middle Ages.[2] But apart from the provision of dozens of proper prefaces and some other variable parts, the eucharistic prayer was inflexible (and the printing of medieval Missals gave the impression that the Canon began with the post-Sanctus *Te igitur*, not the preface's *Vere dignum*). This Canon remained the sole eucharistic prayer in the Roman Catholic Church after the Reformation until the promulgation of the reformed Roman Mass after the Second Vatican Council.

The Reformation in the sixteenth century produced a proliferation of liturgical orders, each with its own eucharistic or communion texts. Irmgard Pahl has again collected dozens of such texts in her anthology, *Coena Domini*.[3] Yet a patient analysis of the multitude of Reformation church orders reveals a remarkable uniformity within the variety of liturgical orders.[4]

In the Lutheran church orders of the sixteenth and seventeenth centuries, the historical structure of the Mass remained intact and most of the forms for the celebration of Holy Communion can be traced to the two forms provided by Martin Luther: his *Formula Missae* (1523) and *Deutsche Messe* (1526).[5] In those mass-orders which followed the model of the *Formula Missae* the Words of Institution were connected with the preface and sanctus. In those mass-orders which followed the model of the *Deutsche Messe* the Words of Institution were proclaimed apart from the context of prayer and were followed immediately by the distribution of the bread and cup.[6]

The Reformed eucharistic tradition is also less complicated than it might at first appear. The original Reformed liturgies were those composed by the Swiss reformers Zwingli, Oecolampadius, and Farel in the mid-1520s. But the decisive development of Reformed worship occurred in Strassburg under the leadership of Martin Bucer.[7] From here can be traced a succession of Reformed liturgies: from Bucer's German Service (1539) to Calvin's French Service for Strassburg (1540) to Calvin's Geneva Service (1542) to Knox's English version of the Geneva Service for the use of the English exiles (1556) to *The Book of Common Order* of the Church of Scotland (1562).[8] The essential characteristics of the Reformed communion service include an exhortation to the communicants, the Words of Institution recited as a warrant for the celebration, a consecration prayer, the fraction, the ministration of communion, and a post-communion thanksgiving (not always in that exact order).

The Book of Common Prayer of the Church of England was also influenced by Reformation sources from the continent.[9] However, its principal author, Archbishop Thomas Cranmer, crafted an ingenious revision of the Roman Canon for the 1549 Prayer Book and radically revised it in 1552. These two eucharistic liturgies have served as the basis for other Prayer Books in the Anglican Communion.[10] John Wesley, while espousing extempore prayer, also provided a revision of the 1662 *Book of Common Prayer* in *The Sunday Service of the Methodists in North America* (1784).[11] Ironically, American Methodists have used the eucharistic prayer from the English *Book of Common Prayer* while American Episcopalians adopted the eucharistic prayer from the Prayer Book of the Scottish Non-Jurors, which was a text inspired by the Liturgy of St. James.

There have been subsequent revisions in each of these traditions, and in the provincial uses within each of these traditions. But the point is that there was only one eucharistic text used at a time; options were limited to proper prefaces and sometimes to a choice of post-communion prayers. It was therefore a momentous decision when, on

June 20, 1966, Pope Paul VI decided that two or three new eucharistic prayers should be adopted or composed to be used alongside the historic Roman Canon, slightly revised. Four eucharistic prayers were included in the Roman Missal of 1970—numbers II, III, and IV drawing respectively on the anaphora of St. Hippolytus, Mozarabic prayers, and Byzantine anaphoras. However, all of the new prayers were to reflect the *ingenium Romanum* in their common outline.[12]

This immediately provided a model for Protestant worship committees charged with the revision of liturgical rites. Several eucharistic prayers could be provided as options within one eucharistic rite. Several assumptions lay behind this approach. First, Gregory Dix proposed the now-widely held view that the eucharistic prayer originally said all that needed to be said about the meaning of the rite.[13] Second, Yngve Brilioth explored the multiple meanings of the eucharist as an act of thanksgiving, fellowship, commemoration, and sacrifice, with the mystery of the real presence of Christ pervading the entire celebration.[14] Third, historical scholarship has demonstrated the impossibility of finding an ur-anaphora; hence no one eucharistic form can be regarded as more authentic or "apostolic" than any other form.[15] Thus, a consensus was achieved across ecumenical lines that the eucharistic prayer should express the meaning of the celebration; that eucharistic meanings are multiple and may receive different emphases in different times and places; and that there is no one prayer form which is better than the others—although there are certain elements which are common to most eucharistic forms, such as praise, narrative recital, anamnesis, oblation, epiclesis, commemoration and intercession, and doxology.[16]

Before Protestant Churches could get to this point, however, they had to recover the use of a full eucharistic prayer—especially in the Lutheran and Reformed traditions. In both traditions consideration had to be given to the relationship between the Words of Institution and the eucharistic prayer. For Lutherans the Verba functioned as an act of consecration by proclamation of the Word (a view which could appeal to Sts. Ambrose of Milan and Augustine of Hippo). For the Reformed the Verba served as a scriptural warrant for the celebration; but following Calvin Reformed liturgies were able to give a greater role to the Holy Spirit in the form of the epiclesis (a view which could appeal to Sts. Cyril of Jerusalem and Theodore of Mopsuestia).

In the first stages of liturgical recovery in both of these Reformation traditions, elements of eucharistic prayer—such as praise, anamnesis, and epiclesis—were included in prayers which did not include the Verba. The Agenda of the Lutheran Church in Bavaria, 1879, provided three such prayers, one of which was to be used following the preface and sanctus and before the Words of Institution. A similar procedure was followed in the *Mässbok* of the Church of Sweden, 1942. It is possible that the first eucharistic prayer to include the Verba was one proposed by Paul Z. Strodach and later adopted, with some changes, in the *Book of Worship* of the Lutheran Churches in India, 1936.[17] Strodach's work served as the basis of the eucharistic prayer composed by Luther D. Reed and later included in the *Service Book and Hymnal* of the Lutheran Church in America, 1958. A full eucharistic prayer, including the Verba, was also included in *Agende* I of the Evangelical Lutheran Churches of Germany, 1955. Three eucharistic prayers, including the Anaphora of Hippolytus, were included in the *Worship Supplement* of the Lutheran Church—Missouri Synod, 1969. One eucharistic prayer was set in place, with no optional use of the Words of Institution alone, in *Contemporary Worship 2: The Holy Communion*, published by the Inter-Lutheran Commission on Worship, 1970.

A similar history can be chronicled among the Reformed Churches, although the resistance to including the Verba within the eucharistic prayer has been stronger among the Reformed than among Lutherans. A splendid eucharistic prayer was provided in *The Book of Common Order* of the Church of Scotland, 1940. A form in close agreement with the Scottish prayer was included in *The Book of Common Worship* of the Presbyterian Churches in the U.S.A., 1946. The *Dienstboek* of the Reformed Church in The Netherlands, 1955, tried to blend the didactic character of its Calvinist heritage with traditional elements of eucharistic prayer, such as preface, sanctus, anamnesis, and epiclesis—without including the Verba within this framework. The same approach can be seen in the 1969 Communion Service of the Reformed Church in America and in the 1972 *Worshipbook* of the Presbyterian Churches in America.[18] The *Supplemental Liturgical Resource 1: The Service for the Lord's Day*, 1984, of the Presbyterian Church (U.S.A.) and the Cumberland Presbyterian Church allows the option of including the Verba within the prayer or in relation to the breaking of the bread.

These achievements were possible because of the weight of historical scholarship in uncovering and analyzing sources in the history of Christian worship. This scholarship was also brought to bear on the Anglican Churches. In the Church of England we may note the texts for eucharistic prayers in the provisional Communion Services, Series B (1967) and Series C (1973). The Episcopal Church in the U.S.A. authorized the *Liturgy for the Lord's Supper* (1967) for three years' experimental use. This was followed by *Prayer Book Study 21* (1970), which contained two eucharistic rites—one in traditional and the other in contemporary speech—with no fewer than nine forms of eucharistic prayer between them. Some commonality in the composition of eucharistic prayers in the Anglican Communion was achieved at the Lambeth Conference in 1968 in a statement listing the basic elements of eucharistic prayer.

The time around 1968 saw the proliferation of eucharistic prayers, especially in private collections emanating from Roman Catholic authors and communities. The most important of these were the table prayers of Huub Oosterhuis, fifteen of which were included in the collection *In het voorbijgaan* (Amsterdam, 1968). These are the prayers of a Dutch poet actively involved in a faith community. Prayers generated out of similar pastoral work were published by Jean-Thierry Maertens and his group in *Livre de la prière* (Paris, 1969). The Oosterhuis prayers were especially influential on several American collections: *The Underground Mass Book,* ed. by Stephen W. McNierney (Baltimore, 1968); *The Experimental Liturgy Book,* ed. by Robert F. Hoey (New York, 1969); and *Eucharistic Liturgies,* ed. by John Gallen (New York, 1970).[19] There have not been similar private collections of eucharistic prayers among Protestants, probably because the eucharistic prayer has not been such a focus of devotion in Protestantism. However, a noteworthy quasi-official collection of material from the work of a Church of Sweden commission for pastoral and liturgical questions, *Svensk mässa,* ed. by Anders Ekenberg (Uppsala, 1971), contained fifteen eucharistic prayers, some Swedish and others translations of traditional and contemporary sources.

These private and quasi-official publications were important for the great work of liturgical revision that was to ensue during the 1970s in several of the Western Churches. The authors of these collections were not oblivious to traditional liturgical structures and theological speech; but they wanted to bring the contemporary world into the eucharistic celebration. This required vernacularization in the true sense—reflecting in language the world as it is known, and not as one might like it to be. Vernacularization of liturgical speech required elasticity in liturgical form. A case can be made that much of the official effort in liturgical revision during the 1970s was a tug-of-war between traditional forms and contemporary speech, one not fitting easily into the other. It is possible that the preference for the West Syrian anaphora structure that was shown in many of the new official eucharistic prayers was because its narrative style allowed for including issues from contemporary life within the scope of salvation history, or for retelling the biblical story in such a way as to address it to the concerns of contemporary life. It should be remembered that the 1960s and

1970s were a time when liturgical renewal went hand in hand with concern for the social implications of the gospel. This social concern was highlighted not only in private eucharistic texts, but also in official ones. For example, in Roman Eucharistic Prayer IV:

> To the poor he proclaimed the good news of salvation,
> to prisoners, freedom,
> and to those in sorrow, joy.

Lutheran Book of Worship Eucharistic Prayer II remembers

> . . . the sacrifice of his life:
> his eating with outcasts and sinners,
> and his acceptance of death.

Eucharistic Prayer C in *The Book of Common Prayer* highlights our expanded awareness of the universe.

> At your command all things came to be: the
> vast expanse of interstellar space, galaxies,
> suns, the planets in their courses, and this
> fragile earth, our island home.
> *By your will they were created and have their being.*

But it went on to address the human situation:

> From the primal elements you brought forth the
> human race, and blessed us with memory,
> reason, and skill. You made us the rulers of
> creation. But we turned against you, and
> betrayed your trust; and we turned against one
> another.
> *Have mercy, Lord, for we are sinners in your sight.*

Such images and phrases, however, were really survivals from the previous decade by 1977 and 1978. By the end of the 1970s liturgical commissions were wondering just how vernacular we really wanted our official prayers to be. It was the old case of the particular versus the general. How could commissions address concerns that might prove transitory in texts that had to endure at least several decades of churchwide use? The kind of texts one publishes in provisional, paperback liturgy books are not the same kind of texts one publishes in authorized, hardbound volumes.

The eucharistic prayers studied in this book are all official texts. This book tells the story of their development, analyzes their component parts, and indicates areas of unfinished business requiring ongoing work. The authors of these essays were all members of the eucharistic prayer study group of the North American Academy of Liturgy, an ecumenical professional society of liturgists. Several of the authors— H. Boone Porter, Gail Ramshaw-Schmidt, Gordon W. Lathrop, and James F. White—served on the committees which produced these prayers. The chapters in this book were originally oral or written presentations given at the annual meetings of the study group. Some of the texts studied in this book, especially the Methodist and Presbyterian prayers, were shared with the study group for reactions and suggestions during the time they were being prepared for publication by other members of the group, Hoyt Hickman and Harold Daniels, directors of worship offices in the United Methodist Church and the Presbyterian Church U.S.A., respectively. For the record, Roman Catholic eucharistic texts prepared by the International Committee on English in the Liturgy (ICEL) were also reviewed in the study group, thanks to the work of two other members of the group, James Schellman and Fr. Patrick Byrne.

It is not possible to include analysis of all the eucharistic prayers which have emerged in all of the Christian denominations today. The prayers included for study in this book are limited to those of the Roman Catholic Church, The Episcopal Church in the U.S.A., several Lutheran Churches in North America, The United Methodist Church, and The Presbyterian Church U.S.A. The principle of selection was quite simple: scholars from these Church bodies participated in the work of the eucharistic prayer study group. Even so, about fifty prayers are included in this survey: nine Roman Catholic prayers (four from the order of Mass, two for Masses of reconciliation, three for Masses with children); six Episcopal prayers; five Lutheran prayers; twenty-two Methodist prayers; and eight Presbyterian prayers. The Methodist and Presbyterian prayers are in provisional worship resources and may soon be superseded by more definitive books, orders, and texts.

It is not possible to reprint all of these prayers in this book. Authors quote portions of prayers on which they make comments. But the serious reader will need to have in hand the available collections of prayers. They are:

Eucharistic Prayers. Toronto: International Committee on English in the Liturgy (ICEL), 1980.

The Book of Common Prayer. . . According to the Use of The Episcopal Church. The Church Hymnal Corporation and The Seabury Press, 1977 (proposed), 1979 (authorized), pp. 361–382.

Lutheran Book of Worship, Ministers Edition. Minneapolis: Augsburg Publishing House and Philadelphia: Board of Publication, Lutheran Church in America, 1978, pp. 207–226.

At the Lord's Table. Supplemental Worship Resources 9. Nashville: Abingdon, 1981.

The Service for the Lord's Day. Supplemental Liturgical Resource 1. Philadelphia: Westminster Press, 1984.

Telling the stories of the development of the new eucharistic prayers is important because it enables us to understand the complex factors confronting liturgical committees. It's not just a matter of placating various constituencies, although in the process of getting texts approved that has to be considered. But there are also the intersections of historical tradition and contemporary concerns, worship and culture, piety and theology with which commissions must deal. The texts which emerged reflect all of these factors, and leave us with unsettled questions. For example: How much linguistic variety and metaphorical innovation is tolerable in public prayers?[20] How can concern for gender-inclusiveness be reconciled with masculine names of God in the Christian tradition? How can the view that the whole eucharistic prayer is "consecratory" be brought to bear on historical theological concerns about the juxtaposition of various parts: e.g. institution narrative and epiclesis, offertory and anamnesis-oblation? How much are we bound to particular structures of eucharistic prayers: e.g. Roman or Antiochene?[21]

Many of the new eucharistic prayers follow a similar structure containing similar parts: preface, sanctus, narrative of salvation history, institution narrative, anamnesis and oblation, epiclesis, intercessions and commemorations, and concluding doxology. The second part of this book contains essays dealing with these individual parts, but looking at them across the ecumenical spectrum of prayer texts. While there is an impressive consensus on what should go into a eucharistic prayer, there are still many unresolved questions. What should be the relationship between the preface and the post-sanctus section, especially when the preface does not praise God for his creative work but only for the works of the Son? If God is not praised for his works of creation in the introductory section of the prayer, where will cosmological themes be included?[22] The sanctus has long had a secure place in the eucharistic prayer, but it has also been something of an interruption in the narrative flow. Is there another location for the sanctus? Shall the institution narrative be a biblical text or a liturgical text? Do the bread-word and the cup-word need to be parallel? Should the words of Christ be in the future tense (as in the Roman prayers) or in the present tense (as in the Protestant prayers)? What is remembered in the anamnesis? What is offered? How does the eucharistic memorial link the eucharist with the sacrifice of Christ? Is the metaphor of sacrifice still a viable way to describe communion in Christ? Is the Holy Spirit called down on the people or on the gifts or both? The epiclesis raises the question of "consecration" and is therefore in tension with the Verba Christi in the Roman tradition—resulting in a "split epiclesis." Is there a way to resolve this problem liturgically and theologically? Should intercessions and commemorations be included in the eucharistic prayer (most of the Protestant prayers do not include them)? Can there be intercessions and commemorations in the eucharistic prayer which do not duplicate those of the synaxis? Should the doxology, like the opening act of praise, be addressed to the first person of the Godhead or to the Trinity? The doxology especially raises the question of inclusive God-language in the eucharistic prayer.

Questions of structure, theology, and language are not the only ones which can be raised. The essay by Kevin Seasoltz points out the need to give attention to the physical environment in which the eucharistic prayer is prayed, the musical settings of the prayer, and the postures of the presider and the assembly. The *way* in which the prayer is proclaimed can say as much about the implied theology of the eucharist as the texts themselves. Is the whole assembly involved in the celebration of the eucharist? If so, how shall the assembly be drawn into the eucharist's central action—the great thanksgiving? The lack of attention given heretofore to musical settings, visual environment, and motor rhythms in the work on the new eucharistic prayers suggests additional issues for ongoing study.

Many of these issues are illuminated by fresh historical study and new research into the areas of eucharistic origins. Are there historical traditions yet untapped which can provide us with different structures and theological emphases? The final essay, by David Power, opens up new possibilities touching on the overall structure, individual parts, and character of the eucharistic prayer as a result of some recent historical research, particularly into the Jewish *todah* tradition and the East Syrian Christian anaphoras. These insights also suggest a new relationship between the eucharist and Christian ethical commitments. As we suggested before, vernacularization in the late 1960s and early 1970s sought to bring the world into the eucharistic celebration.

Living in the memory of holocausts and pogroms, in the presence of refugees and starving millions, and in anticipation of possible nuclear conflagration or other catastrophes caused by humankind's abuse of nature, "remembrance" of the world in the eucharistic prayer calls for a reappropriation of the language of lament and expressions of confession and repentance. What should be celebrated is the world as God meant it to be and its promised destiny in God's kingdom, which calls for a reappropriation of the language of eschatology and expressions of acclamation and petition. The text with which this book concludes is a provocative example of directions which might be taken in new or ongoing work on eucharistic prayers. The principal lesson of this book is that there is an ongoing agenda: we have only just begun the work of eucharistic revision and composition.

NOTES

1. Anton Hänggi and Irmgard Pahl, eds., *Prex Eucharistica. Textus e Variis Liturgiis Antiquioribus Selecti* (Éditions Universitaires Fribourg Suisse, 1968).

2. Joseph A. Jungmann, *The Mass of the Roman Rite: Its Origin and Development*, 2 vols., trans. by Francis Brunner (New York: Benziger Brothers, 1951, 1955).

3. Irmgard Pahl, ed., *Coena Domini*, I. *Die Abendmahlsliturgie der Reformations-kirchen im 16./17. Jahrhundert* (Universitätsverlag Freiburg Schweiz, 1983).

4. See Emil Sehling, ed., *Die evangelischen Kirchenordnungen des XVI Jahrhunderts*, 15 vols. (Leipzig: Reisland, 1902ff).

5. *Luther's Works*, American Edition, Vol. 53, ed. by Ulrich S. Leupold (Philadelphia: Fortress, 1965), 15–40, 51–90.

6. See Hans-Christoph Schmidt-Lauber, *Die Eucharistie als Entfaltung der Verba Testamenti* (Kassel: Johannes Staudas Verlag, 1957).

7. See William D. Maxwell, *An Outline of Christian Worship* (London: Oxford University Press, 1936), pp. 87ff, and Bard Thompson, ed., *Liturgies of the Western Church* (Cleveland: World Publishing Co., 1961), pp. 159ff.

8. See William D. Maxwell, *John Knox's Genevan Service Book, 1556* (Edinburgh, 1931).

9. See F. E. Brightman, *The English Rite: Being a Synopsis of the Sources and Revisions of the Book of Common Prayer. . .*, 2 vols. (London: Rivington's, 1915) and E. C. Ratcliff, *The Booke of Common Prayer of the Churche of England: Its Making and Revisions MDxlix–MDclxi* (London: S.P.C.K., 1949).

10. B. Wigan, *The Liturgy in English* (London: Oxford University Press, 1962).

11. Thompson, pp. 409ff.

12. See Hans-Christoph Schmidt-Lauber, "The Eucharistic Prayers in the Roman Catholic Church Today," *Studia Liturgica* 11 (1976), 159–176.

13. Gregory Dix, *The Shape of the Liturgy* (London: Dacre Press, 1945), p. 119.

14. Yngve Brilioth, *Eucharistic Faith and Practice, Evangelical and Catholic,* trans. by A. G. Hebert (London: S.P.C.K., 1965).

15. See Louis Bouyer, *Eucharist,* trans. by Charles U. Quinn (Notre Dame, Ind.: University of Notre Dame Press, 1968).

16. The general instruction of the Roman Missal (no. 55) lists as the chief elements making up the eucharistic prayer: (a) thanksgiving, (b) the sanctus acclamation, (c) epiclesis, (d) institution narrative and consecration, (e) anamnesis, (f) offering, (g) intercessions, and (h) final doxology. W. Jardine Grisbrooke, "Anaphora," in J. G. Davies, ed., *A Dictionary of Liturgy and Worship* (London: SCM Press, 1972), 10–17, concludes that a good eucharistic prayer includes (1) introductory dialogue, (2) preface or initial thanksgiving, (3) sanctus, (4) a transition which may either continue the thanksgiving in a narrative of salvation history and/or take the form of a preliminary epiclesis, (5) institution narrative, (6) anamnesis-oblation, (7) epiclesis, (8) intercessions, (9) concluding doxology, and (10) Amen.

17. See Luther D. Reed, *The Lutheran Liturgy,* 2nd ed. (Philadelphia: Fortress Press, 1959), pp. 756–757.

18. See Joop Bergsma, "The Eucharistic Prayer in Non-Roman Catholic Churches of the West Today," *Studia Liturgica* 11 (1976), 179–180.

19. For an analysis for these contemporary prayers see John Barry Ryan, *The Eucharistic Prayer. A Study in Contemporary Liturgy* (New York, Paramus, Toronto: Paulist Press, 1974).

20. See Gail Ramshaw-Schmidt, "The Language of Eucharistic Praying," *Worship* 57 (1983), 419–437. Originally presented in the NAAL study group meeting.

21. See Frank C. Senn, "Toward a Different Anaphoral Structure," *Worship* 58 (1984), 346–358. Also originally presented in the NAAL study group meeting.

22. See Joseph Keenan, "The Importance of the Creation Motif in a Eucharistic Prayer," *Worship* 53 (1979), 341–356. Also originally presented in the NAAL study group meeting.

PART I

The Development of New Eucharistic Prayers

ALAN F. DETSCHER

1

The Eucharistic Prayers of the Roman Catholic Church

The past twenty years have seen a total revision of the eucharistic liturgy of the Latin Church and the provision of alternative texts, some new and many based on ancient models, for almost every part of the Mass. One of the most important fruits of this reform which was mandated by the Second Vatican Council has been the expansion of the corpus of prefaces to well over eighty and the addition of three general eucharistic prayers, three eucharistic prayers for use with children, and two eucharistic prayers on the theme of reconciliation. This is most remarkable since the Latin Church, and more specifically, the Roman rite, has had only one anaphora for over 1,500 years and in recent times only a very limited number of prefaces.

In this chapter we shall examine the venerable Roman Canon, the three new eucharistic prayers of the Roman Missal, and the new eucharistic prayers for reconciliation. The three eucharistic prayers for children will be treated in another chapter.

I. A Brief History

1. *Hippolytus*

The earliest extant text of an eucharistic prayer used at Rome is that which has been attributed to Hippolytus (c. 215 A.D.). Hippolytus was a presbyter of the Church of Rome who later became an anti-pope. Theologically he was rather conservative; we might describe him as a traditionalist of his day. We have no evidence that his liturgical texts were actually in use during his lifetime.

The eucharistic prayer of Hippolytus, as found in his *Apostolic Tradition*, is given in his rite for the ordination of bishop. Hippolytus notes that the new bishop is not bound to use his prayer, but rather is free to pray in his own words and according to his own capacity.

Although the original Greek version of Hippolytus has been lost we do have a Latin reconstruction of the text. It is clear from the language and expressions of the prayer that Hippolytus is thoroughly imbued with the theology of Irenaeus.

The structure of this prayer is similar to the later Antiochene form:

Dialog
Praise of the Father for the Work of the Son
Institution Narrative
Anamnesis
Epiclesis
Doxology

However, as Adrien Nocent notes, we do not find traces of any other eucharistic prayer of similar structure being used at Rome. In fact, we would be deluding ourselves if we tried "to see in Hippolytus the origin, even vague, of the 'Roman Canon.' "[1]

When we discuss Eucharistic Prayer II we will speak of the anaphora of Hippolytus in greater detail. Our intention here is to merely situate it in relation to the history of the Roman Canon.

2. *Roman Canon*

The first text that seems to have a relationship to the Roman Canon is found in the *De Sacramentis* of Saint Ambrose (d. 397 A.D.), Book 4:13–27 and Book 6:24. When speaking of the consecration of the eucharist, Ambrose says: ". . . praise is offered to God, prayer is made for the people, for kings, for others; when the time comes for the venerated sacrament to be accomplished, the bishop no longer uses his own words, but the words of Christ."[2] It would seem that the "praise" refers to the preface portion of the eucharistic prayer and the "prayer made for the people" points to the intercessions which come before the words of institution. An anaphora of this type, namely, with the intercessions before the words of institution, is of the Alexandrine type of eucharistic prayer.

Ambrose then goes on to quote portions of the anaphora which are similar to the *quam oblationem,* words of institution, *unde et memores, supra quae,* and *supplices te* of the Roman Canon. Verbally the text of Ambrose has many differences from that of the Roman Canon, but it is clear that he is refering to a common text that may still be in the process of evolution. Ambrose may have brought the canon to Milan from Rome.[3]

Gregory the Great indicates that the Roman Canon was composed after the liturgy of Rome began to be celebrated in Latin rather than in Greek, possibly under Pope Damasus (366–385).[4]

The *Liber Pontificalis* notes that Leo the Great (440–461 A.D.) added the words: "sancto sacrificio immaculata hostia."[5] And it is probable that at some time before Leo the two prayers with lists of saints (*Communicantes* and *Nobis quoque*) were inserted into the Canon.[6]

The above text, quoted by Ambrose, most likely dates from the time of Pope Gelasius (492–496 A.D.) and as a witness to this we can turn to the *Stowe Missal* where the Canon is titled: "*Canon dominicus papae gilasi.*"[7]

It would then seem that the Roman Canon was well established by the first half of the fourth century and continued to develop as a relatively fixed form into the sixth century.

The old *Gelasian Sacramentary* gives us the first complete text of the Canon and it remains relatively fixed from that time on until it reaches the form in which we now know it in the thirteenth century.[8]

A few comments are in order regarding the text of the Canon as it is found in the sacramentaries.

The term *preface* (praefatio) is first found in the *Gregorian Sacramentary*. The earlier sacramentaries begin the canon without any title with either V.D. or *Vere dignum.*[9]

The *Verona Sacramentary* and the *Gelasian Sacramentary* have nearly one preface for each Mass, whereas the *Gregorian Sacramentary* reduces them to fourteen and by the fourteenth century they are further reduced to only nine. Eventually the prefaces of the Blessed Virgin Mary, the Dead, Saint Joseph, Christ the King, and the Sacred Heart of Jesus were added to bring the number back to fourteen.[10]

The *Sanctus,* according to the *Liber Pontificalis,* was introduced by Pope Sixtus (c. 530 A.D.).[11] The *Te igitur* is first found in a textual fragment of Arian origin from around the end of the fourth century. This fragmentary text was published by Cardinal Mai in 1828, and although it is not the prayer as we know it it is very similar in many of its phrases.[12] The *Communicantes* is found in both the *Verona Sacramentary* and the *Gelasian Sacramentary*. Some of the *Communicantes* prayers come from the fifth century.[13] This text is given the title *infra actionem* in the *Gelasian Sacramentary*. The *Hanc igitur* is also given the same title in the *Gelasian Sacramentary*. There are a large number of these prayers and they are used as a special form of intercession within the eucharistic prayer. The common text of the *Hanc igitur* is inserted into the Roman Canon in the *Gregorian Sacramentary*.

The cental portion of the Canon begins with the *Quam oblationem*. The final form of this prayer dates from the time of Pope Gregory the Great and a variant form of this text is found in the *De Sacramentis* of Saint Ambrose. It appears to be a form of *epiclesis* but does not refer to the Holy Spirit.[14] The institution narrative is found in an abbreviated version in Saint Ambrose. The *verba* are not taken directly from any one of the scriptural accounts of the institution of the eucharist. The prayer that follows the institution narrative, *Unde et memores*, is given in a simplified form in Saint Ambrose. The next two prayers, *Supra que and Supplices te*, are combined in Saint Ambrose and the "angel" is mentioned before the sacrifices of the patriarchs. These two prayers appear to be a sort of *epiclesis* although, as in the case of the *quam oblationem*, there is no mention of the Holy Spirit.

The *Memento etiam* is the first of the next group of prayers. It is not found in either the *Gelasian Sacramentary* or the *Gregorian Sacramentary*. In the seventh to eighth centuries it is used only in Masses for the dead.[15] Its language is characteristic of pre-Christian burial texts, e.g., "refugerium lucis et pacis."[16] The *Nobis quoque*, the next prayer of intercession, is found in both the *Gelasian Sacramentary* and the *Gregorian Sacramentary*. Dom Bernard Botte is of the opinion that it is a species of embolism of the *Memento* of the living which occurs in the first half of the Canon.[17] The list of saints in the *Nobis quoque* reflects the papal use of the Roman Church.[18]

According to the eighth century *Ordo Romanus XV*[19] the first words of this prayer are the only ones of the Canon said aloud after the Sanctus. The reason for this is that they served as a signal to the subdeacons to rise and bring the patens to the altar for the fraction. From about the eighth century on the Canon was recited silently, and it was not until the Second Vatican Council that the eucharistic prayer was again prayed or even sung in a audible voice.

The next prayer, *Per quem haec omnia*, is a formula that forms the conclusion of a blessing. Some are of the opinion that originally this part of the Canon was used only when oil, milk, etc., were blessed, for example, the blessing of the oil of the Sick on Holy Thursday; others are convinced that it refers to the eucharistic offerings.[20]

The Roman Canon concludes with a doxology which differs from that of the eucharistic prayer of Hippolytus[21] and the prayer cited by Ambrose.[22]

The Roman Canon was the object of much criticism at the time of the Protestant Reformation. Luther, for example, attacked it for its very strong sacrificial language. However these attacks had no effect on the liturgical reforms of the Council of Trent. On the contrary, the Roman Canon remained unchanged up to the pontificate of Pope John XXIII who introduced the name of Saint Joseph into the Canon after that of the Virgin Mary.[23]

3. Vatican II Reforms

During the period of the Second Vatican Council there was much discussion by liturgists about the reform of the Roman Canon. After the promulgation of the Constitution on the Sacred Liturgy the Consilium for its implementation was established. This commission was divided into various working groups each with the responsibility for the reform of a particular area of the liturgy.[24] One such group, *Coetus* X, was given the task of reforming the Canon of the Mass. This working group consisted of nineteen liturgists who ultimately proposed three new anaphoras in addition to a slight revision of the Roman Canon.[25]

A study prepared by Dom C. Vagaggini[26] became the basis for the work of Coetus X. He examined the proposals put forward by Karl Amon and Hans Küng for a total reworking of the Canon.

Amon's proposal consisted of removing all the intercessions before the institution narrative as well as the preconsecratory epiclesis and replacing this material with a brief christological post-sanctus. The anamnesis, *Unde et memores*, is followed by the *Communicantes*. On Sundays the *Quam oblationem* combined with the last part of the *Supplices te* is said, on weekdays it is replaced by the *Te igitur,* and on special occasions both prayers are replaced by the appropriate *Hanc igitur.* The first part of the *Supplices* is then recited. The *Per quem* is said if there is something to be blessed; otherwise it is omitted. The Canon concludes with the *Per ipsum.*[27]

Hans Küng's proposal for the Roman Canon is in many ways less radical than Amon's. It consists of omitting all the intercessory material of the Canon: the second half of the *Te igitur* is omitted as is the *Memento* for the living, the *Communicantes,* and the *Hanc igitur.* The *Te igitur* is followed by the *Quam oblationem*, the institution narrative (with the words "mysterium fidei"), the *Unde et memores*, the *Supra que*, and the *Supplices te*. The *Memento* for the dead and the *Nobis quoque* are omitted. The Canon concludes with the *Per quem* and the *Per ipsum*.[28]

Vagaggini criticizes Küng for omitting the notion of the Church's offering of the gifts before the words of institution and for the duplication which results by having the *Quam oblationem* follow the first half of the *Te igitur*. Further, he points out that Küng omits the intercessions and the commemoration of the saints.[29]

His criticism of Amon's version of the Roman Canon is even stronger. Vagaggini says that Amon has really rewritten the text. He has dropped out the consecratory epiclesis which is found in all eucharistic prayers, and his reworking of the prayers, in general, is less clear than the original texts. Lastly, Amon's prayer lacks a unified picture of salvation through Christ.[30]

Vagaggini makes three proposals regarding the Roman Canon:

(1) The present canon should be retained with some minor modifications.
(2) There should be a second eucharistic prayer for use with variable prefaces.
(3) There should be a third anaphora with a fixed preface. This would follow the Eastern tradition of giving a synthesis of salvation history in the eucharistic prayer. After the words of institution the prayer would be the same as the Roman Canon.[31]

These proposals were generally accepted by the Consilium. Ultimately, the Consilium turned to the anaphora of Hippolytus and the Alexandrine version of the anaphora of Saint Basil. These two texts became the basis for the second and fourth eucharistic prayers respectively. In addition, it was decided to compose a new anaphora.

The three new anaphoras manifest a common structure:[32]

Preface (Variable in II and III, fixed in IV)
Sanctus
Post-Sanctus (Brief in II and III, long in IV)
Epiclesis I (For the consecration of the gifts)
Institution Narrative
Memorial Acclamation
Anamnesis and Oblation
Epiclesis II (For fruitful communion)

Commemoration of the Saints and Intercession (or vice versa)

Doxology

The major difference between the structure of the Roman Canon and the new eucharistic prayers lies in the placement of the intercessions. In the new prayers the intercessions and commemoration of the saints are all grouped before the doxology, whereas in the Roman Canon some precede the first "epiclesis" and others follow the second "epiclesis." The new anaphoras have an Antiochene structure while the Roman Canon is basically Alexandrine in its structural pattern. In addition, the new prayers follow the Roman practice of an epiclesis before the institution narrative and a second epiclesis for a fruitful reception of communion after the anamnesis.[33]

The ultimate reason for the decision to have three new canons lies on the practical level. The second eucharistic prayer is very brief, simple, and clear in structure and content. It is an adaptation of the anaphora of Hippolytus.[34] The third eucharistic prayer is of medium length, clear in structure, and can be used with any of the variable prefaces.[35] The fourth eucharistic prayer follows the Antiochene anaphoral tradition of presenting a synthesis of the history of salvation in the preface and post-sanctus. The preface praises God and focuses on his act of creation. The post-sanctus speaks of the creation of humanity and the redemptive work of Christ up to Pentecost. Since the preface and post-sanctus form a unity, this prayer may not be used with any other preface.[36] The fourth eucharistic prayer is the longest of the three new texts and the richest in its imagery.

The Consilium also had to face two questions in regard to the words of institution. First of all it was decided to change the words for the bread found in the Roman Canon so as to conform them to 1 Corinthians 11:24f: *Hoc est (enim) corpus meum quod pro vobis tradetur*. This text was to be used in all the eucharistic prayers including the Roman Canon. The second decision was to remove the words *mysterium fidei* contained in the *verba* since they are not found in the New Testament and exist only in the Roman Canon; furthermore, their meaning is far from clear.[37] These words were removed from the *verba* and were transformed into an invitation which elicits the new memorial acclamation of the congregation before the anamnesis.

These new memorial acclamations, three in number,[38] have as their model the acclamations in the Eastern anaphoras.[39] However, the acclamations in the eucharistic prayers of the Eastern Churches come after the anamnesis rather than before it.

Finally the Consilium decided to provide a variety of embolisms or

insertions into the intercessions of the second, third, and fourth anaphoras for the dead and for the occasions of ritual Masses for baptism,
marriage, etc.[40] In a sense, this continues the tradition of the Roman
Canon with its proper *Hanc igitur* texts. New *Hanc igitur* prayers have
also been introduced for corresponding occasions. It should be noted
that Eucharistic Prayer IV does not provide a special embolism for the
dead. The new eucharistic prayers were approved by Pope Paul VI
and promulgated by the Congregation of Rites on May 23, 1968. On
June 2, 1968, Cardinal Gut, president of the Consilium, sent a copy of
the new prayers along with eight new prefaces[41] and a booklet containing a catechesis on the prayers to the conferences of bishops.[42]

After the publication of the new eucharistic prayers there was an
expressed desire in parts of Europe, notably Holland, for other anaphoras. Many unofficial texts were composed and used by priests
without authorization. Consequently the Congregation for Divine
Worship, at the request of Pope Paul VI, reexamined the question of
whether other eucharistic prayers should be approved.[43] After a year
and a half of work the Congregation for the Doctrine of the Faith expressed a negative judgment on the possibility of episcopal conferences approving new eucharistic prayers and, as a result, a "circular
letter" was sent to the presidents of episcopal conferences.[44] Nevertheless the letter did open the way for conferences to ask the Apostolic
See for approval of new eucharistic prayers. In 1974 Rome authorized
the use of a new prayer for the occasion of the Swiss Synod and shortly
thereafter other prayers were approved.

4. Eucharistic Prayers for Children and Reconciliation

In October of 1973 Pope Paul VI requested the Congregation for Divine
Worship to prepare two or three eucharistic prayers for use at liturgies
with children and also an anaphora that could be used during the Holy
Year of 1975.[45] In October of 1974 the new prayers were approved by
the Pope—three for children's Masses and two for the Holy Year on
the theme of reconciliation.[46] Each episcopal conference was to choose
one of the prayers for children and one of the ones for reconciliation.
The prayers were translated into the vernacular and were authorized
for experimental use for a period of three years.[47] Quickly further authorization was given for the use of all five prayers by any conference
that made the request.[48]

In 1977 the Congregation for Divine Worship authorized the continued use of the eucharistic prayers for children and reconciliation for

another period of three years and in 1980 permission was given for a further indefinite period.[49]

The Latin Church thus now has eight new official eucharistic prayers in addition to the Roman Canon. We might close this historical overview by summarizing the basic reasons for this great departure from the ancient Roman tradition of one eucharistic prayer by using the words of the Consilium:

> Why this new departure? To consider the variety of anaphoras in the tradition of the universal Church is to realize that one anaphora alone cannot contain all the pastoral, spiritual, and theological richness to be hoped for. A multiplicity of texts must make up for the limitations of any one of them . . . .
>
> In adding three new anaphoras to the Roman Canon, the Church's intent here too has been to enrich the Roman liturgy pastorally, spiritually, and liturgically.[50]

II. The Roman Eucharistic Prayers

Now that we have briefly examined the development of the Roman Canon and the new eucharistic prayers, we are ready to face our main task, namely, an individual examination of each of the anaphoras. We shall content ourselves with pointing out the structure, significant features, and some of the theological concerns to which each prayer gives rise.

1. The Roman Canon

We have already made some comments regarding the history of the venerable Roman Canon and the development of its parts. In its present form the prayer appears to be a series of distinct prayers which precede and follow the institution narrative.[51]

The Roman Canon has the following structure:

1. Dialog
2. Preface (variable)
3. Sanctus
4. Prayer for the Acceptance of the Offerings and the Church (Te igitur—We come to you, Father)
5. Commemoration of the Living (Memento, Domine—Remember, Lord, your people)

6. Commemoration of the Saints (variable) (Communicantes—In union with the whole Church)
7. Prayer for Those for Whom the Offering Is Made (variable) (Hanc igitur—Father, accept this offering)
8. Epiclesis I (Quam oblationem—Bless and approve our offering)
9. Institution Narrative for the Bread (Qui pridie—The day before he suffered)
10. Institution Narrative for the Cup (Simili modo—When supper was ended)
11. Memorial Acclamation (Mysterium fidei and Mortem tuum—Let us proclaim and Christ has died)[52]
12. Anamnesis and Oblation (Unde et memores—Father, we celebrate)
13. Prayer for Acceptance of the Offerings (Supra quae—Look with favor)
14. Epiclesis II (Supplices te rogamus—Almighty God, we ask)
15. Commemoration of the Dead (Memento etiam—Remember, Lord, those who have died)
16. Prayer for the Ministers and Commemoration of the Saints (Nobis quoque—For ourselves too)
17. Blessing of the Gifts (Per quem—You give us all these gifts)
18. Doxology (Per ipsum—Through him)

The Canon thus has a sequence of praise and intercession interrupted by the institution narrative. The praise begins the prayer (nos. 1–3) and ends the prayer (no. 18). The initial praise is followed by four prayers of intercession (nos. 4–7).

The final prayer of praise, the doxology (no. 18), is preceded by two prayers of intercession (nos. 15 & 16). This structure of praise and intercession before the institution narrative and intercession after it is similar to the sequence found in the Alexandrine anaphoras and is quite different from the Antiochene tradition where the intercessory prayers are grouped together after the epiclesis near the end of the eucharistic prayer.

The Roman Canon also shows another structural aspect that is of interest. Unlike the Eastern anaphoras, the Roman Canon manifests a certain degree of variability as is evidenced by the prefaces and to a lesser degree by the special *Hanc igitur* and *Communicantes* prayers. This represents a compromise between the almost total variability of the Gallican and Spanish anaphoras and the invariability of the Eastern anaphoras, "but most striking of all, it is a solution unique in the history of eucharistic rites."[53]

Any examination of the Roman Canon must evaluate its merits along with its disadvantages, and of course this is what the *Coetus* for the revision of the Roman Canon did. Father Vagaggini provides us with a summary of the work he did for the *Coetus* in this regard.[54]

Merits

He first describes the merits of the Roman Canon as follows:

1. *Antiquity of the text and its traditional character and use in the West.*[55] The Roman Canon has been in constant use from at least the fifth century, and by the tenth to eleventh centuries had replaced even the Gallican eucharistic prayers.

2. *The variable prefaces of the Roman Church* are another positive aspect of the Roman Canon.[56] They provide variety to the celebration and allow for mention of the particular mystery being celebrated within the eucharistic prayer itself. This is especially true when the present *Roman Missal* is used with its more than eighty prefaces.

3. *Theology of offering the gifts.*[57] Vagaggini says: "As distinct from all the other anaphoral traditions, it is characteristic of the present Roman Canon that, from the *Te igitur* onward, it is directed toward the offering of our gifts, their acceptance by God and their consecration."[58] In the Canon the unconsecrated gifts are offered and then sanctified and these sanctified or consecrated gifts are offered to God. That is to say:

> Bread and wine are chosen from among the gifts God has given us and are offered to him as a symbol of the offering of ourselves, of what we possess and of the whole of material creation. In this offering we pray God to accept them, to bless them and to transform them. . . into the body and blood of Christ, asking him to give them back to us transformed in such a way that through them we may. . . be united to Christ and to one another, sharing in fact in the divine nature."[59]

This is basically the notion of the "sacrum commercium" (sacred exchange of gifts) which figures prominently in many of the Roman prayers over the gifts.

4. *Stylistic merits.*[60] The Roman Canon reflects classical Latin liturgical style, especially the *cursus*, that is, the pattern of stressed and unstressed syllables which gives a unique rhythm to the text. In addition, the Latin text exemplifies Roman religious language, e.g., "benedictam, adscriptam, ratam, acceptabilemque" (bless, approve, and make acceptable to you). This language reflects the Roman sobriety in its concise expression of theological concepts. When contrasted with the non-Roman Western liturgies it becomes clear that the language of the Roman Canon (and prefaces) is clear and to the point.

Defects

In spite of the merits of the Roman Canon, there are many criticisms which have been made of the prayer.

1. The impression is given of an agglomeration of features with no apparent unity.[61] Prayers of offering and intercession are intermixed. The Canon does not appear to be one prayer but rather a series of distinct prayers, many with the customary conclusion: "per Christum Dominum nostrum. Amen."

2. There is a lack of logical connection of ideas within the text.[62] The prayers do not seem to flow from one another. The preface and sanctus appear to be divorced from the remainder of the prayer. The English translation has remedied this somewhat by introducing the phrase, "We come to you, Father, with praise and thanksgiving," as a means of connecting the ideas of praise of thanksgiving in the preface with the offering of the gifts found in the *Te igitur*. The *Memento* for the living, the *Communicantes,* and the *Hanc igitur* are all logically unconnected even though they follow one another.

3. The prayers of intercession are assembled in a very unsatisfactory manner.[63] Rather than placing all the intercessions together in one place, the Canon divides them up before and after the institution account. As a result the connections between the hierarchy and laity, the saints, the living and the dead are obscured. In addition, the relationship between the epiclesis and the intercessions which is so clear in the Eastern anaphoras is obscured: the Church is nourished and united by the body and blood of Christ and thus it can pray for itself (clergy and laity), recall those who have died in the faith (the saints), and can intercede on behalf of those who have died. These relationships are not easily seen in the Roman Canon because of the split intercessions.

4. There is an exaggerated emphasis on the idea of the offering and acceptance of the gifts.[64] The theology of offering of the gifts is at one and the same time a merit and a defect of the Roman Canon. For the Canon not only states the theme of offering, but repeats it over and over again.

It is interesting to see that at least three times before the institution narrative the Canon repeats that the bread and wine (the oblations or offerings) are being offered, but identifies the offering itself with the body and blood of Christ only once after the institution narrative.[65] As a result we lose sight of the central notion of the eucharistic celebration, namely, that what is offered is Jesus Christ, and that we join ourselves to him in this his sacrificial act.[66]

5. A theology and role of the Holy Spirit is lacking in the Roman

Canon.[67] The Canon does not specifically refer to the Holy Spirit except in the final doxology. There is no mention of the sanctifying work of the Holy Spirit nor is there an explicit epiclesis of the Holy Spirit. Many have tried to see the *Quam oblationem* as a consecratory epiclesis, but there is no actual invocation of the Holy Spirit on the offerings nor later upon those who will receive the consecrated gifts. The *Supplices* with its reference to the offerings being brought to the heavenly altar by the hands of an angel may be a veiled reference to the action of the Holy Spirit. It may well be that at one time this prayer was a complete epiclesis; however as it now stands it does not fulfill that function.

6. There are several defects in the Institution Narrative.[68] The Roman Canon lacks the Pauline or Lucan reference at the end of the words over the bread, namely, "quod pro vobis tradetur." Since all the other rites include these words the Roman text stands alone. This omission tends to break the parallelism between the texts for the bread and the wine and ultimately has led to an emphasis on the breaking of the bread as a sacrificial act rather than on the sacrifice being that of Christ himself whose body is handed over and broken for us.

The words of institution do not directly follow the scriptural texts but instead are a free rendering of them in a liturgical context. However, the addition of the words "*mysterium fidei*" (the mystery of faith) to the words of Christ do not have a scriptural basis and are not clear as to their meaning. Furthermore, they are not found in any other liturgy.

7. The Canon lacks an overall presentation of the history of salvation.[69] Unlike the Eastern anaphoras with their trinitarian structure, the Roman Canon does not clearly present the action of the persons of the Trinity in the history of salvation. The Eastern prayers usually begin with praise of God in himself and for his act of creation (in the preface), then speak of the work of Christ (post-sanctus, institution narrative, and anamnesis), and finally call upon the Spirit to make the celebration of the eucharist effective for the Church and those who receive it (epiclesis and intercessions).

The Roman Canon, on the other hand, must by the nature of the text restrict this recalling of God's saving acts to the preface. For the Canon itself is almost devoid of salvation history except in the anamnesis. The preface, however, is variable and more often than not Christocentric. The result is that there is no synthesis of the salvation history that is minimally presented.

The Present Roman Canon

The merits of the Canon led the revision committee to a decision that this venerable text could not be discarded, yet the committee felt that the defects of the Canon required certain revisions in the prayer.

1. More prefaces have been provided. In the 1985 edition of the *Sacramentary* there are now eighty-nine prefaces. This allows for a greater expression of the mysteries and history of salvation in Christ and provides a variability in the anaphora which is characteristic of the Latin Church.

2. The conclusions (*Per Christum Dominum nostrum. Amen.*) of the *Communicantes, Hanc igitur*, and the *Memento etiam* have been made optional. This allows for a smoother flow of the prayer without the interruptions occasioned by the conclusions of these prayers.

3. The whole Canon is now to be said aloud so as to be heard by all present.

4. The long lists of the saints in the *Communicantes* and the *Nobis quoque* may be abbreviated.

5. The words *Mysterium fidei* have been removed from the words of institution for the cup and are now used as an introduction for the memorial acclamation of the people which has also been introduced in the other eucharistic prayers.[70]

6. The epicletic gesture of the priest extending his hands over the offerings has be moved from the *Hanc igitur* to the *Quam oblationem* where it is more appropriate.

It was decided that the other defects of the Roman Canon could not be corrected without doing violence to the prayer, and so the three new eucharistic prayers were introduced. The first anaphora in the *Sacramentary* is identified as: Eucharistic Prayer I (Roman Canon); the remaining prayers are simply called Eucharistic Prayer II, III, IV. The second prayer has its own preface but may be used with another preface, the third prayer must be used with a variable preface, and the fourth prayer has a fixed preface and may not be used with a variable preface.

2. Eucharistic Prayer II

In the light of the difficulties encountered with the revision of the Roman Canon, the Consilium committee on eucharistic prayers[71] decided to proceed with the preparation of the ancient Roman anaphora of Hippolytus.[72] The committee quickly realized that the prayer could not be used as it stood but would have to be adapted. These adaptations were to be of two types: structural and theological.

Structure of the Anaphora

The eucharistic prayer of Hippolytus has a structure quite unlike that of the Roman Canon and is much more similar to the anaphoras of the Western Antiochene tradition.

Hippolytus	*Eucharistic Prayer II*
Dialog	Dialog
Thanksgiving	Preface
	Sanctus
	Post-Sanctus
	(Epiclesis I)
Institution Narrative	Institution Narrative
	Memorial Acclamation
Anamnesis	Anamnesis
Epiclesis	Epiclesis II
	Intercessions
Doxology	Doxology

From the above outline it should be clear that two elements of the later Antiochene tradition are absent from Hippolytus, namely, the sanctus and the intercessions.

In Hippolytus the thanksgiving praises God for what Jesus has done and the last reason for giving thanks is what he did at the Last Supper. The institution narrative is not so much a separate element of the prayer but rather is the final portion of the thanksgiving.[73] The theme of thanksgiving continues into the anamnesis and epiclesis.

Sanctus and Post-Sanctus

The insertion of the sanctus into the prayer of Hippolytus gives rise to a new problem, as it has the effect of dividing the prayer in half. The sanctus leads directly into the institution narrative without there being any connection between it and what follows. Therefore it was necessary to insert a brief transitional prayer or post-sanctus to take up the theme of the sanctus and lead into the words of institution.

Epiclesis I

This newly composed post-sanctus has an additional function which was based on a decision made by *Coetus X*. It was determined that the pattern of the Roman Canon of two epiclesis prayers, one before the institution narrative which asks that through the action of the Holy Spirit the bread and wine may become the body and blood of

Christ, and the other after the anamnesis which asks the Spirit to transform those who share in the body and blood of the Lord. The first epiclesis is consecratory and the second sanctificatory. The theological basis for this decision lies in the traditional Roman understanding of the words of institution as being consecratory.[74]

This insertion of a post-sanctus that is also a consecratory epiclesis is not unique. "In the non-Roman Latin liturgies the post-sanctus is often epicletic in the sense that it accepts the theme of the invocation of the Father so that he might sanctify the bread and wine and make them the body and blood of Christ."[75]

Unlike the *Quam oblationem* of the Roman Canon which serves as a form of consecratory, or, rather, pre-consecratory epiclesis, the new post-sanctus of Eucharistic Prayer II specifically mentions the Holy Spirit: "Let your Holy Spirit come upon these gifts to make them holy . . . "

Dom Adrien Nocent points out that there is a strict bond between the intervention of the Spirit in regard to the oblation and the action of the Spirit upon those who participate in the reception of the consecrated gifts. He rightly notes that a split epiclesis fails to show "why we participate in the bread and wine which the Holy Spirit has transformed, that we are transformed and reunited in one body."[76]

Institution Narrative

The words of institution of the second eucharistic prayer are not those of Hippolytus. For purposes of uniformity in the eucharistic prayers the revised form of the Roman Canon is used in this prayer and all the new anaphoras.

Memorial Acclamation

The words of institution are followed by the memorial acclamation which was introduced into the Roman Canon. This acclamation introduces the anamnesis and provides additional congregational participation in the eucharistic prayer.

Anamnesis and Epiclesis II

The anamnesis and epiclesis II essentially are as in Hippolytus with no major changes.

Intercessions

After the second epiclesis of the prayer intercessions have been introduced. They consist of prayers for the Church, the hierarchy, the departed, and a commemoration of the saints.

Although some might object that the intercessions duplicate the general intercessions, it does seem both natural and appropriate that in the midst of the Church's greatest prayer, we pray for the Church itself, for those who have died and were united to it in faith, and finally that we unite ourselves in communion with the saints who have gone before us.

The intercessions flow from the epiclesis and are a natural outcome of its petition that those who share in the eucharist be united and transformed in Christ.

Provision is made in the text for the insertion of a special intercession for the dead with a particular mention of the deceased person. This prayer is intended for use at funerals and other special Masses for the dead. In addition, the *Sacramentary* provides other special intercessions for use on the occasion of ritual Masses, that is, a Mass during which a sacrament or other rite is celebrated, such as baptism, marriage, religious profession, etc.

Doxology

The doxology of Eucharistic Prayer II is not that of Hippolytus; rather it is that which concludes the Roman Canon. The reason for abandoning the distinctive doxology of Hippolytus was not theological, but merely practical. The text of the Roman Canon was chosen because it was more easily sung to the traditional chant.[77]

It should be noted that this eucharistic prayer may be used with any of the variable prefaces in the *Sacramentary*, and in actual use this is the case. However, when this is done only a small part of the original anaphora of Hippolytus is actually used since the preface of Hippolytus contains much of the theological content of his anaphora.

Theological Changes

At the beginning of our examination of Eucharistic Prayer II we noted that the changes made in the anaphora of Hippolytus were of two types: structural and theological. The theological changes in the text are not extensive and the "prayer remains faithful to Hippolytus, except for those terms and expressions which in today's theology would not be understood correctly."[78] The major changes in the prayer are found in the thanksgiving-preface portion of the prayer.

Thus, *dilectum puerum tuum* is changed to *Filium dilectionis tuae* for the sake of clarification. Other phrases are omitted because they are difficult to explain. Often they are based on the theology of Irenaeus which permeates the prayer. Hence, *terminum figat* and *vincula diaboli dirumpat et infernum calcet* are simply omitted.[79]

The addition of this adapted form of the anaphora of Hippolytus to the corpus of Roman eucharistic prayers is extremely significant. Along with Eucharistic Prayer III it has virtually replaced the Roman Canon in daily use. Furthermore, the prayer of Hippolytus is now being used in one form or other in almost every Church that has revised its eucharistic liturgy. It is, in a sense, a common prayer of the Churches.

3. Eucharistic Prayer III

The third eucharistic prayer was intended as an alternative to the Roman Canon, especially for use on Sunday.

Although one is not able to point to any one individual as the author of this prayer it is clear that much of its content and manner of expression can be traced to Dom Cipriano Vagaggini, O.S.B. The first of his two proposed anaphoras which were published in *The Canon of the Mass and Liturgical Reform*[80] is very similar to Eucharistic Prayer III. Nevertheless the final text of this prayer is the work of the entire committee.[81]

Structure

Post-Sanctus

Epiclesis I

Institution Narrative

Memorial Acclamation

Anamnesis

Epiclesis II

Intercessions

Doxology

This eucharistic prayer is to be used with the variable prefaces of the *Sacramentary* and unlike Eucharistic Prayer II and Eucharistic Prayer IV it does not have its own preface.

It is usual to say that it "borrows its scheme from the best elements of the ancient Gallican and Mozarabic tradition"; however, in reality, this is not true. The structure of the anaphora is Antiochene with the Alexandrine addition of a consecratory epiclesis before the words of institution. The Gallican and Spanish (Mozarabic) anaphoras are composed of a series of prayers which are independent of each other and can be interchanged; only the central portion containing the words of institution remains unchangeable.[82] It is clear that Eucharistic Prayer III is not of this type. Its only variable portion is the preface.

Post-Sanctus

The post-sanctus takes up the theme of the sanctus by initially praising the Father for his holiness: "Father, you are holy indeed, and all creation rightly gives you praise." In Latin, the prayer begins, *"Vere sanctus"* (Truly holy), and in many of the non-Roman Western liturgies the post-sanctus is called the *"Vere sanctus."* To the praise of the angels in the sanctus is thus added the praise of all creation for the very holiness of God.

The post-sanctus concludes with a quotation from the prophet Malachi (1:11) which is often used by the Fathers in writing of the eucharist:[83]

> From age to age you gather a people to yourself,
> so that from east to west
> a perfect offering may be made
> to the glory of your name.

Epiclesis I

The Father is then asked to send the Spirit to sanctify the gifts in order that they may become Christ's body and blood. This explicit epiclesis with its strong expression of the action of the Holy Spirit is a welcome addition to the Roman liturgy. The epiclesis leads directly into the institution narrative by recalling that we celebrate the eucharist at Christ's command.

Institution Narrative

The institution narrative of the third eucharistic prayer is the same as that of the Roman Canon. However, the introductory words to the narrative for the bread in the first three eucharistic prayers vary somewhat:

> *Eucharistic Prayer I*
> The day before he suffered
> he took bread in his sacred hands
> and looking up to heaven,
> to you, his almighty Father,
> he gave you thanks and praise.
>
> *Eucharistic Prayer II*
> Before he was given up to death,

a death he freely accepted,
he took bread and gave you thanks.

Eucharistic Prayer III
On the night he was betrayed,
he took bread and gave you thanks and praise.

This variation in the introduction to the words of institution in each canon gives variety to texts that are essentially the same for all the prayers.

Memorial Acclamation

The invitation to the memorial acclamation is the same as in all the other eucharistic prayers as are the congregational acclamations. It is a bit curious that the second, third, and fourth acclamations are addressed to Christ, whereas the first is not. Normally prayers are not addressed to Christ in the Roman liturgy and the only other instances of acclamations addressed to Christ are found in the acclamations of the third form of the penitential rite, "You came to heal the contrite of heart: Lord, have mercy," and before and after the Gospel reading.

The first acclamation, "Christ has died," has also been used in the eucharistic prayers of many other Churches.

Anamnesis

The anamnesis recalls the death, resurrection, ascension, and second coming of Christ and leads into the oblation or offering: "we offer you in thanksgiving this holy and living sacrifice."

The meaning of this phrase is explained by the next part of the prayer:

Look with favor on your Church's offering,
and see the Victim whose death has reconciled us to yourself.

The sacrifice of the Church is identified with Christ. The Father is asked to see in this sacramental action Christ himself, whose sacrifice reconciles us to the Father. There is no question here of a new sacrifice of Christ, but only of that one saving act of Christ on the cross present before us in a sacramental manner.

Vagaggini describes the meaning of the eucharistic sacrifice in these terms:

What is being offered in sacrifice to God is the bread and wine—taken from among the gifts he has given us, and considered as symbols of ourselves and of all things—but also, and at the same time, it is Christ in person. . . .

Profound reflection on the theology of the *commercium* will show that, for us, offering Christ and his service to God means consciously uniting ourselves to the offering which Christ, our head, makes of himself, of us, and of the whole world to God. Such an offering cannot therefore take place without our offering ourselves; and inversely we cannot offer ourselves in sacrifice without offering Christ—which we do by uniting ourselves in heart and mind to the offering he made, and never ceases to make, of himself, of us, and of the whole world. Indeed, no offering is acceptable to God unless it is made part of the offering which Christ makes of himself and of us to the Father.[84]

Epiclesis II

The epiclesis prays that by sharing in the body and blood of Christ we may be filled with the Holy Spirit and be united as one body in Christ. That is, we pray that our sharing in the eucharist may be the means of uniting the Church. The reception of communion means that we are united with Christ and in Christ.

If the first epiclesis and the second epiclesis are seen together, a clear picture of the role of the Holy Spirit in the celebration of the eucharist is seen:

> And so Father, we bring you these gifts.
> We ask you to make them holy by the power of your Spirit,
> that they may become the body and blood
> of your Son, our Lord Jesus Christ. . . .
>
> Grant that we, who are nourished by his body and blood,
> may be filled with his Holy Spirit,
> and become one body, one Spirit in Christ.

The Spirit who transforms the gifts also transforms those who receive the gifts. The Spirit who causes the bread to be the body of Christ also causes those who receive the sacramental body of the Lord to be the body of Christ, the Church.

Intercessions

The epiclesis naturally leads into the intercessions which begin with a commemoration of the saints. United in and with Christ we are also united with the wider Church of the saints: the Mother of God, the apostles, martyrs and all God's holy ones. The commemoration of the saints concludes with the specifically Catholic notion of the intercession of the saints, "on whose constant intercession we rely for help." This phrase is based on an understanding of the Church in heaven being united with the Church on earth in such a way that those in the presence of God can do nothing other than pray for those who seek "to share in the inheritance of the saints."

The intercessions then turn to the Church on earth. The prayers begin with a request for the peace and salvation of the world. The Church is then commemorated beginning with its spiritual leaders: the Pope, the bishops, the clergy, and concluding with all the people of Christ, all those who are assembled for this celebration, and finally all of God's people.

The intercessions for the Church may be concluded on the occasion of baptism, consecration to a life of virginity, religious profession, anointing of the sick, and the dedication of a church by a special intercession related to the occasion being celebrated.

The intercessions end with a general commemoration of the dead. In Masses for a particular deceased person a more specific intercession may replace the general prayer. This special intercession is worth quoting:

> Remember N.
> In baptism he (she) died with Christ:
> may he (she) also share his resurrection,
> when Christ will raise our mortal bodies
> and make them like his own in glory.
> Welcome into your kingdom our departed brothers and sisters,
> and all who have left this world in your friendship.
> There we hope to share in your glory
> when every tear will be wiped away.
> On that day we shall see you, our God, as you are.
> We shall become like you
> and praise you for ever through Christ our Lord,
> from whom all good things come.

This prayer is filled with hope and confident faith. Once again we see that the third eucharistic prayer envisions the heavenly and the earthly Church as united through the eucharistic celebration.

Doxology

The canon ends the common doxology taken from the Roman Canon and the Great Amen by which congregation affirms and ratifies that which has been proclaimed.

4. Eucharistic Prayer IV

The fourth eucharistic prayer is the longest of the new eucharistic prayers although, in reality, it is shorter than the Roman Canon.

Unlike the other eucharistic prayers this anaphora has a fixed preface and may not be used with the variable prefaces of the *Sacramentary*. Accordingly it may be used only on those days that do not require a proper preface.

Eucharistic Prayer IV is unique among the new anaphoras since it derives from the Eastern anaphoral tradition. It takes much of its inspiration from the Alexandrine anaphora of Saint Basil. The actual formulation of the text "derives most often from the 'projects' for new canons, which had been prepared by Vagaggini."[85]

Although the prayer takes its origin from the Egyptian liturgical tradition, its basic structure is decidedly Syro-Antiochene with the addition of an epiclesis before the words of institution as in the Roman Canon and following the Alexandrine fashion.[86]

This prayer, in a different translation and with the epiclesis restored to its original position after the anamnesis, is used by the Episcopal Church and several Protestant Churches under the title, *Common Eucharistic Prayer*.[87]

Structure

The structure of the prayer takes this form:

Dialog
Preface (Celebration of Divine Praise)
Sanctus
Post-Sanctus (Anamnesis of salvation in Christ)
Epiclesis I
Institution Narrative
Memorial Acclamation
Anamnesis
Epiclesis II
Intercessions
Doxology

Eucharistic Prayer IV is a beautiful synthesis of salvation history from creation through the second coming. It is crafted in such a way as to show the salvific activity of the Father as Creator, the Son as Redeemer, and the Holy Spirit as the one who unites and sanctifies the Church.

Preface

The preface of the prayer begins in the usual way with the traditional dialog in the Western form, *The Lord be with you*, etc.

The preface is addressed to the Father and is a wonderful hymn of glory and thanksgiving to the one, living, and true God. God is praised as the "source of life and goodness, who has created all things."

A second theme of the preface is that of light. God lives "in unapproachable light" and leads all people to "the joyful vision" of his light. And the angels look upon God's splendor and praise him "night and day."

Thus God is the life-giving Creator of all things who calls his creation to praise and thank him and contemplate the light of his glory.

The preface ends on the interesting note that we join our praise with that of the angels, and in the name of all creatures we too praise God. We who were given authority over all creatures now speak God's praise in the name of all that he created. Here we have constant echoes of the creation stories of the Book of Genesis.

Sanctus

The sanctus follows the preface as in all the other eucharistic prayers. The sanctus constitutes the first acclamation of the people during the prayer. It fits more naturally into this anaphora since it is an expression of our common act of praise of God along with the angels.

Post-Sanctus

The post-sanctus is the longest section of this eucharistic prayer. It takes up the second part of salvation history, that which deals with the redemption of humankind. It begins by continuing the creation theme with an account of the creation of man and the first act of disobedience. Yet God does not abandon humanity, but rather makes covenants and sends prophets to bring his people back on the way to salvation. Thus the major themes of the Old Testament are summarized in the first part of the post-sanctus.

The prayer then turns to the second act in the drama of redemption. In words echoing the scriptures the incarnation of Christ is proclaimed. And what did Christ come to do?

> To the poor he proclaimed the good news of salvation,
> to prisoners, freedom,
> and to those in sorrow, joy.
> In fulfillment of your will
> he gave himself up to death;
> but by rising from the dead,
> he destroyed death and restored life.

The post-sanctus thus proclaims, in phrases reminiscent of the creed, the very mysteries of our creation and redemption in Christ. The work of Christ is not complete, however, until his Church is established by the action of the Holy Spirit. The Christological anamnesis of the post-sanctus concludes with the Pentecost giving of the Holy Spirit "that we might live no longer for ourselves but for him. . . . " The Spirit is sent by Christ from the Father "to complete his work on earth and bring us the fullness of grace."

Epiclesis I

This recalling of the sending of the Spirit naturally leads into the first epiclesis:

> Father, may this Holy Spirit sanctify these offerings.
> Let them become the body and blood of Jesus Christ our Lord
> as we celebrate the great mystery
> which he left us as an everlasting covenant.

One of the beauties of this anaphora is the way in which each element leads into the next. The preface flows into the sanctus and post-sanctus, the post-sanctus leads into the epiclesis, and the epiclesis prepares us for the institution of the new covenant in the body that is broken and the blood that is shed.

Institution Narrative

The theme of the new covenant, a covenant of love, forms the basis of the introduction to the words of institution:

> He always loved those who were his own in the world.
> When the time came for him to be glorified by you, his heavenly Father
> he showed the depth of his love.

The actual words of institution are the same as those of the other eucharistic prayers and are, in actuality, a modified form of the institution narrative of the old Roman Canon.

Memorial Acclamation

The congregation's acclamation is introduced by the same text as in all the other prayers: "Let us proclaim the mystery of faith." The four acclamations, which may be used *ad libitum,* are those common to the other canons.

Anamnesis

Like the post-sanctus, the anamnesis takes the form of a creedal proclamation. Christ's death, descent among the dead, resurrection, ascension to the right hand of the Father, and his coming in glory are all mentioned.

The anamnesis concludes with the oblation or offering. The General Instruction of the Roman Missal (no. 55f) speaks of the offering in this manner:

> . . . in this memorial (anamnesis), the Church—and in particular the Church here and now assembled—offers the spotless victim to the Father in the Holy Spirit. The Church's intention is that the faithful not only offer this victim but also learn to offer themselves and so to surrender themselves, through Christ the Mediator, to an evermore complete union with the Father and with each other, so that at last God may be all in all.[88]

As we have noted above, this offering is none other than the sacramental participation in the one sacrificial offering of Christ accomplished for our salvation on the cross.

In the fourth eucharistic prayer the offering or oblation is in the following words:

> . . . we offer you his body and blood,
> the acceptable sacrifice which brings salvation to the whole world.

Although the oblation is not usually spoken of in such direct terms, namely, the body and blood of Christ and usually terms such as "this sacrifice" or "the life-giving bread and saving cup" are used, the language is understandable in this prayer. For it speaks of the covenants God has made with us, and most especially of the new covenant in the blood of Christ. We join ourselves, as the General Instruction of the Missal reminds us, to Christ's self-offering of his body and blood which inaugurates the new covenant of love.

Epiclesis II

As we ask God to accept the sacrifice, we also ask him:

Lord, look upon this sacrifice which you have given to your
   Church;
and by your Holy Spirit, gather all share this one bread and one cup
into the one body of Christ, a living sacrifice of praise.

By our reception of the bread and cup we pray that the Holy Spirit may transform us into the living body of Christ and that we may accordingly be a living sacrifice of praise. The oblation and the epiclesis can only be seen in relationship to one another, for the sacrifice is offered only through the power of the Holy Spirit who transforms the bread and cup which we offer, and transforms us who receive the body and blood of Christ, that we may offer ourselves as a living sacrifice. The anaphora thus echo the teaching of Saint Paul in Corinthians and Romans.

Intercessions

The intercessions of this prayer are rather brief in comparison to those of Eucharistic Prayer I and III. They begin with a commemoration of the Church: the Pope, bishops, clergy, those present, all God's people, and "all who seek you with a sincere heart." This latter expression is derived from the Second Vatican Council.[89]

The prayer has a general intercession for the dead but does not admit a more particular intercession as do the other eucharistic prayers. Note that the prayers of the Church are not only for those who have died "in the peace of Christ," but also for "all the dead whose faith is known to you alone."

As does the second eucharistic prayer, so also this anaphora concludes the intercession with a commemoration of the saints. This allows the prayer to end on a decidedly eschatological note:

Then, in your kingdom, freed from the corruption of sin and death,
we shall sing your glory with every creature through Christ our Lord. . . .

Eschatology has been a weak point of the Roman liturgy and this and other references in the new canons are welcome additions to the liturgy.[90]

Doxology

The anaphora concludes with the common final doxology from the Roman Canon.

Eucharistic Prayer IV is an excellent addition to the euchology of the Latin Church. It provides a grand overview of salvation history and fulfills in an unique way the function of the eucharistic prayer as a proclamation of the *mirabilia Dei* and the faith of the Church. When this prayer is proclaimed the use of any other profession of faith (creed) seems to be redundant.

It is to be hoped that someday the original Alexandrine version of the anaphora of Saint Basil, which is the basis of this prayer, may also find a place among the eucharistic prayers of the Church.

III. Eucharistic Prayers for Masses of Reconciliation

The two anaphoras were originally promulgated for use only during the Holy Year, and each episcopal conference was to choose one of the two prayers. However, these limitations were quickly dropped. The prayers are now authorized for permanent use and are printed in the *Sacramentary* in an appendix along with the three eucharistic prayers for use with children.

Structure

Both of the Eucharistic Prayers for Masses of Reconciliation have the same structure. Like the fourth anaphora these two prayers are constructed according to the Antiochene plan with the addition of an epiclesis before the words of institution. Each prayer has a fixed preface and, therefore, may not be used with a variable preface.

The outline of the prayers is as follows:

Dialog
Preface
Sanctus
Post-Sanctus
Epiclesis I
Institution Narrative
Memorial Acclamation
Anamnesis
Epiclesis II
Intercessions
Doxology

1. Eucharistic Prayer for Masses of Reconciliation I

Preface

The preface begins with thanks and praise to the Father who calls us "to a new and more abundant life." This new and fuller life is explained to be the love, mercy, and forgiveness of God as manifested in Christ. It is through Christ that we are reconciled with God and by opening our hearts to the Holy Spirit we are reconciled in service to one another.

The preface, thus, has a trinitarian theme: through Christ and in the power of the Holy Spirit we are forgiven and reconciled to our loving Father.

The preface concludes in a somewhat different way which serves to emphasize the basic theme of the whole preface:

> In wonder and gratitude,
> we join our voices with the choirs of heaven
> to proclaim the power of your love
> and sing of our salvation in Christ. . . .

The preface is followed by the sanctus.

Post-Sanctus

The post-sanctus is a rather brief prayer that is interrupted by the first epiclesis. The first part of the post-sanctus relates to the sanctus, "that we may be holy as you are holy," and to the preface, "you have always what is good for man." God has shown us his love so that we might share in his holiness.

Epiclesis I

The first epiclesis does not seem to be closely connected to the post-sanctus and, in fact, seems to be an interruption in the prayer. A positive aspect of the epiclesis is how it looks beyond the sanctification of the gifts to their effects on us:

> . . . send forth the power of your Spirit
> so that these gifts may become for us
> the body and blood of your beloved Son, Jesus the Christ,
> in whom we have become your sons and daughters.

The post-sanctus theme then resumes: God who has loved us and desires our sanctification has sent us his Son as a sign of his generous

love even when we were lost in our sins. Christ establishes a new covenant on the cross for us who have broken God's covenants (see preface). The prayer concludes by leading into the institution narrative:

> Yet before he stretched out his arms between heaven and earth
> in the everlasting sign of your covenant,
> he desired to celebrate the Paschal feast
> in the company of his disciples.

Institution Narrative

The introduction to the words of institution for the bread is not especially notable. However, the introduction for the words over the cup
continues the reconciliation theme:

> At the end of the meal,
> knowing that he was to reconcile all things to himself
> by the blood of the cross,
> he took the cup, filled with wine.

Memorial Acclamation

The words of institution are followed by the memorial acclamation
common to all the new anaphoras.

Anamnesis

The anamnesis is rather brief and mentions, first of all, the death
and resurrection of Christ. It then makes a strong eschatological statement:

> and look for the coming of that day
> when he will return to give us the fullness of joy.

The conclusion of the anamnesis contains the words of oblation or offering:

> Therefore we offer you, God ever faithful and true,
> the sacrifice which restores man to your friendship.

The Church thus joins in Christ's offering of himself on the cross by
which he reconciles all things to himself.

Epiclesis II

The second epiclesis makes it clear that the oblation is none other
than the sacrifice of Christ on the cross, for it says:

> . . . look with love
> on those you have called
> to share in the one sacrifice of Christ

By sharing in Christ's sacrifice we are united by the Holy Spirit and "healed of all division."

Intercessions

The intercessions have the unity of the Church as their common basis. They pray first for communion with the Pope and the bishop. Then with a strong eschatological emphasis they continue:

> Help us to work together
> for the coming of your kingdom,
> until at last we stand in your presence
> to share the life of the saints,
> in the company of the Virgin Mary and the apostles. . . .

The communion of the Church on earth leads to communion with the Church in heaven. And finally we pray for communion with our deceased brothers and sisters.

The prayer ends on a final eschatological note which also echoes the ultimate purpose of Christ's reconciling and redemptive sacrifice:

> Then, freed from every shadow of death,
> we shall take our place in the new creation
> and give you thanks
> with Christ, our risen Lord.

The anaphora ends with the customary doxology.

2. Eucharistic Prayer for Masses of Reconciliation II

The second of the eucharistic prayers for Masses of reconciliation, like the first prayer, is intended for use during the season of Lent and for special celebrations which have reconciliation as their theme.

Preface

Contrary to the usual pattern of Roman prefaces which normally speak of some salvific act or mystery of Christ, this preface gives spe-

cial attention to the role of the Holy Spirit in bringing about reconciliation.

In a world that manifests conflict and division, God makes his presence known by the action of the Holy Spirit in our hearts:

> enemies . . . speak to one another,
> those . . . estranged join hands in friendship,
> and nations seek the way of peace together.

The Spirit transforms the individual and by changing individual hearts
the relations between individuals and nations are transformed.

The work of the Spirit is concretely manifested in our lives when,

> understanding puts an end to strife,
> . . . hatred is quenched by mercy,
> and vengeance gives way to forgiveness.

The Spirit is thus the cause and the means by which reconciliation is
accomplished in our world.

The preface concludes by thanking the Father for the action of the
Spirit and by uniting with the hymn of the angels in the sanctus.

Post-Sanctus

The post-sanctus presents the Christological aspect of reconciliation
and is connected to the sanctus by the theme of the benedictus:

> . . . we praise you through your Son, Jesus Christ,
> who comes in your name.

Christ is the saving *Word*, the helping *hand* offered to sinners, and the
way to peace. He leads us back to the Father so that we might "find
our way to one another."

Epiclesis I

The Holy Spirit is asked to sanctify the gifts in order that we might
fulfill Christ's command to "Do this in memory of me."

Institution Narrative

The institution narrative follows the usual form and the introductory sections for the words over the bread and cup are not particularly
significant for the theme of reconciliation.

Anamnesis

The anamnesis follows the memorial acclamation with its usual textual options. The eucharistic action is seen as "the pledge of his (Christ's) love" entrusted to the Church. As we celebrate the death and resurrection of Christ, we bring before the Father the "sacrifice of reconciliation" which is Christ; at the same time we bring ourselves to the Father and ask him to accept both offerings.

Epiclesis II

The Spirit, who was asked to sanctify the gifts, is asked to come upon us by our participation in the eucharistic meal that our divisions may be removed. Clearly the Holy Spirit is given a prominent role in this anaphora. The Spirit transforms our hearts and our world through the gifts which we share in the sacred meal.

Intercessions

Since the Spirit takes "away all that divides us," the Spirit also unites us in a communion of love: Pope, bishop, all the bishops, and all the people. United by the Spirit, the Church becomes "a sign of unity and an instrument of your (God's) peace."

The Church, united at the table of the Lord, is also united in a fellowship of love with the saints.

The eschatological theme, so prominent in the first reconciliation anaphora, is continued in the last part of the intercessions where we pray:

> In that new world where the fullness of your peace will be revealed,
> gather people of every race, language, and way of life
> to share in the one eternal banquet
> with Jesus Christ the Lord.

The eucharist, then, is a foretaste of the eternal eschatological banquet where all divisions cease.

The anaphora concludes with the customary doxology.

These two eucharistic prayers present different aspects of the one mystery of reconciliation: it is accomplished by the death of Christ on the cross and it is made effective in our lives by the Holy Spirit. By our sharing in the saving bread and cup, in the sacrifice of Christ, we are reconciled in the Lord Jesus and given a taste of that final reconciliation of all things in Christ.

Conclusion

Up to the Second Vatican Council the Latin Church prayed one anaphora characteristic of the ancient Roman Church. Now the Church has been enriched with five new eucharistic prayers which help to express the manifold aspects of the eucharistic mystery. Certainly these new prayers do not exhaust our understanding of what we do when we take bread and wine and give thanks and praise. Yet they help us to lift up our hearts to the Lord so that

> through Christ,
> with him,
> in him,
> in the unity of the Holy Spirit,
> all glory and honor is yours,
> almighty Father,
> for ever and ever.
> Amen.

NOTES

1. A. Nocent, "La celebrazione dell'eucaristia secondo il 'canone romano,' " in *Anamnesis*, Vol. 3, part 2, S. Marsili, ed. (Casale Monfito: Marietti, 1983), p. 233.

2. R.C.D. Jasper and G.J. Cuming, ed., *Prayers of the Eucharist: Early and Reformed* (London: Collins, 1975), p. 98.

3. A. Bouley, *From Freedom to Formula: The Evolution of the Eucharistic Prayer from Oral Improvisation to Written Texts*, The Catholic University of America Studies in Christian Antiquity, No. 21 (Washington: The Catholic University of America Press, 1981), p. 205.

4. E. Mazza, *Le odierne pregliere eucaristiche*, Vol. I, (Bologna: Edizioni Dehoniane, 1984), p. 78.

5. Ibid., p. 79.

6. Ibid.

7. Ibid.

8. A. Nocent, p. 236.

9. Ibid., p. 237.

10. Ibid.

11. Ibid., p. 238.

12. A. Bouley, p. 206. See also, L.C. Mohlberg, et al., ed., *Sacramentarium Veronense*, R.E.D., Series Major, Fontes 1 (Rome: Herder, 1956, reprint ed., 1978), p. 201.

13. A. Nocent, p. 239.

14. Ibid., p. 240.

15. Ibid., p. 241.
16. Ibid.
17. Ibid.
18. Ibid.
19. M. Andrieu, ed., *Les Textes (Ordines XIV–XXXIV)*, Spicilegium Sacrum Lovaniense Études et Documents, Fasc 24 (Louvain: Spicilegium Sacrum Lovaniense, 1951, reprint ed., 1974), Nos. 39–40, p. 103.
20. A. Nocent, pp. 241–242.
21.

> All glory and honor is yours,
> Father and Son,
> with the Holy Spirit
> in the Holy Church,
> now and for ever. Amen.

(*Eucharistic Prayer of Hippolytus* (Washington: International Commission on English in the Liturgy, 1983), p. 9.)
22. Text in St. Ambrose, *De Sacramentis*, Book 6:24:

> Through our Lord Jesus Christ, in whom and with whom honour, praise, glory, magnificence and power are yours, with the Holy Spirit, from the ages, and now, and always, and to all the ages of ages. Amen. (R.C.D. Jasper, p. 100.)

23. "in primis gloriosae semper Virginis Mariae, Genetricis Dei et domini nostri Iesu Christi; sed et *beati Ioseph ejusdem Virginis Sponsi.* . . . "
24. The work of the Consilium and the working group is described in Archbishop Armibale Bugininis, *La riforma liturgica (1948–1975)* (Rome: Edizioni Liturgiche, 1983).
25. *Cœtus* X consisted of J. Wagner, A. Franquesa, T. Schnitzler, A. Hänggi, P. Journel, L. Agustoni, P. Gy, A. Jungmann, G. Gelineau, L. Bouyer, H. Wegman, L. Ligier, F. McManus, B. Botte, C. Vagaggini, G. Gellier, G. Patino, S. Famoso, A. Lentini.
26. C. Vagaggini, *The Canon of the Mass and Liturgical Reform* (Staten Island: Alba House, 1967).
27. Ibid., pp. 79–83.
28. Ibid., pp. 76–79.
29. Ibid., pp. 114–118.
30. Ibid., pp. 118–122.
31. Ibid., p. 123.
32. A. Buginini, p. 444.
33. Ibid.
34. Ibid., p. 445.
35. Ibid.
36. Ibid.
37. Ibid., pp. 445–447.
38. The official English text provides two translations of the first Latin acclamation:

> Christ has died,
> Christ is risen,
> Christ will come again.
>
> Dying you destroyed our death,
> rising you restored our life.
> Lord Jesus, come in glory.

39. Ibid., p. 447.

40. Ibid., p. 448.

41. 2 for Advent, 1 for the Sundays of Lent, 2 for Sundays, 1 for the eucharist, 2 common prefaces.

42. Ibid., p. 457.

43. Ibid., p. 460.

44. Ibid., pp. 467–468. The letter was dated April 27, 1973 and was published on June 14, 1973.

45. Ibid., pp. 470–471.

46. Ibid., pp. 473–475. The prayers and the norms for their use were issued in a mimeographed format and the booklet containing them was dated November 1, 1974.

47. Ibid., pp. 474–475.

48. Ibid., p. 474, note 48.

49. Ibid., p. 475.

50. Consilium, *Guidelines "Au cours des derniers mois,"* to assist catechesis on the anaphoras of the Mass, 2 June 1968, in *Documents on the Liturgy, 1963–1979: Conciliar, Papal, and Curial Texts*, International Commission on English in the Liturgy (Collegeville: The Liturgical Press, 1982), p. 616.

51. This impression is given by the conclusion, "Per Christum Dominum nostrum. Amen" which ends five of the prayers.

52. The Latin text provides three texts for the acclamation, whereas the English version has four acclamations (see note 38, above).

53. A. Bouley, pp. 214–215.

54. C. Vagaggini, pp. 84–107.

55. Ibid., pp. 84–85.

56. Ibid., p. 85.

57. Ibid., p. 87.

58. Ibid.

59. Ibid., p. 88.

60. Ibid., p. 89.

61. Ibid., p. 93.

62. Ibid., p. 94.

63. Ibid., p. 95.

64. Ibid., p. 96.

65. Ibid., p. 97.

66. Ibid.

67. Ibid., p. 100.

68. Ibid., p. 101.
69. Ibid., p. 106.
70.

> Priest: Let us proclaim the mystery of faith:
> People: Christ has died,
> People: Christ is risen,
>   Christ will come again.

Or one of the other acclamations.

71. *Coetus* X.
72. This anaphora dates from approximately the middle of the third century.
73. E. Mazza, p. 124, note 10.
74. A comment of Dom A. Nocent is worth noting:

> But, besides this desire to have a likeness between the eucharistic prayers, there was above all, an imperiosity, a certain theological mentality. It needed to leave to the words of Christ, pronounced during the institution of the eucharist, all their consecratory value. (A. Nocent, "La liturgia eucaristia: teologia e storia della celebrazione," in *Anamnesis*, Vol. 3, Part 2, S. Marsili, ed. (Casale Monfito: Marietti, 1983), p. 251.)

75. E. Mazza, p. 125.
76. A. Nocent, "La liturgia," p. 252.
77. Ibid., p. 251.
78. E. Mazza, p. 126.
79. One reading of the passage that contains these terms is:

> Of his own free choice
> he was handed over to his passion
> in order to make an end of death
> and to shatter the chains of the evil one;
> to trample underfoot the powers of hell
> and to lead the righteous into light;
> to establish the boundaries of death
> and to manifest the resurrection.
> (*Eucharistic Prayer of Hippolytus*, p. 9)

80. C. Vagaggini, *The Canon of the Mass and Liturgical Reform.*
81. E. Mazza, p. 167.
82. Ibid., p. 165.
83. *The New Eucharistic Prayers and Prefaces* (Washington: National Conference of Catholic Bishops, 1968), p. 43.
84. C. Vagaggini, p. 175.
85. S. Marsili, "Le nuove preghiere eucaristiche. Problematica e commento," in *Preghiere eucaristiche: testo e commento*, F. Dell'Oro, ed. (Torino: Elle di Ci, 1968), p. 111.
86. E. Mazza, p. 195.
87. Lord, we pray that in your goodness and mercy your Holy Spirit may descend

upon us, and upon these gifts, sanctify them to be holy gifts for your holy people, the bread of life and the cup of salvation, the Body and Blood of your son Jesus Christ.

Grant that all who share this bread and cup may become one body and one spirit, a living sacrifice in Christ, to the praise of your Name.

("Common Eucharistic Prayer" (Eucharistic Prayer D) in *The Book of Common Prayer, 1979* (New York: The Church Hymnal Corporation and Seabury Press, 1979), p. 375.

88. *General Instruction of the Roman Missal,* No. 55f.

89. *Lumen gentium,* no. 16.

90. See also, Eucharistic Prayer III:

We hope to enjoy the vision of your glory, through Christ our Lord, from whom all good things come.

91. E. Mazza, p. 237.

JOHN BARRY RYAN

2

Eucharistic Prayers for Masses with Children

Eucharistic prayers composed for congregations where children form a majority of the worshiping community are the fruit of the principle of adaptation taken to its logical conclusion. The novelty that this represents for our time, while an outcome of the Second Vatican Council, must be set in the larger context of liturgical renewal in our century.

Five years after Pius X affirmed the practice of frequent and daily reception of holy communion, he prescribed the age of discretion as the time to fulfill the precept of holy communion.[1] As a result, in the mid-decades of this century, it was not unusual to see row upon row of children communicate while adults at another Sunday Mass, often in some other place in the larger parishes, went rarely to communion on Sunday, except at the great feasts of Christmas or Easter.

While the priest read the Mass in Latin, religious educators had the children recite prayers, read from small missals or prayerbooks or sing hymns. From around 1940 on, the dialog Mass, in which the congregation responded to the priest in Latin, became an increasingly popular form of active participation.[2] Although even before the Second Vatican Council, there were those who found difficulty with separating children from adults to form a group apart for the celebration of the Sunday eucharist, it was a widespread practice that was tied into the Catholic school system that often had one or more weekday Masses for school children. After the Council, the movement to have families attend worship together on Sunday resulted in the disappearance of the special Sunday celebrations for congregations of children but it still left intact the weekday school celebrations, even if they were now less frequent than before. Since the Constitution on the Sacred Liturgy had said that provisions were to be made for legitimate adaptations to different groups, regions and peoples, it was normal that such weekday children's Masses should be seen as a case in point.[3] It was for such Masses that the *Directory for Masses with Children* was composed.[4] This Directory gave many examples of possible adaptation within the Mass on the principle that children truly experience, in their own way and according to the psychological patterns of childhood, the "mystery of faith . . . by means of rites and prayers" (no. 38). For the eucharistic prayers, it merely said that the four approved for Masses with adults should be used until the Apostolic See makes other provision for Masses with children (no. 52).

But already many proposals had been sent to Rome for permission for special eucharistic prayers for various groups of young people, especially teenagers. In 1970, German-speaking countries had been given permission to adapt one of the adult prayers for use with deaf children, and in 1971 the Philippines had received permission for a children's prayer for first communion. In 1972, a eucharistic prayer for children was approved for use at the International Eucharistic Conference at Melbourne, and in Switzerland Eucharistic Prayers I and IV were adapted for use in Masses with children. Meanwhile, national liturgical committees in various countries were preparing experimental prayers as were individuals having no official backing.

I. Composition of the Children's Eucharistic Prayers[5]

On May 3, 1973, the Congregation for Divine Worship asked Paul VI for permission to prepare one or two eucharistic prayers for Masses with children. On October 23, the Pope replied that two or three such prayers should be prepared. A special group, several of whom had worked on the Directory, was immediately established to work on the desired prayers. The members of this group were Balthasar Fischer, chairman (Germany), Reiner Kaczynski, secretary (Germany), André Haquin (Belgium), Vicenti Pedrosa (Spain), Heinrich Rennings (Germany), Gilberto Agustoni[6] (Switzerland), Philippe Béguerie (France), Peter Coughlan (England), Gottardo Pasqualetti (Italy), Didier Rimaud (France) and, later, Joseph Gelineau (France).

On October 30, 1973, the members of the study group received a fifty-four page booklet that contained thirty-eight different eucharistic prayers for Masses with children. In addition, there were three prayers from the French-speaking International Commission for Translations. These contained prayers from Canada, France and Belgium. Rennings presented a text from the Union of German Catechists and the Liturgical Institute of Trier, West Germany.

At its first meeting, November 13–15, the study group discussed the distinctiveness of eucharistic prayers for Masses with children and how the proposed texts should be evaluated. Since most of the texts in the booklet received heavy criticism, the French-speaking members suggested that their texts be adopted. After discussion, it was decided to choose three texts to form the basis for discussion and possible adaptation. According to Kaczynski, these were Eucharistic Prayers I and II from the French and Eucharistic Prayer III from the German.[7] After being revised, they were translated into English (I, II, and III), Spanish (I and II), Italian (I and II) and French (III) and sent out to experts around the world for their reaction. From this group, thirty-three replies were received.

At the next meeting of the work group, January 16–18, 1974, two observers from the Congregation for the Faith, Benoit Duroux and Marcellino Zalba, were present. Each of the three proposed texts were further studied and amended. They were sent on to Carlo Egger, Substitute for the Secretary of State, who oversaw their translation into Latin. The vernacular and Latin translations were returned to the work group for more observations. On February 27 to March 1, Fischer, Gelineau, Rennings and Rimaud met with Duroux, Zalba and Egger to go over the final editing of the prayers. Peter Coughlan was present at this meeting for the English language version. On March 7, after the translations had been reviewed in minute detail, they were sent on to the Congregation for the Faith. On May 10, Archbishop Hamer, the Secretary for this Congregation, wrote the Congregation for Worship that Paul VI had approved the children's eucharistic prayers as well as the decision of the Congregation for the Faith that one of the children's prayers be published but not inserted into the missal and that this prayer not be translated freely into the vernacular.

On May 15, 1974, Cardinal Knox was named prefect of the Congregation for Worship. He sent Cardinal Villot, the Secretary of State, the three texts of the children's eucharistic prayers and a copy of his answer to the Congregation for the Faith as well as a seven page letter telling why that Congregation's decisions were unacceptable: it had not made any suggestions about the faith but took a position on the number of texts that contradicted the Pope's original permission that had spoken of two or three prayers. Knox's letter concluded with three requests: (1) at least two prayers be approved; (2) the approved prayers be allowed in the appendix of the sacramentary; (3) with the exception of the Lord's words in the institution narrative, a free translation be permitted.

On June 3, the Pope replied through Cardinal Villot that the Congregation for the Faith should be followed. On June 21, the Congregation for Worship made a counter proposal: instead of Rome proposing a single text, let the bishops conferences make the choice from the three texts and, for non-European language areas, permit a free translation. This way out of the impasse was elaborated only after Bugnini, the secretary for the Congregation for Worship, had seen the Pope the day previously and had been told to find a way to resolve the problem.[8]

No immediate answer was made to this proposal, but on September 5, Archbishop Hamer wrote Bugnini that the May 10 communiqué from his office had not included suggestions about the doctrinal content in the children's eucharistic prayers and that a letter would follow. On September 24, the Congregation for Worship received the doctrinal suggestions, which turned out to be minor corrections easily assimilated into the texts. The amended eucharistic prayers were sent the following day to Cardinal Villot with a request that a course of action be taken with regard to the suggestions made in the June 21 letter from the Congregation for Worship.

On October 26, Cardinal Villot wrote the final answer:

(1) the three eucharistic prayers are to be allowed *ad experimentum* for a three year period but not to be published officially and not to be inserted into the missal;
(2) the texts may be sent to the chairmen of the bishops' conferences which request them; one text may be chosen;
(3) the texts may be freely translated but must keep the idea of the Latin text and render the Lord's words faithfully;
(4) it must be decided for which Masses and for which age groups the eucharistic prayers are suitable.

On November 1, the Congregation for Worship made available a booklet containing the prayers and the essence of Cardinal Villot's letter. The English translation of these prayers was prepared by the International Commission on English in the Liturgy. In 1975, the prayers were approved as provisional texts by the Executive Committee of the National Conference of Catholic Bishops. In June, the confirmation of the Apostolic See was obtained and permitted the use of these provisional texts for three years until the end of 1977. On December 19, 1977, at the request of the Bishops' Committee on the Liturgy, permission was sought from the Apostolic See to use the three prayers for an additional three years. The Congregation for the Sacraments and Divine Worship (created in 1975 to replace the existing Congregation for Worship) responded favorably to this request by extending the period of provisional use until the end of 1980, but indicated that at that time the use and effectiveness of the three prayers would be reevaluated by the Congregation in light of the experience of the whole Church. If judged to be acceptable and beneficial, the definitive texts would then be prepared and promulgated by the Apostolic See for insertion into the Roman Missal. In 1981, permission for the continued use of these prayers was given with no specific limiting date attached.[9] They now find their place in the most recent edition of the Sacramentary in English.

II. Commentary on the Children's Eucharistic Prayers Preliminary Remarks

In any discussion of these prayers, it must be remembered that they were first used *ad experimentum*. This in itself is significant, for it means that eucharistic prayers can exist in an in-between zone of not officially publishable and yet actually used in liturgies throughout the world. In some sense, therefore, they form part of the *lex orandi*. This is one reason why they were involved in a very elaborate process of approval.

The prayers are restricted to Masses which are celebrated for children only or to Masses at which the majority of participants are children. The community of children envisaged in the preface to the prayers is one consisting of children who have not yet reached the age of pre-adolescence. Since pre-adolescence generally refers to children around eleven or twelve years old, those who have not yet entered pre-adolescence and still would be gathered for Mass are probably the six to ten year old children. However, in the practical order, any such distinction is probably often not taken into account. The Bishops' Committee on the Liturgy questionnaire of 1977 asked, "With what age group(s) are these Masses with children celebrated?" There were 4,521 responses: pre-school, 5%; primary grades (K-1-2-3), 31%; intermediate (4-5-6), 32%; junior high (7-8-9), 28%; other, 4%.[10]

The children's prayers are meant to lead children to the celebration of Masses with adults, especially those that assemble the entire community on Sunday. Thus, the children's prayers were to be like and unlike the adult's prayers. They are already meant to be a form of catechesis. At the same time, formal catechesis on the eucharistic liturgy and the Christian faith find a natural starting point with these prayers.

1. The Structure of the Prayers

In general, the structure of the prayers remains the same as the 1968 prayers, with a few exceptions. Some elements in the children's prayers and the 1968 prayers are identical in wording: the introductory dialogue, the Lord's words, and the closing doxology. All other elements receive new wording.

In children's prayer I, the expression of communion with the Pope and the bishop, found after the epiclesis on the community in the 1968 prayers, becomes part of the preface and is an expression of a communion of praise throughout the world as well as a vertical movement of praise from earth to that of the saints, with Mary and the apostles and the angels in heaven. Thus, this part of the preface is also an introduction to the sanctus.

The acclamations found after the institution narrative in the 1968 prayers are found after the anamnesis offering in children's prayer I. In children's II, there is an acclamation after each set of the Lord's words. In children's III, the acclamation is found as a brief refrain. Children's II is punctuated from beginning to end with brief responsorial acclamations.

None of the elements which the Roman Church regards as necessary, integral and important for a eucharistic prayer is missing in the children's prayers.

2. The Elements of the Prayers Considered Separately

The Preface

Children's I has a preface divided into three parts. The first part praises and thanks God for his creation; the second part tells what Jesus did for us; the third part joins the children's praise with that of the wider Church and the communion of saints. Each part corresponds to a part of the sanctus-benedictus: the first to "Heaven and earth are full of your glory"; the second to "Blessed is he who comes in the name of the Lord"; the third to "Holy, holy, holy Lord, God of power and might." The English translation of prayer I violates this intended progression when it gives the entire sanctus as the response after the first part.

Children's II is a dialogic hymn of praise around the theme of love.

Children's III is a brief thanksgiving for creation seen in terms of relationships. It comes with a variation for the Easter season.

The Post-Sanctus

Children's I briefly ties in with the holy from the sanctus.

Children's II, using "Blessed is he who comes in the name of the Lord" as its starting point, has a brief Christological development that repeats the benedictus.

Children's III makes use of the transition from the "holy" to introduce a brief Christological prayer. There is a variation for the Easter season.

The First Epiclesis

Perhaps what is most noticeable is the use of the word "change" in children's II and III, for it is not found in the Latin, French, or German, all of which have "that they may become (for us) the body and blood of Jesus. . . . " Nor is the word "change" found in the 1968 prayers. It seems to me to be a word more at home in talking about the eucharist than within the prayer itself.

Children's I takes a cue from the Byzantine anaphora by adding, "Then we can offer to you what you have given to us."

The Institution Narrative

What is most noticeable about this element is the language that is used. Here, as in other parts of the prayers, the name "Jesus" is used without any qualifying titles: "Jesus took the cup" (I). The familiar expressiveness of "Jesus was having supper with his apostles" (I) or "When he was at supper with his disciples" (II) or " . . . he had supper for the last time with his disciples" (III) is not found in the 1968 prayers. Furthermore, each of the children's prayers uses the expression, " . . . gave [the bread] to his *friends* . . . " (my emphasis).

As has already been noted, Children's II introduces acclamations after each set of the Lord's words.

In all the prayers, the use of the introductory words, "Then he said to them," before "Do this in memory of me," is meant to enable children to distinguish more clearly what is said over the bread and wine and what refers to the continuation of the celebration.

The Anamnesis Offering

In each of the prayers the offering is expressed differently. However, each prayer refers to Jesus' offering and the offering of the Church. Prayers I and III also refer to the faithful offering themselves with Christ to the Father: "Jesus brings us to you; welcome us as you welcome him" (I) and "Father in heaven, accept us together with your beloved Son" (III).

While the expression of the anamnesis is short in I and II, it is greatly amplified in III, which divides it by means of a refrain into three parts. In its explicitness and with its distinctions, one is reminded that prayer III was originally proposed by the Union of German Catechists.

The Second Epiclesis

Two things are to be noted about the wording of the epiclesis. First, unlike the 1968 prayers, which purposely stress the unity of the Church in Christ, none of these prayers does so, although II does allude to the concept of unity as it moves from the epiclesis into the intercessions. Prayers I and III ask the Father to fill the communicants with the joy of the Holy Spirit, and prayer II asks that the Holy Spirit be sent to all who share in the meal.

This leads to the second observation. In each of the prayers, there is the same suppleness of language that is found in the institution narrative as well as throughout the prayers. Here it is through the use of the word "table" in I and III and the word "meal" in II.

Intercessions

The intercessions tend to be inclusive: "Remember everyone who is suffering pain and sorrow" (I); "Remember Christians everywhere and all other people in the world" (I); "Remember all those we do not love as we should" (II); "Remember those who have died" (II); "Help all who follow Jesus to work for peace and bring happiness to others" (III).

III. Final Remarks

It must be remembered that motives for thanksgiving may be invited from the children before the dialogue of the eucharistic prayer. Such a practice allows for a contemporary response and for a rootedness in the experience of the children. At the same time, from beginning to end, the children are being led by adults, and these children's prayers are adult's prayers. Thus the values expressed in the prayers are values that adults want to pass on to their children. In effect, the prayers are saying, "This is the Church to which you belong." A creed for children could be constructed from the thought content of the prayers. I do not wish to develop it at length here, but it would look something like this:

I believe in God who is a good and loving Father; he gathers us together at the eucharist; he created the world and us. He sent Jesus.

I believe in Jesus, the Son of God; he healed people, forgave sinners and died for us. He sent the Holy Spirit.

I believe in the Holy Spirit, who is active in the Church and in our eucharist. The Holy Spirit fills us with joy.

I believe in the Church which thanks and praises God and remembers Jesus and is filled with the Holy Spirit. I am part of it with the Pope and the bishop, with my friends and my family, with Mary, the Mother of God, and the apostles and the saints.

In 1977, the Bishops' Committee on the Liturgy prepared a questionnaire to evaluate the use and effectiveness of the 1973 *Directory for Masses with Children* as well as the 1974 (1975) eucharistic prayers. A total of 2,095 questionnaires were returned for tabulation. The summary evaluation was that there was overwhelming acceptance of the new eucharistic prayers for children. Like the proper implementation of the *Directory*, the prayers assist the children in their participation at Mass, but greater familiarity with the texts and additional musical settings for the acclamations would further assist the pastoral usefulness of the new prayers. The BCL report concludes with two new musical settings for the acclamations in each of the three eucharistic prayers.[11]

NOTES

1. "The Daily Reception of Holy Communion" and "The Age for Admission to First Communion" in R. Kevin Seasoltz, *The New Liturgy: A Documentation, 1903–1965* (New York: Herder and Herder 1966), 11–15 and 17–22.

2. Gerald Ellard even assembled a whole book about it, *The Dialog Mass: A Book for Priests and Teachers of Religion* (New York: Longmans, Green and Co. 1942).

3. *Constitution on the Liturgy*, no. 38 in *Documents on the Liturgy, 1963–1979: Conciliar, Papal, and Curial Texts* (Collegeville, MN: The Liturgical Press 1982), 12.

4. *Directory for Masses with Children* in *Documents on the Liturgy*, 676–688.

5. The information in this section is found in two accounts that cover more or less the same ground, that of Reiner Kaczynski, "Direktorium and Hochgebetstexte für Messfeiern mit Kindern," *Liturgisches Jahrbuch* (1979), 157–175 and Annibale Bugnini, *La riforma liturgica (1948–1975)* (Rome: CLV—Edizioni Liturgiche 1983), 470–475.

6. Bugnini has L. Agustoni. Luigi Agustoni like Gilberto Agustoni was a

consultor from Switzerland, but Kaczynski is clear in identifying Gilberto Agustoni as a member of this particular group, Kaczynski, 167, Bugnini, 471.

7. Bugnini says that Eucharistic Prayer I was from a Belgian-Dutch model, but according to Kaczynski's account it was from a French Canadian model, Bugnini, 471, Kaczynski, 168–169.

8. Bugnini, 473.

9. *Notitiae* 17 (1981), 23.

10. *BCL Report: The Directory for Masses with Children* and *Eucharistic Prayers for Children* (Washington, D. C.: Bishops' Committee on the Liturgy 1979), 15.

11. *BCL Report*, the summary evaluation is on p. 9 and the musical settings on pp. 19–36.

H. BOONE PORTER

3

Episcopal Anaphoral Prayers

For the study of prayers of consecration in Christian liturgy, the Book of Common Prayer of the Episcopal Church in the United States offers a substantial amount of data. The Episcopal Church is part of the Anglican Communion, and the American Prayer Book is related to other versions of the Book of Common Prayer, but the present American book, adopted in 1979 after many years of preliminary work, is the most extensive revision of the Book of Common Prayer to have taken place anywhere in the English speaking world. In it, there are no less than six complete prayers provided for use as the Great Thanksgiving in the Holy Eucharist, and there are two additional less complete forms. All of this material is in current use. Thus we have a significant flowering of this particular genre of solemn corporate prayer.[1]

I. Historical Background and Liturgical Context

The liturgical position of the Episcopal Church in America is unique in the Anglican Communion in that it entered the twentieth century without any living memory of the use of the Communion Office of the classic English Prayer Book. The Episcopal Church had adopted its own Prayer Book in 1789. The eucharistic prayer of consecration in the American book was based on the distinctive prayer of the Scottish Non-jurors, which was inspired by the Liturgy of St. James. In Amer-

63

ica it was fitted into a liturgy of the English type. The adoption of such an anaphoral prayer was partially due to the influence of the first American bishop, Samuel Seabury of Connecticut, who was consecrated in Scotland, but others also desired it. Such a prayer met the standards of church leaders who had studied John Johnson's *Unbloody Sacrifice* (1714 and 1724)[2] and similar Anglican writings. At the same time, the American prayer was so moderately worded that it did not fall within the arena of serious controversy between Evangelicals and High Churchmen. During the decades which followed, in America as elsewhere, the knowledge of older Anglican sacramental teaching eroded, but Americans were glad to have an anaphoral prayer which was more expressive and more traditional than that of their British and Canadian cousins. The American eucharistic prayer was reaffirmed in the revisions of the American Prayer Book in 1892 and 1928.

When Prayer Book revision again began to be seriously addressed by the standing liturgical commission of the Episcopal Church in the 1960s, the major goal for the Holy Eucharist was to make it a suitable vehicle for the normal public worship on Sunday of all members of the Episcopal Church, of all schools of thought. A rehabilitation of the pro-anaphora was undertaken, with an Old Testament lesson, psalmody, and a three-year lectionary. A mitigation of the previously pervasive atmosphere of penitence, the addition of flexible and varied intercessions, more opportunity for lay participation, and fuller articulation of the church year were all seen as needed. We may perceive a significant shifting into the eucharistic liturgy of themes and emphases formerly associated in Anglican usage with Morning and Evening Prayer and the Litany: creation, the history of Israel, the incarnation, and intercession for those outside of the church. Successive drafts of parts of the projected new Prayer Book were published from 1966 to 1975. Baptism, Confirmation, Marriage, and Burial all appeared, not as they had been in the context of choir offices, but in specialized forms of the pro-anaphora. The rest of the Eucharist can, and usually does, follow. So too is the case with special rites for Ash Wednesday and Palm Sunday. Although extensive space is devoted to the daily offices, the new American Prayer Book is eucharistically centered. It may also be noted that Morning or Evening Prayer may serve as the pro-anaphora, the liturgy continuing with the offertory and consecration.

All of this, it must be understood, has had a direct bearing on the anaphoral prayer. The historic American prayer was recognized by many as too lengthy to hold the attention of worshipers. At the same time, in the context of the projected new liturgy, many additions were called for. If the Old Testament was a regular element in the reading and preaching, should it be ignored in the climactic prayer of the service? If frequently used after Baptism and other parochial occasions, must not the anaphora reflect a wider range of intentions? Finally, could any one prayer possibly be short enough for constant use and at the same time also include these added themes?

Before such a question could be answered, it was decided that, whereas the new American Prayer Book as a whole was to be in modern English, Morning and Evening Prayer, the Holy Eucharist, and Burial would have a Rite One in the traditional sixteenth century Prayer Book idiom, as well as a Rite Two in contemporary speech. Generally speaking, Rite One resembles similar revisions elsewhere in the Anglican Communion. Rite Two is a more thorough revision, and is not unlike contemporary Lutheran and Roman Catholic liturgies. In both rites, the rubrics are very flexible, and permit many different combinations of materials. Some of these variations may be reflective of the church year. Even further variation is possible in an Order for Celebrating the Holy Eucharist (sometimes incorrectly referred to as "Rite Three") designed to guide those who are planning services for unusual or less formal occasions, or for use in private houses or various secular settings.

II. Rite One

The first anaphoral prayer of the first rite, given in traditional Prayer Book English, continues in wide use. The material contained in it has been discussed many times. The importance of the prayers in Rite One for our present analysis is that they show how traditional forms, in a slightly altered context, can acquire new depths of meaning.

Eucharistic Prayer I is printed in a place in Rite One (pp. 333–36. All page citations in the text are to the Book of Common Prayer, New York, 1979)[3] with the salutation and sursum corda immediately following the offertory. It is in fact the very prayer which has appeared in all editions of the American Prayer Book for nearly two centuries. Following the pattern inherited from the Non-jurors of Scotland, it has post-sanctus leading to words of institution, anamnesis (containing "we now offer unto thee"), invocation rather mildly worded, and long prayer of acceptance (including self-oblation of the worshipers) leading to final Amen. These words have not been changed. What is new is the extensive provisions for proper prefaces, the restoration of the "Blessed is he who comes" and the rubric for the manual acts.

No less than twenty two proper prefaces are now provided (pp.

344–49). These cover all special seasons, feasts, and such occasions as Baptism and Marriage. Ferial weekdays in the periods after Epiphany and Pentecost are the only times when a proper preface might not be used. Thus a far more animated relationship to the history of salvation is brought about.

For ordinary Sundays after Epiphany or after Pentecost, there is a choice of three prefaces, one referring to the creation and light, another speaking of the resurrection "on the first day," and the third referring to "water and the Holy Spirit." Assuming that each of these will be used many times every year, a foundation is laid for expressing the relation of the eucharistic consecration to creation, to Sunday, to the resurrection, to Baptism, and to the community renewed by the Holy Spirit. Such a relationship remains, however, somewhat implicit, and it hardly thrusts itself on the uninformed worshiper.

As to the manual acts, a new rubric occurs immediately before the words of institution, and it is repeated in each of the other anaphoral prayers in the Proposed Book. This rubric is deliberately permissive. Imposition of the hand on the bread and cup or a modest elevation is equally legitimate. The breaking of bread is now delayed until after the Lord's Prayer and is emphasized. The sequence of offertory, The Great Thanksgiving (so described by a section heading in the text), fraction, and administration of Holy Communion is very clear. Gregory Dix's teaching about the consecratory prayer as primarily a thanksgiving had been gladly received among American Episcopalians as a helpful elucidation of their own prayer, the source of which had been framed as a thanksgiving by the Non-juror divines. Thus we see, in the case of Eucharistic Prayer I, that an old formulary has indeed been renewed and enriched by a new frame of reference.

Some pages later (pp. 340–43), Eucharistic Prayer II is provided as an option for Rite One.[4] The introductory part and proper prefaces are identical with Prayer I. The rest of it is a revision and shortening of Prayer I. Added material includes a reference in the post-sanctus to creation and the incarnation ("... to take our nature upon him"), and reference to the second coming in the anamnesis. The invocation is more objective ("that they may be unto us the Body and Blood ..."). Prayer II is very closely related, in content if not in language, to Eucharistic Prayers A and B of Rite Two which we will consider.

III. Rite Two

We now come to the primary objects of our consideration in this essay, the rich theological and literary material of the four complete anaphoral prayers for the Holy Eucharist in contemporary language. All four of these prayers are to begin right after the offertory, with the same salutation and sursum corda. All use the ICET sanctus with "Blessed is he who comes." All have the same rubric for the manual acts. All are followed by the Lord's Prayer and the breaking of the bread. Eucharistic Prayer A, which is most frequently used, is printed at the proper point in Rite Two (pp. 361–63). Prayers B, C, and D are given as alternatives some pages later (pp. 367–75). The rubrics do not indicate whether certain of these are especially suitable to particular times or occasions. Such a judgment is left to the priest or others planning the service. Some opinions will be expressed, however, by the present author.

Let us then consider Prayer A.[5] After "Hosanna in the highest," the priest continues with a relatively brief post-sanctus referring to the creation and fall of man, and the redemption achieved by Christ on the cross. There follow words of institution, congregational acclamation, anamnesis (with "we offer you these gifts"), epiclesis (with "sanctify them by your Holy Spirit to be the Body and Blood . . ."), petition for salvation, and concluding doxology and Amen.

Although inspired by the historic American prayer and an earlier proposed revision of it authorized for use in 1967, this relatively brief prayer was drafted as a fresh composition in 1969, at Evanston, Illinois, in circumstances directly involving the present author. As it was intended that proper prefaces would be used with this prayer on all major occasions of public worship, it was not deemed necessary to develop at length within the fixed part of the prayer those themes which would frequently be expressed in the prefaces. In other words, not everything needs to be said on every occasion. Rite Two also has twenty-two proper prefaces, differing little from those of Rite One, including the three commonly used prefaces for ordinary Sundays. In Rite Two the word "Creator" does not occur in the first Sunday preface, however, because this word is in the fixed part of the preface.

In regard to the atonement, the intention was to replace Cranmer's rather juridical imagery by what is essentially a suggested visual picture of Christ on the cross, the one in whom the image and likeness of God is perfectly disclosed, lifted up and drawing all mankind unto himself. "He stretched out his arms upon the cross, and offered himself, in obedience to your will, a perfect sacrifice for the whole world." There is no attempt here to explain or define sacrifice, but rather to express and celebrate the reality of that sacrifice, allowing it to have its own impact. The allusion to God's will was intended by the original drafter as a cue tying the prayer to Hebrews 10:9–10 and Psalm 40.

Christ's command to remember him is carried out in the acclamation in which the people join the priest, and in the brief paragraph following. This is a drastic condensation of the historic American anamnesis, but it differs from the latter in closely associating "this sacrifice of praise and thanksgiving" with the offering of the gifts.

In the epiclesis, a reference to "holy food and drink" amplifies the designation of Christ's Body and Blood, and emphasizes the acts of eating and drinking. The action of the Holy Spirit in the worshipers as well as in the elements is implied in the phrase, "Sanctify us also. . . ." The effects of communion, for this life and the life to come, are then-briefly indicated.

Eucharistic Prayer B[6] is in many ways similar to A. It has the same opening preface as A, and utilizes the same proper prefaces. The words of institution and the concluding doxology are also the same.

While remaining within the framework of A, B was intended to have emphases different from the former and to provide a significant option for various times of year. Whereas the post-sanctus of A reflects the historic Anglican preoccupation with the crucifixion, B calls attention to the history of Israel, culminating in the incarnation, and the Virgin Mary is referred to. In this prayer, as in A, the influence of the *Apostolic Tradition* is obvious. This prayer seems especially suitable in the Christmas and Epiphany seasons.

The acclamation of priest and people in the long form "We remember his death . . . " is an integral part of the anamnesis: the priest does not repeat a reference to the death, resurrection and second coming. The bread and wine are presented "to you, from your creation."

The epiclesis is rather objective in relation to the gifts. The sanctification of the worshipers is in terms derived from Romans 15:16, indicating their self-oblation through Christ. Again it is the intention to be suggestive rather than restrictive in speaking of the eucharistic mystery. The eschatological petition is based in part on 1 Corinthians 15:23–28. The reference to the saints makes the prayer particularly useful on saints' days. The accumulation of titles of Jesus Christ, "the first born of all creation, the head of the Church, and the author of our salvation," reflects Colossians 1:15–20, again a remarkably suggestive passage. This prayer as a whole is strongly Pauline in character, but in a different way from Cranmer's eucharistic prayers.

Prayer C[7] was first published in 1970 for experimental use within the order for an informal liturgy. It was composed by Howard Galley, an evangelist of the Church Army, who was engaged in editorial work for the standing liturgical commission. Its widespread acceptance led to its later inclusion in Rite Two. This is a prayer unique both in its style and in its arrangement. After the usual sursum corda, it proceeds as follows, without proper preface, continuing the alternation between the chief celebrant and the congregation.

> God of all power, Ruler of the Universe, you are
>   worthy of glory and praise.
>
> *Glory to you for ever and ever.*
>
> At your command all things came to be: the vast
>   expanse of interstellar space, galaxies, suns, the
>   planets in their courses, and this fragile earth,
>   our island home.
>
> *By your will they were created and have their being. . . .*

The litany-like exchange between priest and congregation throughout this prayer gives it, in actual use, a remarkable dramatic movement. The extended references to creation in the lengthy and unchanging preface reflect the scientific interest of many people and the desire to see God's purposes carried out in man's stewardship of the natural world. This prayer has proved especially effective for out-of-doors celebrations at summer camps, on the seashore, and so forth.

After the sanctus, the gifts are presented and the Spirit is invoked that "they may be the Body and Blood. . . . " The epiclesis prior to the words of institution resembles those in some other Anglican rites and in the Roman rite. It marks a willingness on the part of the Episcopal Church to recognize that its own historic Non-juror type of prayer is not the only acceptable pattern. At the same time, the reader will notice the careful arrangement. Here the elements are "brought before" God prior to the invocation, not during the anamnesis after the words of institution. In the latter "this sacrifice of thanksgiving" is offered, rather than bread and wine. The concluding petition for the benefits of communion is a striking expression of twentieth-century spiritual aspirations.

Eucharistic Prayer D[8] is a great piece of liturgical literature, but it is not unique to the Episcopal Prayer Book. In 1975, a group of liturgical scholars of several churches in North America met to formulate and propose a eucharistic prayer which could be used, at least on some occasions, within all of their respective communities. The Episcopal tradition was represented by the Rev. Professor Marion J. Hatchett of the University of the South in Sewanee, Tennessee, who was chairman. Rather than formulate a new prayer, it was decided to adopt Eucharistic Prayer IV from the new Roman Missal, recognizing this prayer as having a style and spirit of great beauty and spiritual depth, and deriving primarily from the ancient and justly respected anaphora attributed to St. Basil. This ecumenical group published its version of the prayer as "A Common Eucharistic Prayer." The text is for the most part a new translation of the Latin Roman prayer, except for features we will note.

Proper prefaces are not used with this text. The exact phraseology of the words of institution was left to each church to determine. In the Episcopal version, the words spoken by Jesus are given as in Prayers A, B, and C.

In the Roman Catholic prayer, the epiclesis was transferred to a position before the words of institution, in conformity with the usual teaching of that Church about consecration. Since the elements were accordingly viewed as being consecrated during those words, the oblation during the subsequent anamnesis was drastically reworded to be an oblation of Christ's body and blood, no longer of bread and wine. The ecumenical group agreed that the preliminary epiclesis should be deleted, and a somewhat abbreviated form of the epiclesis of St. Basil was restored to its historic position after the anamnesis. In the latter, the original offering of the elements of bread and the cup was accordingly restored. The epiclesis prays for the descent of the Spirit on the people and on the gifts, "sanctifying them and showing them to be holy gifts for your holy people . . . the Body and Blood. . . ."

In the later parts of the prayer, there are intercessory clauses which are bracketed and made optional. Similarly, the references to "the Blessed Virgin Mary, with patriarchs, prophets, apostles, and martyrs" are bracketed and optional, although certainly widely used. The Episcopal version also added a bracketed option for inserting the name of a particular saint, as on a saint's day.

Because of its comprehensive character, Prayer D is especially suitable for major feasts and for ecumenical occasions. In its patristic source, and in the Christian humanism of its literary style, this is a type of prayer which, in the opinion of some, should have found a place in Anglican Prayer Books at an earlier date. It is interesting that the most popular of all Anglican private prayer books, Jeremy Taylor's *Holy Living* (1650), offers the non-sacramental parts of the anaphora of St. Basil for private recitation on Sundays and feasts.

IV. Order for Celebrating

This third arrangement for the Holy Eucharist in the American Book of Common Prayer is an outline of the liturgy intended to guide persons planning services in special circumstances. As a rubric states, "It is not intended for the principal Sunday or weekly celebration of the Holy Eucharist" (p. 400). For the great Thanksgiving, any one of the six prayers which we have discussed may be used, or one of two forms provided in this order.

Form 1 (p. 402)[9] has the usual contemporary salutation and sursum corda, but the preface and post-sanctus are left to be filled in, and the sanctus itself is optional. Rubrics direct thanksgiving for creation and God's disclosure of himself before the sanctus, if it is used and, when appropriate, expressions of particular intentions are suggested, and the adaptation or incorporation of the proper preface if desired. After the sanctus, or following the above, thanksgiving for salvation through Christ is directed. Extemporaneous material, or something composed for a unique occasion, or material from other ancient or modern liturgies might legitimately be used. The words of institution, much as in Prayer C, are preceded by this brief invocation:

> And so, Father, we bring before you these gifts. Sanctify them by your Holy Spirit to be for your people the Body and Blood of Jesus Christ our Lord.

After the words of institution there is an anamnesis including "By means of this holy bread and cup, we show forth the sacrifice of his death. . . . " This would seem to be the closest any Episcopal prayer comes to offering to the Father the elements after both words of institution and invocation have been said. The self-oblation of the worshipers is expressed in the petition "Make us a living sacrifice of praise." The concluding part of the prayer is very brief.

Form 2 (p. 404)[10] has, following the sursum corda, the same rubrics for thanksgiving to be expressed by the chief celebrant. Here the usual American order of words of institution, anamnesis, and invocation are resumed. There is, on the other hand, no explicit verbal offering of the elements, only "Accept, O Lord, our sacrifice of praise, this memorial of our redemption." The invocation follows, and then a rubric directs the priest to provide further petitions.

It should be recognized that these two forms, which are not authorized for the principal Sunday Service, have less authority than the eucharistic prayers of Rite One and Rite Two. These forms must be interpreted in the light of the others, not vice versa.

V. Conclusion

The recent revision of the Book of Common Prayer in the United States was pluralistic in approach. For the Great Thanksgiving in the Holy Eucharist, the old form has been retained and new prayers have been provided which offer alternative literary forms and alternative emphases, to be used according to local preference, or in keeping with the intentions of particular seasons or occasions. Apart from the two forms in the Order for Celebration, there is considerable consistency in this variety. The thanksgivings of the preface and post-sanctus are often similar. The anamnesis always contains an oblation of the elements, except when, in Prayer C, they are presented earlier. The action of the Holy Spirit is always petitioned. Interestingly enough, all six prayers speak of a "sacrifice of praise and thanksgiving," except for C which simply has "sacrifice of thanksgiving." What does the expression mean in this edition of the Book of Common Prayer?[11] There does not seem to be any desire either to define it or to limit it. It would seem to refer broadly to the whole action of taking bread and wine, giving thanks over them, breaking the bread, and eating and drinking as Christ commanded. More narrowly, it seems to refer to the thanksgiving for creation and redemption through him, a thanksgiving involving thoughts and intentions expressed in words, and also involving the use of bread and wine. The offering of this sacrifice is expressed by the presentation both of the words and of the elements to God the Father, through Jesus Christ, in the power of the Holy Spirit. In Anglican tradition, all this is closely associated with the self-oblation of the worshiping church. This theme is expressed in various ways in these prayers. A frequently used post-communion in Rite Two gives thanks that God has "graciously accepted us" (p. 365).[12]

It is assumed that the Holy Spirit hallows the elements themselves, and also enables the worshipers to receive them to their salvation. At the same time, this takes place in a context of thanksgiving. The operative verb, "sanctify," which appears in most of these prayers, may be understood in this context. What does it mean for bread and wine to be sanctified so as to be the body and blood of the Lord? Older Anglican prayers, laboriously emphasizing his death and passion, indicate that it is the immolated flesh and blood we receive. These newer prayers and their prefaces have a much wider range of reference. It is the body and blood of Jesus who was born as a child for us, who manifested God's glory, who died, rose, ascended, and who is still our great High Priest. But these prayers go even further. They speak of the creation of all things and the fashioning of humankind and the history of an ancient community of faith on the one hand. On the other hand, they speak of the souls of the redeemed who remain members of Christ's body as they praise him in their heavenly country for all eternity. This bread and this cup are now related to all of this. This whole story has been invoked upon them. Here is the food and drink of a renewed creation, the manna and living water of a new Israel, and the medicine of the immortality to come. No single eucharistic text can say all that deserves to be said, yet the effort to bring all our vision into unity, to bring together past and future, to find the center point of it all, the still point around which all revolves—this is the work of sacrifice. For the Christian, it is the cross which is "that Centre of Eternity, that Tree of Life in the midst of the Paradise of God."[13] Our sacrifice of praise and thanksgiving is the sacred action in which all that we are and have and know are brought to that center where their true being is perennially rediscovered, renewed, and made fruitful.

NOTES

1. Portions of this essay were included in *The Sacrifice of Praise; Studies. . . in Honour of Arthur Hubert Couratin*, CLV—Edizioni Liturgiche, Rome, 1981, pp. 181–186.

2. Johnson's *Works I*, Library of Anglo-Catholic Theology, Oxford, 1847. See also Richard F. Buxton, *Eucharist and Institution Narrative*, Alcuin Club Collections No. 58, Great Wakering, 1976, Chapter Eight.

3. The prayer is also reprinted in *Latest Anglican Liturgies 1976–1984*, Colin O. Buchanan ed., Alcuin Club/SPCK, London, 1985, pp. 133–35.

4. Ibid., pp. 137–38.

5. Ibid., pp. 142–43.

6. Ibid., pp. 146–47.

7. Ibid., pp. 147–49.

8. Ibid., pp. 149–51.

9. Ibid., p. 155.

10. Ibid., pp. 155–56.

11. See Catechism, Prayer Book, p. 859. "Q. Why is the Eucharist called a sacrifice? A. Because the Eucharist, the Church's sacrifice of praise and thanksgiving, is the way in which the sacrifice of Christ is made present, and in which he unites us to his one offering of himself."

12. Buchanan, op cit. pp. 144–45.

13. Thomas Traherne (c. 1636–74), *Centuries*, several editions, I, 55.

GAIL RAMSHAW-SCHMIDT

4

Toward Lutheran Eucharistic Prayers

In producing the 1978 *Lutheran Book of Worship*, the working committees of the Inter-Lutheran Commission on Worship did not keep detailed minutes. Thus it is an inexact science to tell the tale of how
American Lutheranism got its eucharistic prayers. An initial effort so-
liciting prayers from Lutheran writers achieved nothing of note. A
drafting committee convened in 1974 and produced eight trial prayers.
Published in a booklet in 1975,[1] these prayers met extensive opposition. A second committee altered the work of the first into the six options present in the *LBW*. These two stages represented a major shift
in thought concerning the language of eucharistic praying, and perhaps for this reason alone the process is worth our hindsight.

The original committee, in resisting bland "committee prose," decided that the prayers were to be individual compositions by excellent
writers, even poets, using distinctive styles. The five liturgists on the
committee were lovers of metaphor and creative writers of theology,
besides being students of the history of eucharistic prayers. Liturgical
reform in American English was producing a dull and terse linguistic
style which this committee hoped to counter with individual pieces of
brilliant poetic rhetoric. The committee offered eight prayers which
were criticized by foes and friends alike. Gradually the mind of the
committee itself changed.

Foes there were many. Reformation historians put forward vociferous objection to Lutherans praying a eucharistic prayer at all, basing their arguments on Luther's rejection of the Roman canon and on the Reformation controversy concerning the word "sacrifice."[2] Especially those Lutherans unconvinced by the current ecumenical consensus on the eucharist[3] felt that Lutheran identity would be fatefully diminished by the introduction of eucharistic praying. The Reformation stress on the word had developed into an elaborate distinction between proclamation and prayer, the first God's action and the second the assembly's action, which even dictated the posture of the presider,[4] facing toward the people or "toward God." The eucharistic prayer, then, with its Hebraic combination of proclamation and prayer, did not fit neatly into this distinction. Prayer as human action had been downplayed in Lutheran circles: thus the massive efforts to find appropriate eucharistic prayers were unsettling to those for whom the Lord's Supper is solely God's gift.

But even friends of eucharistic praying were displeased with the committee's eight prayers. The novel forms and the individualistic rhetoric found little support among veteran liturgical scholars whose life had been poured out urging American Lutherans to reclaim their catholic heritage. One critic, for example, accused one option of not being a eucharistic prayer at all because it did not conclude with a classic doxology. Finally the committee members altered their original conviction that liturgical language ought to be highly poetic.[5] When used, the first committee's efforts proved to be too idiosyncratic. The effect was of presiders' reading poetic prose of individual authors, rather than of presiders' praying the church's prayer. A look at the original eight prayers is helpful in demonstrating this change of position toward their final form in the *LBW.*

Trial Prayer I, nicknamed the Prayer of Many Parts, was seven paragraphs of interchangeable options, offering variety within a classic frame, held together with standard cue lines. Finding one's way through the variations, however, was a minor problem compared with that caused by the diction in which the prayer was cast. Nearly every sentence threw words into startling juxtapositions so that attentive praying became a kind of theological adventure. The Spirit was "to vivify this bread and cup." People were called "from nothingness to take the chance of life." The prayer's language mirrored the life of faith by being metaphorically adventurous. Much revised, simplified, and abbreviated by Frank Senn, on behalf of the committee, Trial Prayer I appears in the *LBW* as option II. The idiosyncratic oxymorons have been tamed into more traditional prose; the odd phrases—"our Lord Jesus . . . who had no place to lay his head, and after calling to him the slaves of all nations, entered the wilderness of death, to meet your kingdom"—were all omitted; the existentialist images were dropped. This rewrite has been fit into the cue lines of the *LWB* option I. Thus it comes off as merely an elaboration for Christmas and Easter of the most commonly used eucharistic prayer.

Trial Prayer II was a translation of Hippolytus. Because Lutherans are not yet able "to offer this bread and cup," the translator, Gordon Lathrop, amended the text to read "to lift this bread and cup before you," hoping that the later phrase "your priestly people" would supply the image which Lutherans lack by their refusal of the word "offer." This Trial Prayer II appears in the *LBW* as option IV.

Trial Prayer III was a contemporary revision of the eucharistic prayer published in the 1958 *Service Book and Hymnal*, a prayer compiled originally by Luther Reed from ancient sources. The prayer uses much biblical language, which helps legitimate it among Lutherans. Many Lutherans had grown to love this prayer, and, barring thee's and thou's, wanted it retained. With most of the revisions rescinded, the prayer appears in the *LBW* as option III.

Now come Trial Prayers IV through VIII, none of which is represented in the *LBW*. Trial Prayer IV was a newly composed eucharistic prayer with an invariable preface. It was typical of many eucharistic prayers of that decade, a gentle variation on classic language, neither particularly bad nor exceptionally good. Trial Prayer V, based on the images in the Exsultet, was composed in rhythmic and poetic rhetoric. With a system of cues more clever than profound, the congregation participated repeatedly in the classic Easter affirmations: "He is risen indeed" and "Thanks be to God." Understandably, reactions to this prayer were mixed, some vehemently negative, other enthusiastically positive. Trial Prayer VI, using the Birkat-ha-Mazon as a type of corporate prayer, was especially appropriate for eucharist at table, something that occurred more in 1975 than it does now. The prayer used Old Testament typology and thought of meal, instead of sacrifice, as its primary metaphor for meeting God. Trial Prayer VII was the Common Eucharistic Prayer as published in 1975 by Marion J. Hatchett. Inspired by St. Basil's prayer, it uses an eastern exalted rhetoric. Neither its profuse praise nor its ecumenical implications caught on among Lutherans. Finally, Trial Prayer VIII was a translation of a eucharistic prayer written by Dutch Roman Catholic T. Naastepad in 1968. The prayer is an imaginative development of biblical and religious images. Grace is multiplied; Lady Wisdom sets the table; and we beg that God will not forget the Messiah. Lutherans were not prepared for such a fabric of prayer, a tweed with various colors popping in and out, and merely complained about how God "peopled the waters with reverence." There is no way to know how many Lutherans used these five prayers how many times.

In summary:

Trial Prayers IV through VIII were dropped.
Trial Prayer I became a source for *LBW* option II.
Trial Prayer II became *LBW* option IV.
Trial Prayer III became a source for *LBW* option III.

Political efforts to pacify those Lutherans who believed strongly that no eucharistic prayer could be Lutheran led to the inclusion of two more options: the recitation of the words of institution following the Sursum corda, the preface, and the sanctus (which had been an option in the Common Liturgy of the *Service Book and Hymnal*); and (for those desiring some eucharistic prayer, but not with the words of institution included in it) a four-sentence thanksgiving translated from the 1942 Swedish Massbook placed between the sanctus and the words of institution. Both of these options are, unfortunately, included in the pew edition of *LBW* and are used exclusively by some Lutherans.

Finally, we come to *LBW* option I, the only eucharistic prayer printed out in full in the pew edition and thus the one most often used of the four. This prayer is a revision of the one in the Inter-Lutheran Commission on Worship's 1970 publication of a trial eucharistic liturgy,[6] which had received wide exposure in congregations, at workshops, and at synod conventions. The final prayer was expanded from its original form by a committee, and, while avoiding all idiosyncratic expression, elaborates a little on the minimalist vocabulary and style which marked liturgies of the 1960s. Still there is not one dispensable word. The committee was under considerable pressure to obtain the conventions' imprimaturs by eliminating all possibly controvertible phrases. The committee hoped that were this first option acceptable to all, the *LBW* could forego offering as options the naked verba and the short detached prayer. Unfortunately the committee lost to popular prejudice and ended up with both a minimalist prayer and the no-eucharistic-prayer options as the ones printed in the pew edition.

One criticism must be directed especially at Lutherans. Granting the agreements reached in the Lutheran–Roman Catholic dialogues on the eucharist, and granting current scholarship on the metaphoric use of the word "sacrifice" in the Christian tradition,[7] it is no longer defensible for Lutherans to continue their eccentric refusal to speak the language of offering and sacrifice in the eucharist. Merely repeating late medieval quarrels, which surfaced in a far different situation than our own and were carried on in Latin and European languages, keeps Lutheranism in a linguistic time warp and turns the Lutheran movement in the church catholic into an anachronistic sect. Such fundamentalistic interpretation of religious language does not commend the descendants of Luther, who ought to know a good deal about the riches of Christological metaphor.

While Lutherans have come a long way quickly toward acceptable eucharistic praying, the question of rhetoric remains a challenge for all Christian speakers of American English. At the least, the Lutheran drafting committee must be commended for attempting to discover appropriate rhetoric for praise. But the antidote to the primer prose of the 1960s need not be bizarre or individualistic writing styles. The prayers of American Orthodox Jewry give an example of a far richer style than was adopted by the Christian liturgical reform:[8] prose which like music lifts the listener; images which depict what abstract nouns cannot; lists of synonyms which attest to the inadequacy of any of our words. There must be something of the babble of the infant, the ecstasy of the lover, and the stuttering of the maimed, as well as the formal request of the subjects, in our corporate prayer. Something there must be of the going beyond the mind into the soul: the Berthier chants prayed at the Taizé community capture this quality so lacking in western prayer. While it is true that Christians must pray in their vernacular, it does not follow that our eucharistic praying must be cast in the prose of the slowest reading group. Contemporary American English is a wondrously vulgar tongue; we need more work to discover how this our language can speak of the things of God.

NOTES

1. *The Great Thanksgiving* (New York: Inter-Lutheran Commission on Worship, 1975). The drafting subcommittee consisted of John W. Arthur, Robert W. Jenson, Gordon W. Lathrop, and Gail Ramshaw-Schmidt.

2. See for example Oliver K. Olson, "Contemporary Trends in Liturgy Viewed from the Perspective of Classical Lutheran Theology," *The Lutheran Quarterly* 24 (May 1974), 110–57.

3. *Lutherans and Catholics in Dialogue, IV, Eucharist and Ministry.*

4. Luther Reed, *The Lutheran Liturgy* (Philadelphia: Fortress, 1947).

5. See for example Gail Ramshaw-Schmidt, "Liturgy as Poetry: Implications of a Definition," *Living Worship* 15 (October 1979), no. 8, and "The Lan-

guage of Eucharistic Praying," originally published in *Worship* 57 (1983), 419-437. This paper was originally presented at an NAAL meeting.

6. *Contemporary Worship 2* (New York: Inter-Lutheran Commission on Worship, 1970).

7. David Power, "Words That Crack: The Uses of 'Sacrifice' in Eucharistic Discourse," *Worship* 53 (September 1970), 385–404.

8. See for example *Mahzor for Rosh Hashanah and Yom Kippur*, ed. Rabbi Jules Harlow (New York: The Rabbinical Assembly, 1972).

JAMES F. WHITE

5

United Methodist Eucharistic Prayers: 1965–1985

The United Methodist eucharistic prayers of the past two decades are distinguished both by their large number (surpassing the quantity authorized in any other western church) and by their radical departure from the past Methodist tradition. In this chapter, we shall examine the process by which change came about and then look at the products of such change. Our examination of the development of the new prayers is intended to be a guide to the origins and revisions of each of the sixty published versions of these prayers. The analysis will be confined to the most frequently-used prayers for common use. It is intended that this chapter provide a chronicle of how United Methodists have learned to give thanks through the Lord's Supper in recent years.

Since I was directly involved in much of this process, I shall not hesitate to use first person, singular or plural, where it is natural. No one else has produced accounts of these processes and the only published documentation is the prayers themselves. I shall direct the reader in each instance to material in print. The publisher in every case is Abingdon Press or the United Methodist Publishing House of Nashville. For convenience, I shall use a few abbreviations: EP for eucharistic prayer to avoid constant repetition, ALT for *At the Lord's Table* (1981), BOS for *Book of Services* (1985), and SWR for *Supplemental Worship Resources* (1972–1984).

I. Development of the Prayers

No time could have been worse for publishing a new service book than 1965 when the Methodist Church published its second *Book of Worship*. My own contact with the Commission on Worship began at a service dedicating that new book in the spring of 1965. No one realized then that this was the final expression of a venerable but restricted tradition. The book contained a single EP; indeed the idea of multiple EPs was scarcely considered in western churches at the time. Basically the EP in the *Book of Worship* preserved the 1662 Anglican prayer which is virtually that of the 1552 *Book of Common Prayer*. Wesley had passed on to American Methodists the 1662 prayer in 1784, omitting only a redundant single word: "one." The 1965 text included a few minor modernizations. The only theological change was the substitution of the petition: "may be partakers of the divine nature through him" where 1662 and Wesley had "may be partakers of his most blessed body and blood." This change dates from 1932, reflecting the liberal theology of the time in its reading: "may also be partakers of the divine nature through him."

The most notable feature of the prayer, dating from 1552, is its division into two portions with the oblation and doxology placed after the communion. This second half had been preserved almost unchanged from 1552. Thus the 1965 Methodist prayer represents over four hundred years of the Anglican-Methodist tradition. Nor were we expecting any great change in the near future.

But everything, it now seems, began to change after Vatican II. It became increasingly apparent that the work of the Commission on Worship, only recently completed, would need to be done over again. Those who had borne the burden of the revisions of 1965 could hardly be expected to be enthusiastic about starting again, but at a meeting of the executive committee in Chicago in September 1970 and of the full Commission at United Theological Seminary in Dayton in November 1970, a few of us were able to convince the veterans that the work must commence anew. This was especially ironic in that *The Companion to the Book of Worship* had just appeared earlier that year and Commission members were ready for a well-deserved rest.

The process began with the formation of a Committee on Alternate Rituals, consisting of ten people and chaired by Professor H. Grady Hardin, Perkins School of Theology. I was chosen to be the writer for the first service, the eucharist. The process involved the writer producing a text, the committee meeting to discuss it, and then the writer revising it on the basis of what had been decided. In the meantime, each text was given limited testing in actual use. The first text was ready for a March 14–15, 1971 meeting in Chicago. At this meeting, Professor David Buttrick, then at Pittsburgh Theological Seminary, and Professor Laurence Stookey of Wesley Theological Seminary were present as consultants. Other meetings followed in St. Louis in May where a fourth text was presented. Two fifth texts were reviewed in Arlington, Vermont in July and a sixth text in Denver in August. Two subsequent revisions followed before it was sent to the printers. Several revisions were circulated by mail to the committee. Altogether the whole rite went through eight revisions between the fall of 1970 and its final publication in the spring of 1972. The first official use was at the 1972 General Conference in Atlanta.

In the process, a few changes were made in the structure of the rite (dropping the Kyrie, not printing the Gloria, changing the creed, adding the invitation, and dropping the offertory prayer). Much of the rite (three lessons and psalmody, the kiss of peace, the fraction) was new to modern Methodists. But the 1972 EP was certainly the most significant change and is especially important since it became the model for all our subsequent EPs.

In the process of revision of the entire rite, the EP did not differ much from the first text I had prepared for the 1971 meeting in August. The preface was shortened somewhat. There were slight changes in the post-sanctus. A significant revision was made in the words of institution. Professor Fred D. Gealy, a New Testament scholar from Perkins School of Theology, convinced the committee that anamnesis was better translated as "experience anew" than as "to recall me" as I had translated it. The words were also conflated so it only appears once. At one of the stages we added the words: "the presence of the Lord Jesus Christ/and look forward to his coming in final victory." The oblation was improved somewhat by making it "Christ's offering" which made it possible to speak of our "holy surrender of ourselves." In the fourth version, the epiclesis prayed: "Make this bread and wine be for us the presence of Christ." This proved too strong for some of the committee and after the sixth text this reverted to "Help us know/in the breaking of this bread/and the drinking of this wine/the presence of Christ." By the fifth text, the doxology has dropped the traditional "Through him" in favor of the wording of Hippolytus.

One of the most significant decisions made during this process involved the preface. We began convinced of the value of proper prefaces. (*The Book of Worship* had included four.) But we were equally convinced of the importance of referring to God's works of the old covenant in the preface. Rather than trying to include both Old Testament narration in the preface and prayer proper for each special occasion, we came eventually to see the need for entirely new EPs for special seasonal and ritual occasions. This allowed us to do justice to salvation history in the old covenant in the prefaces and at the same time to give the whole prayer the flavor of a proper. This had immense consequences since it led to the production of a larger number of eucharistic prayers (nearly three score) than other western churches have found necessary. However this solitary path (as far as modern western churches are concerned) has led us into the company of various Gallican missals and Ethiopian anaphoras, I suspect for similar reasons. Certainly it is proved to be a viable possibility and given us both possibilities: to proclaim the Old Testament witness and to declare the present occasion.

Upon the publication of the service in 1972, we expected a short run of maybe fifty or sixty thousand copies. But it soon proved far more popular than we had ever dreamed, eventually selling over two and a half million copies. A quick change between printings soon removed the words "men" and "mankind" (twice) which had crept in as we revised the texts although these words were not in the first version.

In the summer of 1974, I taught at St. John's University and submitted the service to several distinguished Roman Catholic liturgists teaching there. That winter I collated their comments which, to my surprise, were more literary than theological. These included chiefly transitions into the post-sanctus and oblation. During this time, the service was being widely used and we collected comments from every source. In 1976, we named the new services "Supplemental Worship Resources" with the 1972 rite being volume one. Three further volumes appeared in that year. By 1980, we were able to do a second-generation version of the eucharist appearing together with baptism, marriage, and funerals in *We Gather Together* (SWR #10). The changes in the EP were slight: "God and King" in the preface becoming "Sovereign God," improvement of the transitions just mentioned, and a slight change in the epiclesis. Apparently we had done as well as we could with this prayer. It was published separately in 1981 as "The Sacrament of the Lord's Supper: Revised Edition 1981."

Translations were made into Spanish appearing in 1978 as *El Sacramento de la Santa Cena* and in 1981 in the collection, *Congregado en Su Nombre*, and a revised text into Japanese, appearing in 1982 in *A Sunday Service: English-Japanese Parallel*. The wide acceptance of the 1972 eucharist, by both conservative and progressive congregations, by rural and city churches, helped firmly establish the 1972 service and its EP as those most familiar to United Methodists. The 1972 EP also provided the structure and some of the wording for other prayers as we developed them. The rest of the rite has not evolved in significant ways except for a rather firm suggestion of placing the acts of confession after the sermon rather than as in the opening rite. Except for this and some minor changes in the closing rite, the service has remained little altered since 1972.

This initial success encouraged other work, especially on seasonal EPs, ritual EPs, and additional EPs for common use.

An important event for United Methodist worship was the appointment in 1972 of the Reverend Hoyt L. Hickman to the staff of the newly-organized Section on Worship of the Board of Discipleship. A member of the Western Pennsylvania Annual Conference and former President of the Order of St. Luke, Dr. Hickman holds degrees from both Yale Divinity School and Union Theological Seminary. He served as secretary of the Commission on Worship in its final years while working as pastor of Cascade United Methodist Church, Erie, Pennsylvania. In the years from 1975 to 1985 he was to become both the leading United Methodist authority on the EP and most prolific author of new prayers.

Since the decision had been made against variable prefaces, flexibility had to be found in another way, namely the development of complete prayers for various seasonal and ritual occasions. In 1974, Dr. Hickman began developing a series of seasonal EPs. These were eventually published in four-page leaflets by Discipleship Resources, the publishing agency of the Board of Discipleship. The format was the same in each case: a colorful cover, followed by an order for the service of the word with the EP occupying pages three and four (except in the Christmas text). The EP was printed in full and intended for congregational use, the dialogue, sanctus, acclamation, and doxology being printed in bold face type. Eventually we stopped encouraging the congregation to recite the doxology except for the concluding Amen.

The prayers for "Advent," "Christmas," and "Epiphany" appeared in 1974; 1975 brought "Lent," "Maundy Thursday," "Eastertide," "Pentecost," "A People under God," "The Communion of Saints," and "Thanksgiving." All were subtitled: "A Service of Holy Communion."

The structure of each EP followed very closely that of the 1972 common prayer, often including the very same wording in many places. Different, of course, were portions of the preface, post-sanctus, and (in some instances) epiclesis which were directed to the season or occasion at hand. For Advent, prophecy in the preface leads to the coming of Emmanuel, narrated in the post-sanctus. The Christmas prayer omits the sanctus and most of salvation history to focus on the nativity, culminating in a extended doxology.

The Epiphany prayer is notable for our first use of the Luke 4:18 (Isaiah 61:1–2) passage: "He preached good news to the poor," which became prominent in many EPs thereafter. Lent lacks any clear anamnesis-oblation. Maundy Thursday lacks a sanctus but gives a full narration of the Last Supper. Eastertide balances creation in the preface and the new creation in the resurrection in the post-sanctus. A similar recital occurs for Pentecost in the Old Testament works of the Holy Spirit interrupted by the sanctus before leading to the New Covenant works of the Spirit. "A People under God" is somewhat ambiguous, being designed for use on any national or civic occasion, and culminates with intercession for justice and peace. Categories of the saints form the preface for "The Communion of Saints" with a long congregational oblation and intercession at the end. Harvest bounty is the theme of the preface of "Thanksgiving."

A second generation of some of these prayers appeared in 1979 in a book dealing with the seasons of Lent and Easter: *From Ashes to Fire* (SWR #8). This volume was largely the work of Prof. Don E. Saliers of Emory University although revised by members of the Editorial Committee of the Section on Worship. Six EPs are included. That for Ash Wednesday is a new prayer, later to appear in a revised version "Lent II" in *At the Lord's Table* (SWR #9), published in 1981. The Palm/Passion Sunday EP was apparently the work of Professor Saliers and does not appear elsewhere. The oblation is brief but the epiclesis lengthy. For Maundy Thursday, the EP is a later version of the 1975 leaflet EP with the sanctus not included and some changes in the post-sanctus. The eucharistic prayer for the Easter Vigil was drawn from "The Common Eucharistic Prayer." It contains a long and glorious post-sanctus narration from both convenants, two acclamations, and a long epiclesis with intercession for the church. It is both the longest and most joyful of all the Methodist EPs. Another EP is provided by Saliers for Ascension, with mention of the Ascension concluding the post-sanctus. The EP for the Day of Pentecost is a reworking of that in the 1975 leaflet with an expanded intercession for the Church.

A major advance was the publication in 1981 of *At the Lord's Table* (SWR #9), largely the work of Hoyt Hickman who edited the volume and most of the prayers in it. Essentially it is a collection of twenty-two EPs, published for use at the altar-table. We shall examine here the eleven seasonal ones. (#10–20). Most of these EPs are second generation texts of those in the leaflet series. A second EP has been added for Lent and several changes made in the titles. The most conspicuous change is that all of the prayers have come to conform more closely to the structure of the 1972 prayer and in most of them the words of institution and oblation are similar to those in the 1972 except that the words over the bread and cup are not conflated and "remembrance" replaces "experience anew." The wording of the preface, post-sanctus, anamnesis, and epiclesis have all been reworked without great changes in the content. The doxologies are no longer congregational. In short, what has happened has been to standardize on the 1972 structure and certain portions of its contents. The changes in wording seem mostly in the direction of stronger images (mostly biblical) and in moving to more terse expression. The new prayers for Lent (I and II), are interesting, especially Lent I which in a long preface dwells on the imagery of "forty days and forty nights" in scripture. New names have appeared: "All Saints and Memorial Occasions," "The Gift of Food," and "Christ the King or Civic Occasions."

A third generation of some of the seasonal prayers occurred in 1984 in *From Hope to Joy* (SWR #15), largely written by Don E. Saliers. This volume provides services for occasions from just prior to Advent through the Epiphany Season, and contains seven EPs. These include All Saints' Day, Christ the King, and Thanksgiving all taken from ALT. The Advent EP from ALT does not appear in this volume but that for Christmas Eve and Day does. A new EP has been produced by the Reverend Kenneth Bedell for use with the Covenant Service, a Methodist tradition dating from John Wesley. This EP is unusual in that it uses different words for the words of institution, has no anamnesis-oblation, and has a congregational doxology. It is more a ritual EP than a seasonal one although Methodists have tied the Covenant Service generally to the beginning of the civil year. With the Epiphany prayer we are back on familiar ground; it is ALT #12 only slightly changed. Transfiguration has a new prayer, the work of Don Saliers. It contains a very long post-sanctus plus a long series of intercessions. Saliers seems to favor inclusion of intercessions for the church, saints, and individuals, living and dead.

The next stage of seasonal EPs, some eleven in their second, third, or even fourth generations, appear in *Handbook of the Christian Year* (1986). Prof. Saliers and Dr. Hickman made revisions in the seasonal prayers that originated in the leaflet series or *From Ashes to Fire* and *From Hope to Joy*. These include the Advent Prayer (ALT #10), Christmas (ALT #11), but none for the Covenant Service, Epiphany (ALT #12), and Transfiguration (*From Hope to Joy*). When we come to Lent, Ash Wednesday has none, but one is provided for the Sundays of Lent

(ALT #13). Passion/Palm Sunday has ALT #14 heavily revised. ALT #15 forms the basis for Maundy Thursday. The Easter Vigil EP is largely a new prayer, incorporating portions of ALT #16 plus the 1984 common prayer. No Ascension Day EP appears. Pentecost is ALT #17 with the new covenant narration moved from the preface to the post-sanctus, and other changes in wording. For Trinity Sunday and Christ the King the 1984 common prayer is provided. ALT #18 provides the basis for the All Saints' Day EP and Thanksgiving Day is based on ALT #19. In general, the prayers in *Handbook of the Christian Year* tend to stress biblical images and are more consistent than ALT in placing the narration of the new covenant in the post-sanctus, thus leaving the preface more free to narrate more of the old covenant. It is likely that the eleven seasonal prayers as revised in *Handbook* will appear in a new edition of ALT in 1987.

The list of ritual EPs is briefer. The first to appear was that in the wedding service, a new departure for United Methodists. Indeed, the 1965 *Book of Worship* advised "When the Sacrament of the Lord's Supper is requested, this service should be provided at a time other than the service of marriage." Thus provision of a EP as part of the rite itself was a major advance. The new EP was written by Hoyt Hickman and first appeared in 1979 in *A Service of Christian Marriage* (SWR #5). It follows the 1972 structure except for adding intercessions as the occasion strongly suggests. The same text of this prayer appeared as ALT #21. A second generation appears in BOS, largely accommodated to the 1984 common prayer.

A similar history can be traced for the funeral and memorial service EP. It, too, was written by Hoyt Hickman and first appeared in 1979 in *A Service of Death and Resurrection* (SWR #7). This EP represents an even greater change for United Methodists who had no tradition of the eucharist at funerals. The same prayer appeared as ALT #22. It follows basically the 1972 prayer in structure. In the BOS version, the wording appropriates more that of the 1984 common prayer.

If United Methodists were unfamiliar with the eucharist at such occasions, there was an irony in a similar absence of the ordination rite since John Wesley's rites explicitly provide that "all that are ordained shall receive the holy Communion." *An Ordinal* "adopted for official Alternative Use by the 1980 General Conference" was published in 1980 and takes the eucharist for granted. The EP was written by Dr. John D. Grabner, currently pastor in Pasco, Washington. It follows the familiar 1972 structure with narration of the sending of the apostles in the preface. This EP has not been revised.

Blessings & Consecrations (SWR #14), published in 1984, is largely the work of Professor Roy Reed of the Methodist Theological School in Ohio. It includes one EP three times in: "An Order for Organizing a Church," "An Order for the Consecration of a Church Building," and "An Order for the Consecration of a Dwelling." All prayers are the 1984 common prayer although in the third instance the congregational portions are eliminated.

An EP was also necessary for ministry to the sick and dying. Brevity was of importance in this instance. Two versions appeared, both by Hoyt Hickman as ALT #8 and #9, the chief difference being the omission of responses in the latter. The same urgency shapes two versions in BOS of the 1984 prayer: the "Brief Text" and the "Minimum Text," the latter of which also has no responses.

The development of prayers for common use other than the 1972 EP occurred over a decade. All but the 1984 EP are collected in ALT. The first, ALT #1, is simply the 1972 prayer in the revised form which appeared in *We Gather Together* (SWR #10) in 1981 and in leaflet form, "The Sacrament of the Lord's Supper: Revised Edition 1981" (SWR #1). It is identical in all three of these books.

ALT #2 is simply the eucharistic prayer from the 1965 *Book of Worship* reunited (after four centuries of division) so that the oblation and doxology follow immediately after the words of institution. The four proper prefaces from the *Book of Worship* are also provided. An EP "In Traditional Language," ALT #3, is Hoyt Hickman's effort to use familiar Cranmerian prose to express newer theological concepts. It was written while he was still a pastor in Erie, Pennsylvania (before his move to Nashville in the summer of 1972), and is referred to as the "Erie" EP. It represents our last effort to use traditional language for composing new prayers. The structure involves a long preface combining parts of the traditional Methodist prayer and new material. The post-sanctus, words of institution, oblation, and doxology come from the traditional prayer with a new anamnesis and epiclesis added.

Sources outside Methodism contribute to ALT #4. This prayer is drawn from the Consultation on Church Union service, published as *Word Bread Cup* by Forward Movement Publications in 1978. It appears as EP II in that publication. The preface is from the "Common Eucharistic Prayer." Dr. Richard Eslinger, at that time on the staff of the Section on Worship, was involved in its composition, as also was Don Saliers. The "Common Eucharistic Prayer," ALT #6, was produced by an ad hoc committee convened in 1974 by Professor Marion Hatchett of St. Luke's School of Theology, University of the South, Sewanee, Tennessee. Hoyt Hickman and Don Saliers were the United Methodist representatives. Most of it is a new translation of the Latin Roman

Catholic EP IV, itself a shortened version of the Alexandrian EP of St. Basil. Certain additions from ancient manuscripts appear and the remembrance of the pope is deleted. Unlike other Roman Catholic EPs, it has no proper preface. The same prayer appears as EP D in the 1979 *Book of Common Prayer* except the words of institution are an Episcopal version, just as in ALT they follow the 1972 United Methodist words. In the Presbyterian *The Service for the Lord's Day* (Westminster, 1984), this prayer is EP E with yet another set of words of institution. Thus this prayer ties United Methodists into a broad euchological tradition. Parts of the Common EP soon appeared in other Methodist EPs, especially the use of Luke 4:18.

Once we had made up our minds about the theology and structure, we turned our attention again to problems of language. New concerns had also come into our consciousness since 1972, particularly environmentalism and feminism. In 1977 I wrote a second EP, giving it the title "A Lyrical Prayer" to suggest that poetry was an important quality in such prayers. The "Lyrical Prayer" was discussed in the EP study group at the 1978 meeting of the North American Academy of Liturgy and revised thereafter. It appears in ALT as #5. It has a more cosmic preface, translates anamnesis as "know anew," has a stronger oblation, and uses language from Wesley in the epiclesis. A structural change was the move of the acclamation to a position after the oblation, thus ending the commemoration of Christ's work and introducing the invocation of the epiclesis. This reordering makes the Trinitarian shape of the prayer even more apparent and was used in later prayers.

At about the same time, Hoyt Hickman produced an EP "For General Use" which appears as ALT #7. It focuses on the work of Christ in the preface. A favorite theme of Dr. Hickman, the Luke 4:18 passage, appears. At that time, he favored mention of the Emmaus meal after the words of institution. From the oblation on, ALT #7 is close to the 1972 EP. We have already mentioned ALT #8 and #9 as ritual prayers designed for use in the sick room. They are condensed versions of ALT #7, "For General Use."

One additional prayer remains to be mentioned but it is of major importance. We have already referred to it as the 1984 EP. Work was begun in the early 1980s on revising the five basic services that appear in *We Gather Together*. Most of this work was done by the staff of the Section on Worship with some assistance from consultants. Although changes were minor in the eucharist as a whole, there were some major changes in the EP. The new EP that emerged was largely the work of Hoyt Hickman and includes some of his characteristic phrases. The structure, except for relocation of the acclamation, is the same as the 1972 EP, as is some of the wording, especially in the preface, oblation, and epiclesis. But there are significant improvements: anamnesis becomes "in remembrance" and the bread and cup words are not conflated, at last the epiclesis uses ontological language "make them be for us the body and blood of Christ" rather than cognitive terms, and the eschatological dimension is clearer and comes at the end of the prayer. The acclamation comes between the oblation and epiclesis.

In many ways it is still recognizable as the 1972 EP, improved considerably. The eucharistic rite with this prayer included was accepted as part of the official "Ritual" of the United Methodist Church at the 1984 General Conference. It was published as a leaflet, "A Service of Word and Table: Complete Text 1984 Edition." It is included in *The Book of Services* (1985). This publication also includes the sick room versions mentioned previously, "Brief Text" and "Minimum Text." The present (1985) likelihood is that this EP, perhaps slightly fine tuned, will be part of the next *Book of Hymns*, expected to be approved by General Conference in 1988 and published in 1989. Thus the process, begun in 1970, will reach a conclusion after two decades. Although many improvements have been made in the wording of the 1972 EP, its structure has remained virtually intact. The original content is still quite present, only made more clear. Either we have learned little in the intervening years or we did our work well the first time!

II. Analysis of Selected Prayers

We turn now to analyzing the content of the 1972 EP and its 1984 successor. Obviously, much of this has come out in our chronicle of the development of these prayers but it is appropriate to examine them in a more systematic fashion. We had four intentions in mind while developing the 1972 rite: contemporary liturgical language, classical and ecumenical shape, flexibility, and contemporary theology. Of "flexibility," little need be said except that we obtained it by multiplicity of prayers plus abbreviated versions for two.

In 1970, it was not yet clear to anyone just what "contemporary liturgical language" meant in English. The Committee winced at that first meeting in Chicago in 1971 when they saw the first text. Not only had all obsolete words been eliminated, but the sentence structures had been changed to avoid parallelisms and to achieve a terse straightforward presentation. But what seemed strange and unfamiliar in 1971 had become conventional a decade later. The change in cadences was probably more significant than the alteration in vocabulary. In time, the 1972 wording became familiar and even beloved.

Fresh problems arose as we became sensitive to inclusive language problems. We had no standards when we approached the task nor did any other church at the time. Eventually I drew together the results of our experiences in this area as the basis for several periodical articles and for the first text of *Words That Hurt, Words That Heal* (1985). We soon realized that terms such as "men," "mankind," and "man" no longer meant what we intended and they were replaced. We soon eliminated third-person pronouns referring to God except for Jesus Christ.

At the first meeting in Chicago, we decided to use ICET (International Consultation on English Texts) texts for such items as the sursum corda and sanctus. Although we altered the sursum corda slightly ("The Lord is with you") we eventually conformed to ICET. The "him" in the sursum corda became "to give our thanks and praise" in the 1984 EP; "he who comes in the name of the Lord" has remained consistently. Dr. Fred D. Gealy's version of the Lord's Prayer was used but changed to the ICET translation in 1980. The familiar *Book of Common Prayer* text is still the most widely-used version.

The greatest problem on inclusive language arose over five key Christian images: Father, Son, Lord, King, and Kingdom. Although controversial for some, these were retained in the conviction that the Church has, at present, no viable alternatives. An effort was made to add feminine metaphors whenever possible. But it was thought important that the EPs be addressed to the Father explicitly and that the doxology also conclude with this term.

It was less difficult to decide what was the "classical and ecumenical shape" for the EP. In the early 1970s these were probably equivalent terms, for everyone was using Hippolytus and other ancient sources. It must be remembered that in 1972 other churches were, or recently had been, involved in similar processes of revision. I always kept within reach the new Roman Catholic prayers as well as the latest productions of the Episcopal Church, Inter-Lutheran Commission on Worship, the Consultation on Church Union, the Presbyterian Joint Commission on Worship, the United Church of Christ, the Church of England, and the Church of South India. Most of these churches were then moving from a single EP (which had sufficed in most instances for four hundred years) to several. Ancient sources, especially the Byzantine rite, were plundered when needed.

Hippolytus could tell us much about the contents but could not give us an adequate structure. That was found in the Antiochene EP tradition. Such prayers could accommodate the full breath of commemoration of God's work from creation to final consummation, quite an advance beyond the passion narrative which had seemed sufficient for westerners for many centuries. This form could also make the EP our basic creedal statement by proclaiming through prayer the faith that unites the Church. Of course, it was not easy to compress the Old Testament into something as short as the preface, but we did cover much in just fifty words. And we could add eschatology and pneumatology, totally lacking in our existing prayer.

The other churches were restoring the *benedictus qui venit*. Against opposition, I was able to prevail in a committee meeting by pointing out to objectors that this passage was from Psalm 118:26. Somehow the Old Testament text made it acceptable. We took the doxology directly from Hippolytus and the acclamation that had been incorporated in the 1970 Roman missal from the Liturgy of St. James. We have tended to develop the post-sanctus more than some churches have although certainly no more than the "Common EP." Fortunately, we were free from the theological compromises that necessitated a preliminary epiclesis.

This classical Antiochene shape has served us well and persists from the 1972 EP through the 1984 prayer. Perhaps we should have tried a few exotic experiments such as intercessions in the preface but we preferred not to do so. Such intercessions as we have are chiefly in the wedding and funeral ritual EPs where they are almost inevitable and in the prayers for All Saints' Day and Transfiguration. Most of the time, we have preferred to allow the prayer of the faithful to fulfill this function. Thus, we avoid any sense of a more holy moment in the EP for the intercessions and make them less clerical.

An attempt was made to solve a peculiarly Methodist problem— the infrequency of the eucharist—by suggesting that every Sunday service conclude with a prayer of thanksgiving. As a means of providing models for this, the EPs in ALT and the 1984 EP are printed with a vertical line in the left margin beside those portions that pertain only to eucharist. The possibility is presented of using the remainder of these prayers as non-eucharistic thanksgivings on Sundays when the holy communion is not celebrated. This does not seem to have been widely done and teaching the idea of thanksgiving as the logical response to the hearing of the good news has proved difficult.

What we meant by "contemporary theology" slowly evolved as we worked on the 1972 prayer. We wished to be current in our expression of the Christian faith and yet faithful to our own tradition. We tried to recover much that was in the Wesleyan heritage, particularly in the 166 eucharistic hymns by John and Charles Wesley. These are Methodism's greatest contribution to eucharistic theology and in many ways they are still ahead of our apprehension of them. Much of this is because John Wesley was a patristics scholar and a very catholic person even when restricted by the limitations of the western tradition. Recent studies such as Geoffrey Wainwright's *Eucharist and Eschatology* (Epworth, 1971) and John McKenna's *Eucharist and Holy Spirit* (Alcuin, 1975) have stimulated our theological reflection.

I shall try briefly to outline the main theological emphases in the 1972 prayer, all of which remain prominent in the 1984 EP. It would be difficult to say there has been a major shift anywhere except to make the expression of some concepts more clear or graphic.

We were determined to move away from the penitential mood which the 1662 BCP prayer transmitted from late medieval piety. The eucharist is expressed throughout in joyful terms of thankfulness for what God has done, not in apologetic terms for what humans have done amiss. The tone is more Easter than Good Friday, more directed to proclaiming God's works than bewailing ours. This effort was successful in some of the seasonal prayers which focus on some particular work of God, for example, Christmas or Epiphany.

We are greatly concerned to widen the scope of the commemoration of those works for which we give thanks. For the first time, creation as well as redemption enters our thanksgiving. No longer are we limited to the few hours of the passion. The commemoration sweeps on past Jesus' ministry on earth to "his coming in final victory." We are led to recall thankfully the entire sweep of time, an important escape from the narrow confines of a thousand years of the western euchological tradition. Narration forms the preface and post-sanctus in a thankful recital, proclaiming God's acts. The Luke 4:18 passage, added in 1984, is effective in summarizing Jesus' mission in the words of Isaiah 61:1–2.

Our tradition has had a strong sense of the eucharist as fellowship but this was little expressed in the EP. The 1972 rite has a separate and distinct fraction for the first time but we were also able to articulate this action in the EP: "Make us one with Christ,/one with each other,/and one in service to all the world." The 1984 EP changed "service" to "ministry" but keeps the passage which is essentially an attempt to summarize 1 Corinthians 12.

We found an important resource in Wesley for our treatment of the eucharist as sacrifice, notably in the twelve hymns on "The Holy Eucharist as it implies a Sacrifice." Protestantism in general has been most negative on this concept and the old Methodist prayer was certainly defensive even while praying. By employing Hebrews 9 and 13, Romans 12, and Augustine, we were able to produce a strong positive statement of eucharistic sacrifice. The sequence of the lines has been somewhat shuffled in the 1984 EP but it is better tied to the anamnesis.

Another important element in the Wesleyan eucharistic hymns is the frequent use of imagery about the work of the Holy Spirit. Of course with no epiclesis, the old Methodist prayer had not even the slightest suggestion of the Spirit's work. We were able to remedy this lack with an epiclesis directed to both the congregation and gifts. The 1984 EP dropped the phrase "out of love for you" but gained explicitness in identifying "these gifts" as "of bread and wine." The location of the acclamation after the oblation also gives the final portion of the EP a more distinct role, focusing entirely on the pouring out of the Holy Spirit here and now, not as past commemoration or future hope but as present reality.

In 1972, we did not succeed in stating the presence of Christ in anything stronger than cognitive terms: "Help us know/in the breaking of this bread/and the drinking of this wine/the presence of Christ." Objections to something stronger eventually dissipated and the 1984 EP invokes the Spirit to "Make them be for us the body and blood of Christ." The translation of anamnesis also reverted to "in remembrance" but it is questionable whether this is as strong as "experience anew" or "know anew." Since we had to invent a post-communion prayer (not having one in our tradition other than part of the misplaced canon), we were able to say: "You have given yourself to us, Lord," thus further expressing the presence experienced by the worshiping community.

Eschatology is a strong theme in Wesley's twenty-three hymns on "The Sacrament a Pledge of Heaven." This was expressed in 1972 at the end of the commemoration of the works of God the Son: "[we] look forward to his coming in final victory." A major improvement was moving this phrase to the end of the epiclesis so that it directly follows the Spirit's present activity and is the last word before the doxology: "until Christ comes in final victory/and we feast at his heavenly banquet."

All of these theological factors seem, as far as I can judge, integrated with each other and function well in an oral style. The 1972 EP and its 1984 revision represent for United Methodists an entirely different way of thinking about what it means to give thanks in the eucharist.

I. Presbyterian Historical Antecedents

The three denominations which originally agreed to cooperate in this project had worked closely together in the past. The *Book of Common Worship* 1946 was used broadly by all three.

The *Worshipbook*, 1970, 1972 had had the cooperation of the three denominations during the time of its formation in the late 1960s. The three denominations, with the Reformed Church in America, had shared a common hymnal, *The Hymnbook*, 1955.

The *Worshipbook* had made several notable contributions both within Presbyterianism and ecumenically. It was the first denominational book of services which did not use Tudor English as its medium of expression. It was committed to the use of contemporary language and utilized the interim texts from the International Consultation on English Texts for the Lord's Prayer, the Apostles' and Nicene Creeds, the dialogue introducing the Eucharistic prayer, etc. The language of the hymns included in the *Worshipbook* (with hymns), 1972 was altered in order to make it contemporary. There was an attempt at "the straight-forward use of words and language in current, contemporary use in the last third of the 20th century." Also, the framers of the *Worshipbook* avoided, if possible, the King James version of the Bible, employing newer translations.

The *Worshipbook* recovered and set as the norm for Sunday worship among Presbyterians, the "Word–Table" structure of the service for the Lord's Day. This was substantiated by citing historical precedents, both with reference to the structure of the service and the frequency of its celebration. The eucharist was to be celebrated "as often as each Lord's Day," though there was the expectation that this goal would perhaps be slow in realization. However, even if the Lord's Supper was not celebrated on a given Sunday, the "Word–Table" structure would prevail. No alternative form was provided for a "preaching service" or "daily prayer service" to take place on the Lord's Day.

The *Worshipbook* was the first non-Roman Catholic resource to include an adaptation of the three-year Roman Catholic lectionary. The committee responsible for the *Worshipbook* indicated that the scripture selections in that three-year lectionary, together with their manner of organization, "were remarkably in harmony with the teaching of the Reformation." The lectionary provided alternate readings for the deutero-canonical selections in the Roman Catholic lectionary, and in this altered form the lectionary was recommended for use in Presbyterian churches.

There were four primary concerns that led to the decision to write

In many ways these EPs pick up important but overlooked parts of Wesleyan theology and of the wider Christian tradition, certainly for more than the single EP of 1965 could. In this, they bring us closer to the worship of Christians at all times and places, both past and present.

ARLO D. DUBA

6

Presbyterian Eucharistic Prayers

In 1979 the Joint Office of Worship (of the United Presbyterian Church USA and the Presbyterian Church US), responding to an overture and recommendation from a group of Presbyterian Churches in Oregon, developed a proposal for the formation of new liturgical resources for Presbyterians. The 1980 United Presbyterian General Assembly authorized the development of a plan which would provide supplemental liturgical resources and also authorized contact with other Presbyterian denominations in the United States which might be invited to participate in the project.

In the fall of 1980, the Division of National Missions of the Presbyterian Church US (often referred to as the Southern Presbyterian Church) and the Board of Christian Education of the Cumberland Presbyterian Church became full partners in the process of the development of the new liturgical resources.

The process would involve the appointment of a number of task forces representative of the three denominations and the production of a series of Supplemental Liturgical Resources for interim and provisional use with a view to the eventual production of a new liturgical book about 1990.

The United Presbyterian Church USA and the Presbyterian Church US merged in the spring of 1983, becoming the Presbyterian Church (USA). The task of coordinating the liturgy project was centered in the

Office of Worship of this denomination in Louisville, Kentucky, under the direction of the Rev. Dr. Harold M. Daniels.

The Office of Worship functioned through an Administrative Committee which had the prerogative of reviewing the work of all the task forces. Harold Daniels, as the Director of the Office, functioned as the primary resource person for all task forces and provided resources on such matters as historical and theological antecedents, both ancient and modern, and the biblical and pastoral concerns of the church. Through his personal contact with persons and worship offices of other denominations he shared information and reactions from those sources with each task force.

The task force on "The Service for the Lord's Day" was charged with the production of a manuscript which would embody the following guidelines:

1. Liturgical text for The Service for the Lord's Day (service of Wor and Lord's Supper) for use in congregational worship.
2. A book of not more than 96 pages containing:
   a. background support material of a historical, theological a practical nature;
   b. alternate liturgical texts;
   c. annotated bibliography.
      The resource will be faithful to the Reformed perspectiv worship and the sacraments, and reflect an understandir the directories for worship of the respective denominat The resource will incorporate insights from contempor turgical scholarship (historical, theological and pa within the broad ecumenical arena.
3. The resource will reflect pastoral sensitivity by showing for the diversity within the churches and be usable in a v riety of situations.

Additional guidelines were provided for the task force wi ence to inclusiveness. The resulting publication was to dem awareness of and utilization of materials from various ethnic tives, the utilization of sex inclusive language and, finally, demonstrate that the drafters were "familiar with the curre Word and Lord's Supper of other denominations, togethe theological/historical/practical rationale of the rites."

a new service for the Lord's day, three of which had to do with perceived weaknesses in the *Worshipbook* and one which was a matter of ecumenical development. These four areas are:

1. the issue of language;
2. the eucharistic prayer;
3. the need for additional resource materials;
4. the ecumenical climate among the Christian churches.

Language. The International Council on English Texts (ICET) moved beyond the interim drafts which were utilized in the *Worshipbook.* The *Worshipbook* inclusion of these provisional texts had been premature and they were soon superseded.

Immediately after the *Worshipbook* was published the issue of inclusive language came to the fore. While the language of the *Worshipbook* was contemporary, it was markedly sexist. The bias was evident both in the liturgies and in the hymns. Thus, the ink had hardly dried when a great hue and cry arose concerning the justice issue of inequality and non-inclusiveness.

Eucharistic prayer. At the time the *Worshipbook* was drafted, the sixteenth century ideal of "one fixed canon" for the eucharistic prayer prevailed in virtually all Christian communions. Thus, the *Worshipbook* provided only one eucharistic prayer. Especially in those churches which were celebrating the eucharist more and more frequently, there was a desire for a broader repertoire for eucharistic praying. Furthermore, by the time of its publication, the Roman Church had expanded its number of official eucharistic prayers, thus establishing a new norm.

A paucity of resources. There was a desire for a broad range of liturgical resources which moved beyond the rather narrow range provided in the *Worshipbook.* Resources for the Christian year, a variety of prayers of confession, alternate forms for the prayers of the people and other similar resources were being requested.

Ecumenical developments. Resources developed by churches of other traditions were being used by individual pastors to fill the perceived gaps. There was a strong desire to have resources made available in one place for pastors and congregations, resources that could be drawn together from the new liturgical books of other traditions and which could be made available in one place.

The action of the General Assembly in 1980 was an attempt to respond to those needs and to create a process by which additional resources could be provided for the churches.

II. The Work of the Task Force

The task force met during 1981 and 1982, with the last meeting held in March of 1983. Two study papers were provided for the committee, both by David Pfleiderer. The first one dealt with "liturgical issues" (July 1981) and outlined twelve areas for study and discussion. There were; 1. theology (lex orandi, lex credendi), 2. to whom is the liturgy addressed, 3. symbolism, 4. language, 5. the Bible, 6. the comparative roles of clergy-laity, 7. sacrifice and offering, 8. Christ–real presence, memorial, mediator, 9. the Words of Institution, 10. seasonal variants, 11. rubics, 12. the peace.

A second paper "Reflections on 'Blessings' and 'Offering' " (February 10, 1982) dealt with the role of the pastor in blessing, and it raised questions concerning the appropriateness of including the offering of possessions together with the "offering" of the gifts of the bread and the cup. It also suggested the appropriateness of a ritual response of alms-giving and commitment, following the receiving of the eucharist, rather than preceding it.

The discussion of these issues guided the task force as it made its decisions concerning the development of a total service. In response to the needs expressed by pastors in the church it was decided to provide numerous options at several points, including several eucharistic prayers. Each person on the task force wrote at least one eucharistic prayer which was shared with the entire group. In addition, eucharistic prayers which were written by others were also considered.

The basic work of the task force was completed by January 1983. This work was shared with the eucharistic prayer sub-committee of the North American Academy of Liturgy (NAAL) in January of 1983, providing the first outside reaction to and evaluation of the work of the committee. However, because of the lateness of this sharing, very little of the Academy evaluation was incorporated into the preliminary manuscript of the task force which was completed early that spring.

The completed manuscript was sent out to the churches accompanied by a letter from Harold M. Daniels dated July 1983. The manuscript was a type-script, field testing document that was sent to congregations of Presbyterian churches as well as to individuals both within and beyond the Presbyterian denomination.

Churches were asked "to incorporate the liturgical text into the worship as you are able, and use the order that is suggested." Committees from field testing sites and individuals were asked to react and to make suggestions concerning (1) the order of worship, (2) the interpretive material, (3) the liturgical text, and (4) the title of the resource. The

II. The Work of the Task Force

The task force met during 1981 and 1982, with the last meeting held in March of 1983. Two study papers were provided for the committee, both by David Pfleiderer. The first one dealt with "liturgical issues" (July 1981) and outlined twelve areas for study and discussion. There were; 1. theology (lex orandi, lex credendi), 2. to whom is the liturgy addressed, 3. symbolism, 4. language, 5. the Bible, 6. the comparative roles of clergy-laity, 7. sacrifice and offering, 8. Christ–real presence, memorial, mediator, 9. the Words of Institution, 10. seasonal variants, 11. rubics, 12. the peace.

A second paper "Reflections on 'Blessings' and 'Offering' " (February 10, 1982) dealt with the role of the pastor in blessing, and it raised questions concerning the appropriateness of including the offering of possessions together with the "offering" of the gifts of the bread and the cup. It also suggested the appropriateness of a ritual response of alms-giving and commitment, following the receiving of the eucharist, rather than preceding it.

The discussion of these issues guided the task force as it made its decisions concerning the development of a total service. In response to the needs expressed by pastors in the church it was decided to provide numerous options at several points, including several eucharistic prayers. Each person on the task force wrote at least one eucharistic prayer which was shared with the entire group. In addition, eucharistic prayers which were written by others were also considered.

The basic work of the task force was completed by January 1983. This work was shared with the eucharistic prayer sub-committee of the North American Academy of Liturgy (NAAL) in January of 1983, providing the first outside reaction to and evaluation of the work of the committee. However, because of the lateness of this sharing, very little of the Academy evaluation was incorporated into the preliminary manuscript of the task force which was completed early that spring.

The completed manuscript was sent out to the churches accompanied by a letter from Harold M. Daniels dated July 1983. The manuscript was a type-script, field testing document that was sent to congregations of Presbyterian churches as well as to individuals both within and beyond the Presbyterian denomination.

Churches were asked "to incorporate the liturgical text into the worship as you are able, and use the order that is suggested." Committees from field testing sites and individuals were asked to react and to make suggestions concerning (1) the order of worship, (2) the interpretive material, (3) the liturgical text, and (4) the title of the resource. The a new service for the Lord's day, three of which had to do with perceived weaknesses in the *Worshipbook* and one which was a matter of ecumenical development. These four areas are:

1. the issue of language;
2. the eucharistic prayer;
3. the need for additional resource materials;
4. the ecumenical climate among the Christian churches.

Language. The International Council on English Texts (ICET) moved beyond the interim drafts which were utilized in the *Worshipbook*. The *Worshipbook* inclusion of these provisional texts had been premature and they were soon superseded.

Immediately after the *Worshipbook* was published the issue of inclusive language came to the fore. While the language of the *Worshipbook* was contemporary, it was markedly sexist. The bias was evident both in the liturgies and in the hymns. Thus, the ink had hardly dried when a great hue and cry arose concerning the justice issue of inequality and non-inclusiveness.

Eucharistic prayer. At the time the *Worshipbook* was drafted, the sixteenth century ideal of "one fixed canon" for the eucharistic prayer prevailed in virtually all Christian communions. Thus, the *Worshipbook* provided only one eucharistic prayer. Especially in those churches which were celebrating the eucharist more and more frequently, there was a desire for a broader repertoire for eucharistic praying. Furthermore, by the time of its publication, the Roman Church had expanded its number of official eucharistic prayers, thus establishing a new norm.

A paucity of resources. There was a desire for a broad range of liturgical resources which moved beyond the rather narrow range provided in the *Worshipbook*. Resources for the Christian year, a variety of prayers of confession, alternate forms for the prayers of the people and other similar resources were being requested.

Ecumenical developments. Resources developed by churches of other traditions were being used by individual pastors to fill the perceived gaps. There was a strong desire to have resources made available in one place for pastors and congregations, resources that could be drawn together from the new liturgical books of other traditions and which could be made available in one place.

The action of the General Assembly in 1980 was an attempt to respond to those needs and to create a process by which additional resources could be provided for the churches.

In many ways these EPs pick up important but overlooked parts of Wesleyan theology and of the wider Christian tradition, certainly for more than the single EP of 1965 could. In this, they bring us closer to the worship of Christians at all times and places, both past and present.

ARLO D. DUBA

6

Presbyterian Eucharistic Prayers

In 1979 the Joint Office of Worship (of the United Presbyterian Church USA and the Presbyterian Church US), responding to an overture and recommendation from a group of Presbyterian Churches in Oregon, developed a proposal for the formation of new liturgical resources for Presbyterians. The 1980 United Presbyterian General Assembly authorized the development of a plan which would provide supplemental liturgical resources and also authorized contact with other Presbyterian denominations in the United States which might be invited to participate in the project.

In the fall of 1980, the Division of National Missions of the Presbyterian Church US (often referred to as the Southern Presbyterian Church) and the Board of Christian Education of the Cumberland Presbyterian Church became full partners in the process of the development of the new liturgical resources.

The process would involve the appointment of a number of task forces representative of the three denominations and the production of a series of Supplemental Liturgical Resources for interim and provisional use with a view to the eventual production of a new liturgical book about 1990.

The United Presbyterian Church USA and the Presbyterian Church US merged in the spring of 1983, becoming the Presbyterian Church (USA). The task of coordinating the liturgy project was centered in the

Office of Worship of this denomination in Louisville, Kentucky, under the direction of the Rev. Dr. Harold M. Daniels.

The Office of Worship functioned through an Administrative Committee which had the prerogative of reviewing the work of all the task forces. Harold Daniels, as the Director of the Office, functioned as the primary resource person for all task forces and provided resources on such matters as historical and theological antecedents, both ancient and modern, and the biblical and pastoral concerns of the church. Through his personal contact with persons and worship offices of other denominations he shared information and reactions from those sources with each task force.

The task force on "The Service for the Lord's Day" was charged with the production of a manuscript which would embody the following guidelines:

1. Liturgical text for The Service for the Lord's Day (service of Word and Lord's Supper) for use in congregational worship.
2. A book of not more than 96 pages containing:
   a. background support material of a historical, theological and practical nature;
   b. alternate liturgical texts;
   c. annotated bibliography.
      The resource will be faithful to the Reformed perspective on worship and the sacraments, and reflect an understanding of the directories for worship of the respective denominations. The resource will incorporate insights from contemporary liturgical scholarship (historical, theological and pastoral) within the broad ecumenical arena.
3. The resource will reflect pastoral sensitivity by showing respect for the diversity within the churches and be usable in a wide variety of situations.

Additional guidelines were provided for the task force with reference to inclusiveness. The resulting publication was to demonstrate awareness of and utilization of materials from various ethnic perspectives, the utilization of sex inclusive language and, finally, it was to demonstrate that the drafters were "familiar with the current rites of Word and Lord's Supper of other denominations, together with the theological/historical/practical rationale of the rites."

I. Presbyterian Historical Antecedents

The three denominations which originally agreed to cooperate in this project had worked closely together in the past. The *Book of Common Worship* 1946 was used broadly by all three.

The *Worshipbook*, 1970, 1972 had had the cooperation of the three denominations during the time of its formation in the late 1960s. The three denominations, with the Reformed Church in America, had shared a common hymnal, *The Hymnbook*, 1955.

The *Worshipbook* had made several notable contributions both within Presbyterianism and ecumenically. It was the first denominational book of services which did not use Tudor English as its medium of expression. It was committed to the use of contemporary language and utilized the interim texts from the International Consultation on English Texts for the Lord's Prayer, the Apostles' and Nicene Creeds, the dialogue introducing the Eucharistic prayer, etc. The language of the hymns included in the *Worshipbook* (with hymns), 1972 was altered in order to make it contemporary. There was an attempt at "the straight-forward use of words and language in current, contemporary use in the last third of the 20th century." Also, the framers of the *Worshipbook* avoided, if possible, the King James version of the Bible, employing newer translations.

The *Worshipbook* recovered and set as the norm for Sunday worship among Presbyterians, the "Word–Table" structure of the service for the Lord's Day. This was substantiated by citing historical precedents, both with reference to the structure of the service and the frequency of its celebration. The eucharist was to be celebrated "as often as each Lord's Day," though there was the expectation that this goal would perhaps be slow in realization. However, even if the Lord's Supper was not celebrated on a given Sunday, the "Word–Table" structure would prevail. No alternative form was provided for a "preaching service" or "daily prayer service" to take place on the Lord's Day.

The *Worshipbook* was the first non-Roman Catholic resource to include an adaptation of the three-year Roman Catholic lectionary. The committee responsible for the *Worshipbook* indicated that the scripture selections in that three-year lectionary, together with their manner of organization, "were remarkably in harmony with the teaching of the Reformation." The lectionary provided alternate readings for the deutero-canonical selections in the Roman Catholic lectionary, and in this altered form the lectionary was recommended for use in Presbyterian churches.

There were four primary concerns that led to the decision to write reason for the last item was some concern about the use of the masculine term "Lord" in the title.

The document included seven eucharistic prayers, only three of which were entirely new for this resource, prayers A, E, and G. Prayer A provided an option of a number of seasonal prefaces. Prayer B was a revision of the eucharistic prayer found in the *Worshipbook*. Prayer C was an adaptation of the eucharistic prayer originally drafted by Henry Van Dyke based on the 1621 *Book of Common Prayer* and published in the *Book of Common Worship*, 1906, altered in the *Book of Common Worship*, 1932, and still in wide use. Prayer D was a translation of the eucharistic prayer of Hippolytus. Prayer E was a new composition based on John Calvin's 1542 communion exhortation. Prayer F was from the eucharistic liturgy of Taizé. Prayer G was a very brief prayer, not for use in Sunday congregational worship, but "was designed for use in house communions or in informal situations," or with the sick.

The response to the field testing document was voluminous. In addition to responses from pastors, local church committees and individuals within the Presbyterian tradition, responses were received from a number of persons from other traditions. As a result, Harold Daniels, in consultation with the Administrative Committee of the Office of Worship, began the process of forming the final draft.

The original prayer A which had been written for this resource was found quite unsatisfactory by virtually all respondents. It was deleted.

The first draft of the *Worshipbook* prayer, done by the Rev. David Romig, was further revised. David Romig was the only person on this task force who had also served on the committee which developed the services for the *Worshipbook* in the 1960s. This prayer became prayer A in the final manuscript.

A new prayer, primarily drafted by the Rev. Dr. Ross MacKenzie, was to embody language which, according to the accepted standards of the time, is entirely "inclusive" with reference to sex-specific words. Neither the people of God nor the deity was referred to by the use of sex-specific words. The word "Father" was avoided as was the word "Son," although masculine pronouns were used with reference to Christ. Some passages from the prayer will illustrate this.

> Holy God,
> in your mercy you sent the One in whom your fullness dwells,
> your only begotten,
> to be for us the way, the truth and the life.
> In Jesus, born of Mary, your Word became flesh
> and dwells among us, full of grace and truth.

We glorify you for your great power and mercy in Christ.
By his suffering and death on the cross,
our sins are forgiven.
In rising from the grave,
he won for us victory over death. . . .

Through Christ, with Christ, in Christ,
in the unity of the Holy Spirit,
all glory and honor are yours, Almighty God,
now and forever.

This became prayer B in the final manuscript.

Harold M. Daniel provided the first draft of the revision of the *Book of Common Worship* eucharistic prayer. As indicated above, this prayer is probably the best known and most used among all Presbyterians. It received a high rate of acceptance in the field testing, and a few suggestions which came from the field testing were incorporated. This prayer became prayer C in the final manuscript.

The first draft of the translation of the prayer of Hippolytus was provided by the Rev. Dr. Horace Allen. This translation was refined primarily on the basis of the discussion which took place at the North American Academy of Liturgy. In addition to the work done on this prayer by Horace Allen and Harold Daniels of the task force, the significant work of Professor Gordon Lathrop should be mentioned as should Father Patrick Byrne and other members of the Eucharistic Prayer Group of the North American Academy of Liturgy. The prayer of Hippolytus became prayer D in the final manuscript.

The eucharistic prayer from the liturgy of Taizé received very little acceptance. It was entirely deleted. In its place, the Administrative Committee decided to include what has come to be known as "the common eucharistic prayer," which was drafted in 1974, modeled after the Alexandrine liturgy of St. Basil. This prayer was published by the Consultation on Church Union, was considered by the Inter-Lutheran Commission on Worship, has been authorized by the United Methodist Church, and appears also in the *Book of Common Prayer*, 1977. A very similar prayer is found in the Roman Sacramentary. This prayer became prayer E in the final manuscript.

It was also decided to include the eucharistic prayer developed by the Commission on Worship of the Consultation on Church Union which appears in its publication, *The Sacrament of the Lord's Supper: A New Text 1984*. This is eucharistic prayer F in the final manuscript.

The Rev. Dr. David Pfleiderer had drafted the eucharistic prayer which was inspired by John Calvin's communion exhortation of 1542.

This draft was left virtually unchanged from the field testing document. This rather short prayer which includes the reformed epiclesis "lift our hearts and minds on high . . . " became eucharistic prayer G in the final document.

The brief prayer for small, informal celebrations was drafted by Ross MacKenzie and revisions were made in consultation with Professor John Burkhart. In twenty-three brief lines this prayer seeks to cover what is necessary in eucharistic praying. This became eucharistic prayer H in the final manuscript.

When *The Service for the Lord's Day* was printed, it included these eight eucharistic prayers. The final copy was completed in the spring of 1984 and it was rushed into print so that the published book could be available at the Presbyterian General Assembly which met in Phoenix, Arizona, May 29–June 6, 1984. The first books arrived from the printer after the first several days of the Assembly were past. These were immediately purchased from the bookstore and soon were in evidence among participants at the Assembly. The book, entitled *Service for the Lord's Day*, Supplemental Liturgical Resource 1 (Westminster Press, 1984), had immediate and wide circulation.

III. Issues with Reference to the Prayers

We will look first at the consistency manifested in the prayers, then at the centrality of the eucharist, then at four structural items, then at five major theological themes with several sub-themes, and finally we will conclude with some comments on the reception which the book has received. A chart is appended which will both summarize the discussion and provide a graphic display of the comparisons which will be made.

The Issue of Consistency. One of the issues that becomes evident from reading the minutes of the committee as well as from a survey of the services themselves is that the committee was not reaching for consistency. The services and the eucharistic prayers within them are electic in nature, generally reflecting theological emphases from the Reformed tradition, but at the same time very much alert to, and expressive of, the ecumenical consensus which is forming within Western Christendom.

The prayers may be criticized for this lack of consistency, although the resulting variety may also be lauded by some. Analysis becomes difficult because there is no evident theology driving the composition of the prayers. There seems to be no "canon within the canon" as in other eucharist prayer collections. There is no consistent wording for the institution narrative as one finds in Prayers 1–3 in the *Lutheran Book of Worship,* or in prayers A, B and D of Rite II in the *Book of Common Prayer,* 1977. The wording of the institution narrative is different in each of the prayers written for this resource. This will without doubt create difficulty for those who preside at the eucharist.

The memorial acclamation of the mystery of faith is not consistent in its form or in its placement. Several forms are provided, with a preference for:

> Christ has died,
> Christ is risen,
> Christ will come again.

The acclamation which is found in the text of the Common Eucharistic Prayer (E) is:

> We praise you, we bless you,
> We give thanks to you,
> And we pray for you, Lord our God.

This acclamation is not found among the four memorial acclamations on page 119, raising a question about the interchangeability of the acclamations.

There is no common "cue line" for the congregation to bring them into the acclamation. And the acclamation varies in its placement. In prayer A, C and G it is after the anamnesis while in prayer B it immediately follows the institution narrative. In prayer F it follows an extended anamnesis and is placed immediately before the epiclesis.

There is no common oblation as one finds in the United Methodist prayers, which words ring clear in every prayer written specifically for Supplemental Worship Resource 9, *At the Lord's Table:*

> . . . we ask you to accept this our sacrifice
> of praise and thanksgiving
> which we offer
> in union with Christ's sacrifice for us,
> as a living and holy
> surrender of ourselves.

As intimated before, this latitude can be attributed to an affirmation of diversity in the church. However, it also militates against coherent theological teaching and against ease in presiding. C.S. Lewis said that one is not dancing when one still must count the steps. The danger here is that these liturgies may never be danced because they contain so much variety as to make familiarity very difficult.

Centrality of the Eucharist. Supporting denominational documents and the services themselves demonstrate that it is expected that the eucharist will be celebrated "as often as each Lord's Day." The eucharist is conceived of as the normal service of each Lord's Day and of all Christological festivals. It should be noted that, in keeping with the tradition of Reformed thinking, the eucharist seems not to be recommended for days other than the Lord's Day and Christological festivals. Rather, the daily office is the appropriate worship for other days.

There are differences of opinion within the Presbyterian and Reformed tradition about the weekly celebration of the eucharist. Some will feel that this document does not stress strongly enough the desirability for weekly celebrations. Others will feel that it is too insistent in this emphasis. This is a case of pastoral compromise.

However, the integrity of the Word–Supper unity is never compromised. There is no option of a preaching service which might find its origin in morning prayer, in the revivals of the Great Awakening or in Zwingli's reformation teaching. Even if the eucharist is not celebrated in Sunday worship, the word–table structure prevails. The "Directory for the Service of God" of the Presbyterian Church states that "It is fitting to celebrate the Sacrament as frequently as each Lord's Day, and at least as often as quarterly. Observance should be regular enough that it is seen as a proper part of and not an addition to the worship of God" (The *Book of Order* of the Presbyterian Church, "The Directory for the Service of God," 3.0500). Presbyterian congregations are to be taught that the exclusion of the supper from Sunday worship is an aberration which needs to be remedied.

Another Reformed emphasis is very evident. The word will always be preached before the Lord's Supper is celebrated. However, as can be seen from what has been said above, it is not required that the sacrament be celebrated whenever the word has been preached.

IV. Structural Considerations

The Indispensable Prayer. Whenever the eucharist is celebrated there shall be an eucharistic prayer. "The presiding minister stands behind the table with the elders on either side," and, beginning with the dialogue, leads the people in the Great Prayer of Thanksgiving (*Service for the Lord's Day*, p. 166).

The Roman Rite. There are lively discussions among scholars concerning whether the West Syrian model for eucharistic praying should monopolize the eucharistic services of the Western church. In the Reformed tradition the Mercersberg liturgy provided the possibility of two prayers divided by a declaration of the words of institution. Some have suggested a prayer modeled after Jesus' high priestly prayer in John 14–16. Some have suggested the inclusion of a Byzantine or Oriental model for Western eucharistic praying.

The decision of this committee was an affirmation of the West Syrian model and of the western (Roman) rite as providing the common and uniform structure for the Presbyterian eucharistic prayers.

Words of Institution. The sixteenth century reformers insisted that the words of institution be announced audibly and directed declaratively to the congregation. This practice has prevailed in virtually all documents coming from the Reformed tradition until after the second world war. The earliest eucharistic prayer of the Reformed Community in Taizé, France once again included the words of institution within the eucharist prayer. However, the *Worshipbook* had no provision for inclusion within the prayer.

There was significant discussion in the committee as to whether the words of institution would be within or outside of the prayer proper. There was further discussion as to whether the institution narrative, being included within the prayer, would be in the form of a credal declaration of the words.

The committee had an obvious preference for the inclusion of the words within the prayer; however, the option of the use of the words of institution outside the prayer, usually with the fraction, is still permitted. "The reason for including this institution narrative in some of the prayers is to move us beyond the theological debates of the 16th Century, since those issues are not major considerations today. . . . Whether made a part of the prayer or read separately it is important that the narrative be included in each celebration of the Supper" (*Service of the Lord's Day*, pp. 168–69).

The institution narrative is included within the body of the first six prayers. It is outside the prayer in prayer G (fittingly, the prayer taken from John Calvin) and prayer H, the one used in informal, house and hospital communions. Prayers A, B and C have a rubric which would permit the use of the institution narrative outside the prayer.

The Presbyterian prayers, following the pattern of the Roman rite, include the words of institution in prayer form; they address the Father:

> We thank you that on the night before he died,
> Jesus took bread . . . (Prayer A).

> On the night of his betrayal, the Lord Jesus took bread.
> After giving thanks to you . . . (Prayer C).

Only the Lutheran prayers 1–3 consistently use the form of credal declaration, without any address to the Father. The Cranmer prayer, retained in Holy Eucharist I, Eucharistic Prayer I (*Book of Common Prayer*, 1977) and Great Thanksgiving 2: Traditional Anglican-Methodist (*At the Lord's Table*, United Methodist Supplemental Resources 9) also use direct credal declaration.

Intercessions. While the Lord's Day service always includes prayers of intercession before the introduction of the offering, intercessions are listed and provision for free intercessions is provided in prayers B, E and F. There are tacit or implied intercessions in prayer C.

Preface. Proper prefaces are provided in prayers A, B, C and F. The Hippolytus prayer (D), the Calvin prayer (G) and the home communion prayer (H) do not lend themselves to the use of a preface. The common eucharistic prayer (E) could easily be adapted to include a seasonal preface.

A total of thirty-eight prefaces are available in the book. The question is raised as to their interchangeability. They are not presented in the book in such a way that they could be easily interchanged. Perhaps the resource could be further refined to make these prefaces easily interchangeable. This is particularly true of the five general prefaces.

The prefaces themselves are eclectic, some being traceable to Latin sources of the Roman rite, to the *Book of Common Prayer*, the *Lutheran Book of Worship* and the *Book of Common Worship*. Much of the work on these prefaces was done by Harold Daniels.

V. Theological Issues

Both the Christian tradition and the Presbyterian and Reformed confessions and documents provide a number of theological theses which one could expect to find reflected within the eucharistic prayers of the Reformed tradition. There follow five such theological themes with a number of sub-themes, and a brief analysis of how the prayers measure up.

Basic Themes

The Trinity. In Christian history, since Nicea-Constantinople, the Trinity and the present mystery of the Trinity in which we are to participate has been central within the Christian faith. Historically, there has been an integral relationship between the mystery of the Trinity and the eucharist, and this relationship has been particularly emphasized within the Reformed tradition where, from the time of Calvin, the eucharist has been seen as the gift of God through the work of the Holy Spirit.

The committee, in following the model of the Roman rite, wrote eucharistic prayers which are trinitarian in structure and in inspiration. The Father, the origin of all that is, the author of salvation and the fulfillment of all things, is the one to whom the prayer is addressed. The Son is the incarnational center in, with and through whom the eucharist comes into being, is celebrated and fulfilled. The Holy Spirit is the empowering, presence-engendering, actualizer of remembrance.

The Trinity must mark the whole liturgy, but especially the prayer.

It would seem that with this strong centrality of the Trinity, the language of these eight prayers is minimal in its expression of the Trinity, particularly of the Holy Spirit. It is notable that the three prayers adapted from outside sources (the Hippolytus prayer [D], the common eucharistic prayer [E] and COCU prayer [F]) are much more expressive of trinitarian language than the prayers written for this resource.

All eight prayers mention the Holy Spirit at the epiclesis and refer to the Father, Son and Holy Spirit in the closing doxology. In addition, the Hippolytus prayer mentions the Holy Spirit with reference to the incarnation. The common eucharistic prayer speaks of the Trinity (Father, Son and Holy Spirit) with reference to the incarnation, the Holy Spirit as the gift sent by Christ and contains an allusion to "one spirit" as one of the fruits of communion. The COCU text (Prayer F) mentions the Holy Spirit with reference to the incarnation, at Jesus' baptism and as forming the church.

Trinitarian language and mention of the Holy Spirit is also minimal in the prefaces. The Trinity is specifically mentioned only in the Trinity Sunday preface of prayer A. The Holy Spirit is mentioned in the preface of the baptism of Jesus (A), implied at the transfiguration (A), of Pentecost (A, C and F) and as the preface in which baptism is celebrated (A).

Hebrew Scriptures and the Totality of Holy History. The eucharist is a culmination and summary of the whole created order, from the beginning until the consummation. The eucharist is the feast of the Jewish people. The eucharist prayer itself is related to the *berakoth* of Judiasm and gains its emphasis on comprehensiveness from that source.

Three items stand out which it seems should characterize eucharistic praying: (1) the creation, (2) time, and (3) the totality of holy history—the covenants and the prophets, the church, and the parousia.

Is the world present in these eucharistic celebrations? Does God's order challenge the disorders of this world and of our history?

The Creation. All of the prayers with the exception of the Hippolytus prayer (D) specifically refer to God's creation of all things.

There are additional references to creation and the created order in several of the prefaces. However, it seems that the presence of the world could be more convincingly expressed in the prayers, and the gift of God's order to replace the chaos of human disorder should be more evident.

There seems to be a hesitancy about the created order in these prayers which is also characteristic of the prevailing theologies of the recent past.

Time. Time references are particularly limited to the seasons of the Christian year as represented in the variable prefaces. As will be noted from the number of prefaces, this marking of Christian time also includes occasions in human life such as birth, death, marriage, commissioning, etc.

Holy History. While there is an attempt to be aware of the entirety of holy history, it seems that there could be additional references to Israel and to holy history. Promises to the people of Israel are mentioned only in prayer H. The key and seminal covenant of Moses, with the giving of the law and the celebration of the passover, is intimated in the first general preface and in the post-sanctus of prayer F. There is a reference to Christ our Passover only in the second of the three Easter prefaces. There is a reference to Abraham and Isaac and other forebears in the marriage preface (A) and there is reference to the prophets in the pre-sanctus of A, in G and in F (under church). The prophets are also mentioned in the Advent and Lent preface of A and Advent of C.

There are additional biblical allusions but they are not as prominent or prevalent as one would expect within a tradition that has placed so much emphasis on the unity of Scripture and the importance of the Hebrew Scriptures.

References to the apostles and martyrs is generally limited to the pre-sanctus. The preface for All Saints Day says "We praise you today for saints and martyrs, faithful people in every age . . . " (A). The general preface III of prayer A simply says "You set us in families on the earth to live with you in faith." Most people will hear this in terms of nuclear families rather than families of faith. The church in its varied and broad manifestations seems little mentioned.

The present reality of eternal life seems to be confined to eschatological statements. In other words, in these prayers eschatology seems not to be realized in the here and now. For example, in prayer A, "We trust him (Jesus) to overcome every power that can hurt or divide us, and believe that when he comes in glory we will celebrate victory with him."

The presence of eternal life in contemporary Christian living is most graphically stated in prayer A in the sentence which leads to the closing doxology:

> Fill us with eternal life,
> That with joy we may be his faithful people
> Until we feast with him in glory (p. 97).

This is also hinted in prayer B:

> We praise you that Christ our life now reigns with you in glory,
> Praying for us,
> Until all things are made perfect in Christ (p. 99).

> In union with your church in heaven and on earth,
> We pray that you will fulfill your eternal purpose
> In us and in all the world (p. 100).

Christology

Anamnesis. There is an evident attempt on the part of the task force to keep in balance the dual anamnestic dimensions of the past and the future; of the historic sacrifice of Christ (the death-resurrection) and of festive, jubilant participation in the kingdom which is to come.

The prefaces which may be included and the anamnesis which is included in each eucharistic prayer provide excellent historic representation of the person and the work of Christ. For example:

> Like a dove, your Spirit descended on him,
> anointing him as the Christ,
> sent to preach good news to the poor
> and proclaim release to the captives;

> to recover sight for the blind
> and set free the oppressed;
> to announce that the time had come
> when you would save your people. . . .
> > (Preface for the Baptism of the Lord, prayer A)

> Therefore,
> remembering his incarnation and holy life,
> his death and glorious resurrection,
> his ascension and continual intercession for us,
> and awaiting his coming again in power and great glory,
> we claim his eternal sacrifice and celebrate with these
> your holy gifts
> the memorial your Son commanded us to make.
> > (Anamnesis from prayer C)

The festive, jubilant participation in the banquet of the kingdom is portrayed in the first invitation to the Lord's Table, an adaptation of Luke 13:29, which is followed by the Emmaus account of the risen Lord with his disciples:

> Friends, this is the joyful feast of the people of God!
> They will come from east and west
> and from north and south,
> and sit at the table in the kingdom of God.

The task force was also careful to include both the festive and the penitential dimensions of the supper. The second invitation serves to balance the first and lends itself well to a penitential tone:

> Come to me, all you who labor and are heavily burdened,
> and I will give you rest.
> Take my yoke upon you, and learn from me. . . .

The prayers express well and in varied ways the anamnesis of the representation of the historic life and work of Christ. They are effective, but not as lavish, in expressing the anamnesis of the eschatological banquet and of the very presence of the kingdom of Christ (and thus of Christ himself) in our midst.

Christ's presence and the signs of bread and wine. The Reformed tradition has always affirmed that the entire eucharist, and not merely the bread and the cup, together with the historical words of Scripture and of prayer, are necessary components of the bearing of this presence.

Thus, one searches the eucharist, and particularly the eucharistic prayers, for Christ-bearing language, language of Christ's presence.

The entire service should be christopherical and the language itself should be Christ-bearing. An example of such language is in prayer H:

We bless you for creating the whole world,
For your promises to people Israel,
and for the life we know in Jesus Christ your Son.

Born of Mary, he shares our life.
Eating with sinners, he welcomes us.
Leading his followers, he guides us.
Dying on the cross he rescues us.
Risen from the dead, he gives new life. . . .

Unite us in faith, inspire us to love,
encourage us with hope,
that we may receive Christ as he comes to us in this holy banquet (p. 118).

Here the past and the present are totally joined. Christ who comes to us in the banquet is one whom we know now, in our present life, where he welcomes, guides, rescues and gives new life, with faith, hope and love.

In contrast, the first general preface of prayer A expresses the general past tense syntax of that entire prayer:

You commanded light to shine out of darkness,
divided the sea and dry land,
created the vast universe and called it good.
You made us in your image to live with one another in love.
You gave us the breath of life
and freedom to choose your way.
You set forth your purpose in commandments through Moses,
and called for justice in the cry of prophets.
Through long generations
you have been patient and kind to all your children.

Yes, it is assumed that God continues to bring light, that God continues to fill us with the breath of life, that God continues to call for justice and is patient and kind to us today. But the syntax of this prayer does not clearly express this presence and present activity of God, but speaks of it in the past tense. Statement of the presence of Christ waits for the conclusion of that prayer which states:

> Fill us with eternal life,
> that with joy we may be his faithful people
> until we feast with him in glory.

The past tense of the prayer "turns" on these three lines. Suddenly we are at the parousia. Thus, while presence is acknowledged, it would seem that in some of the prayers, this dimension could be more prominently and positively stated.

The bread and the wine. The services and the prayers of *The Service for the Lord's Day* avoid localizing the presence of Christ in the bread and the wine, but the bread and the wine are an indispensable accompaniment of the service in which the presence of Christ is experienced and received. The Constitution of the Presbyterian Church, in its "Directory for the Service of God," lists a number of components: "the Words of Institution . . . the prayer and the responses . . . the invocation of the Holy Spirit . . . the breaking of the bread and the pouring of the wine . . . (and) the distribution and partaking of the elements show the reality of the believers' union with Christ by faith and their willingness that Christ's presence should abide in them" (Directory for the Service of God, 3.05, p. 176).

"Both sacraments . . . declare that Jesus Christ is present" (Directory for the Service of God, 3.01, p. 170).

Christ as host and primary actor. One of the salient Christological doctrines of the Reformed tradition is that Christ is our only high priest, advocate and mediator. Ordained "ministers act not on their own right but on behalf of Christ and the church" (Directory for the Service of God, 3.01, "The Sacraments").

The second Helvetic Confession speaks very specifically about the role of ministers in the celebration of the sacraments. A minister of the church is "commanded to carry out only what he has received in commandment from his Lord, and not to indulge in his free choice" (5.155). The minister is to "carry out everything as the Lord has commanded" (5.159). There is power in the office of the minister, but "this is more like a service than a dominion" (5.159). It is a power only insofar as the minister becomes a steward of the mysteries and permits Christ to work through the present ministry of the church. It is Christ who speaks in the sermon and who acts and is present in the sacraments. Under the section on the sacraments, 5.173 states:

CHRIST STILL WORKS IN SACRAMENTS. And as God is the author of the sacraments, so he continually works in the church in which they are rightly carried out; so that the faithful, when they receive them from the ministers, know that God works in his own ordinance, and therefore they receive them as from the hand of God; and the minister's faults (even if they be very great) cannot affect them, since they acknowledge the integrity of the sacraments to depend upon the institution of the Lord.

The Directory for the Service of God states that in the eucharist, "God's people receive with grateful joy the gifts God has prepared for them. . . . What takes place in the Sacrament is not accomplished by human endeavor, but is done by the grace of God" (3.05, p. 176).

This understanding is highlighted in two prayers composed for this book. The post-sanctus of prayer B says:

> We glorify you for your great power and mercy at work in Christ.
> By his suffering and death on the cross
> our sins are forgiven.
> In rising from the grave,
> He won for us victory over death.
> We praise you that Christ our life now reigns with you in glory,
> praying for us,
> until all things are made perfect in Christ (p. 99).

Similarly, the post-sanctus of prayer G:

> God of mercy,
> in thanks we remember how Jesus invites us to his table,
> imprinting on our hearts his sacrifice on the cross.
> In gratitude we bow before the Righteous One,
> declaring his resurrection and glory,
> and knowing that his prayers alone
> make us worthy to partake of his spiritual meal (p. 116).

It seems that this concept, which again relates to the presence of Christ in the eucharist, could be more vividly stated. An adaptation of the latter part of the anamnesis of eucharistic prayer II in the *Lutheran Book of Worship* would seem to express well Christ's hosting of the supper:

> We cry out (in thanks)
> for the resurrection of our lives,
> when Christ comes
> in beauty and power
> to share with us
> the great and promised feast.

The Holy Spirit and the Church

Epiclesis. The Scots confession voices the strong emphasis on the role of the Holy Spirit in Reformed eucharistic theology. "This union and conjunction which we have with the body and blood of Christ Jesus in the right use of the sacraments is wrought by means of the Holy Ghost, who by true faith carries us above all things that are visible, carnal, and earthly, and makes us feed upon the body and blood of Christ Jesus . . . " (Chapter 21, The Sacraments. 3.21).

Thus, it would seem that the epiclesis will loom large in the eucharistic prayers of the Presbyterian Church. A survey of the prayers shows that this is correct.

However, a review of the prayers also indicates that there is latitude in the interpretation of whether the epiclesis is to be upon the people, upon the gifts or upon both. Prayer A states:

> Gracious God,
> pour out your Holy Spirit upon us,
> that this bread and this cup
> may be for us the body and blood of our Lord . . .

Prayers B and C specifically pray for the outpouring of the Holy Spirit upon both the people and the gifts while prayer G, inspired by Calvin who was uneasy about the blessing of inanimate things, states:

> Almighty God,
> pour out your Holy Spirit upon us,
> that as we receive bread and wine
> we may be assured
> that Christ's promise in these signs will be fulfilled.

The common eucharistic prayer (E) and the COCU prayer (F) each mentions both the people and the gifts whereas the Hippolytus prayer (D) speaks ambiguously:

We ask you to send your Holy Spirit upon the offering of the Holy Church,
gathering into one all who share these holy mysteries,
filling us with the Holy Spirit. . . .

The offering of the holy church may be interpreted as the church itself in its sacrifice of praise and thanksgiving, but it may also be the offering of the bread and the wine. The brief prayer H shares some of this evocative ambiguity:

> Send to us your Holy Spirit
> that this meal may be holy
> and your people may become one.

The fruits of communion. The fruits or benefits of communion that are appended to the epiclesis provide a guard against the subjectivity of some undefined blessing. Just as specific events of holy history are rehearsed within the eucharistic prayer, so the anticipated benefits of communion provide specificity. The epiclesis is not merely for some undefined "special blessing," or for some good feeling. It is that we as the church might be made one with the witness and communion of saints and service to the world, impelled by Christ through the Spirit.

Prayer B speaks powerfully and extensively to this, probably as a result of the inclusion of intercessions within the prayer. The prayer proper expresses the following fruits of the gift of the Holy Spirit:

> That . . . we may know the presence of
>   Christ
> and be made one with him,
> and one with all who come to this table.
> . . . that you will fulfill your eternal purpose
> in us and in all the world.

The intercessions give expression to what we pray will happen in the church as a result of the presence of the Holy Spirit:

> Unite (the church) in the truth of your word
> and empower it in ministry to the world.
> . . . By your spirit renew the face of the earth;
> let peace and justice prevail.

The intercessions continue with prayers for family and friends, the sick and the suffering, the aged and dying, faithful servants who have been called from this life, and it ends with the final benefit:

> Keep us in communion with all the faithful
> from every time and place,
> until we rejoice together in your eternal realm.

Catholicity of the eucharist and of the church. The Directory for the Service of God is very clear that the sacraments are actions of the whole church, and that each individual celebration is a participation in the action of the whole church (p. 176). Just as baptism is initiation into the one, holy, catholic and apostolic church, so the Lord's Supper is larger than the gathered congregation and includes the whole church, the entire communion of saints. The Scots confession says, "This Kirk is Catholic, that is, universal, because it contains the chosen of all ages, of all realms, nations and tongues, be they of the Jews or be they of the Gentiles, who have communion and society with God the Father, and with his Son, Christ Jesus, through the sanctification of his Holy Spirit."

It seems that this catholicity of the eucharist is inadequately stated in all contemporary eucharistic prayers. An unpublished paper by the Rev. William Austin, chaplain of the United Campus Chapel at Radford University in Virginia, indicates that historically, when the diptychs of the living stopped mentioning specific patriarchs and prelates, it was only a matter of time before communion with those branches of the church was broken. Father Austin suggests that the expression of the unity of the church would be best addressed by naming those church bodies and their leaders with whom such unity is affirmed.

The intercessions of prayer B, quoted above, with its prayer for the unity of the church and for the abiding communion with all the faithful from every time and place, comes closest to fulfilling this need.

Mission to the whole world. This is another theme that seems to be much neglected in eucharistic praying. Within this collection of prayers, the most adequate statement is that adapted from the *Book of Common Worship and Prayer* (C):

> Here we offer ourselves to be a living sacrifice,
> holy and acceptable to you.
> In your mercy,
> accept our sacrifice of praise and thanksgiving.
> In communion with all the faithful in heaven and on earth,
> we ask you to fulfill, in us and in all creation,
> the purpose of your redeeming love.

This prayer, which immediately precedes the closing doxology, expresses a theology of creation and of the universal mission of the church, which has both a personal and a communal, cosmic dimension. A similar emphasis is found in the concluding two paragraphs of eucharistic prayer C in the *Book of Common Prayer 1976*.

Justice issues. Many eucharistic prayers speak in general terms of one of the fruits of communion, that we might faithfully serve Christ in the world. This lacks the cutting edge of specificity and of urgency. In the Presbyterian prayers, the dimension of social justice is predominantly found in the prefaces, and is only alluded to in the post-epiclesis. There is nothing equivalent to the eucharistic prayer III in the *Roman Sacramentary:*

> Lord, may this sacrifice,
> which has made our peace with you,
> advance the peace and salvation of all the world.
> Strengthen in faith and love your pilgrim church on earth.

Even stronger is the post-epiclesis of great thanksgiving 20 of the United Methodist *At the Lord's Table,* where we pray that

> The prophets' dream
> shall come to pass,
> when justice shall roll down like waters
> and righteousness
> like an ever flowing stream,
> when nations shall not lift up sword against nation,
> neither shall they learn war anymore.

This emphasis could easily be included as one of the intercessions of prayer B in words such as:

> Remember your lowly ones,
> the oppressed and the burdened,
> and empower us to come to their assistance.

Oblation. There is no consistent oblation in these prayers as there is in the United Methodist collection. The most obvious and beautiful oblation is the one just quoted from prayer C which begins, "Here we offer ourselves to be a living sacrifice." Here the oblation is a part of the fruits of communion, as a result of the empowering by the Holy Spirit.

In prayer B, the oblation,

> We offer ourselves to you to be a living sacrifice
> dedicated to your service,

is a part of the anamnesis.

In prayer G, the only reference to oblation is embodied within the Reformed sursum corda. In prayer G it is in the post-anamnesis, in the simple phrase, "receive our sacrifice of praise."

A question must be raised about whether the oblation of the eucharistic prayer should be individual or communal or both. In each of these cases, the oblation appears to be almost exclusively individualized. The United Methodist formula

> which we offer
> in union with Christ's sacrifice for us
> as a living and holy
> surrender of ourselves,

seems to have a predominantly individual emphasis, though it could be argued that it also can be understood corporately.

The oblation of prayer C cited above does place the oblation in the context of the communion of "all the faithful in heaven and on earth," though it may be deficient in bringing to conscious attention the need for the church as church to offer itself in obedient service to the Lord, empowered and nourished through the Holy Spirit at the Lord's table.

Communion of saints. The prayers written for this resource uniformly set the prayer in the context of the communion of saints, with that communion being mentioned immediately before the closing doxology. That doxology is:

> Through Christ, with Christ, in Christ,
> in the unity of the Holy Spirit,
> all glory and honor are yours,
> Almighty Father,
> for ever and ever.

In prayer B there is a change attributable to the inclusive syntax mentioned above. It states, "All glory and honor are yours, Almighty God . . ."

VI. The Reception of the Document

The Service for the Lord's Day, also known as SLR I (Supplemental Liturgical Resource I), has been received with overwhelming enthusiasm. Pastors have welcomed the return of the prayer from the *Book of Common Worship*. They have commented positively on the variety that is available in the resource, but there has also been a recurring suggestion that there should have been "one service."

This is undoubtedly a criticism of format of this document. The resource has multiple prayers and component parts, arranged in the or-

der of the service for the Lord's Day. For example, there are twenty-
six sets of Scripture sentences that may introduce the service; there are
twelve opening prayers; nine prayers of confession. There are, of
course, eight eucharistic prayers, and the list ends with six optional
blessings for the end of the service. In all, there are two hundred and
forty-seven items, each numbered.

Thus, it is not possible simply to use the book as a "service book,"
moving one page at a time through a specific service. One needs a significant supply of paper clips (ribbons would be impossible!) in order
to move through a complete service.

The placing of all two hundred and forty-seven options on a computer, adding the thirty-eight prefaces and asking the computer to
print out the service for a given Sunday, would be an answer.

It has been emphasized that this resource is an "in process" document, and that the material from the resource is still subject to revision
and re-formating. Critiques and suggestions continue to come to the
Office of Worship, and a final revision process will take place as the
new worship resource is brought into being. In the meantime, this resource seems to be meeting a need and is being widely used across the
church.

Chart 6.1
Presbyterian Eucharistic Prayers: A Structural Comparison

	A Worshipbook Revision	B New For This Resource	C Book of Common Worship Revision	D Hyppolytus	E Common (Alexandrine)	F COCU	G Calvin	H Brief
Creation	Minimal, only in general prefaces I, II, and III.	None, unless in preface.	Good.	Good.	Good.	Good. (In Anamnesis)	Good.	Good.
Variable Preface	Yes (24)	Yes (1)	Yes (6)	No.	No.	Yes. (7)	No.	No.
Hebrew Scriptures	Minimal, only in general prefaces I and II.	Minimal, only by implication.	Negative	Negative.	Only by implication.	Negative.	Negative.	Only by implication.
Angels (Transcendent Language)	No.	Yes.	Yes.	No.	Yes.	No.	No.	No.
Institution Narrative	In or out	In or out.	In or out.	In.	In.	In.	Out.	Out.
Anamnesis Past	"He made you known." Healed the sick. Took up the	Word became flesh. Won for us victory.	Took our nature. Suffered death for our redemption.	Was revealed as your son. Won for you a holy people. Stretched out	Lived without sin. Proclaimed the good news. Gave himself	Born of Mary he shared our live. He reconciled us to God's	Jesus broke the bread.	(Past and present merge.) Born of Mary he shares.

Chart 6.1
Presbyterian Eucharistic Prayers: A Structural Comparison (Continued)

	A Worshipbook Revision	B New For This Resource	C Book of Common Worship Revision	D Hyppolytus	E Common (Alexandrine)	F COCU	G Calvin	H Brief
	cross and died. Overcame death.		Made sacrifice for sin. Gave us this sacrament.	his hands in suffering.	up to death. Instituted the supper.	love. At Jordon the spirit descended on him. He healed the sick.		Eating with sinners he welcomes us.
Present	Is risen to rule. Is friend of sinners.	By his death our sins are forgiven. Now reigns with you, praying for us.		Shatters chains. Leads righteous into light. Fixes boundaries of death. Manifests the resurrection.	We recall Christ's death. We proclaim resurrection and ascension.	Leads us into new creation. We celebrate redemption.	Makes us partakers of his body & blood. Invites us to the table. We bow & declare his resurrection and glory.	Leading disciples he guides us. Dying on the cross he rescues us. Risen from the dead he gives life.

Chart 6.1
Presbyterian Eucharistic Prayers: A Structural Comparison (Continued)

	A Worshipbook Revision	B New For This Resource	C Book of Common Worship Revision	D Hyppolytus	E Common (Alexandrine)	F COCU	G Calvin	H Brief
			We continue this memorial until . . .				We live in him and declare the mystery of faith.	
Future	We overcome and will come in glory.	Until all is made perfect.	he comes again.	None.	We await his coming in glory.	None.	None.	None.
Epiclesis On people (P) or gifts (G)	us	P & G	P & G	Offering.	P & G	P & G	P	To us.
Fruits of Communion	Unity with Christ. Eternal life. Faithfulness.	Know the presence of Christ. Unity with Christ. Unity in the church.	Communion in the body and blood. Communion with all the faithful. Become living sacrifice and fulfill redemptive purpose.	Be filled with the Holy Spirit. Confess faith and give praise & glory.	Sanctify the gifts. Show them to be the body & blood. Oneness. A living sacrifice.	That gifts may be for us the body and blood. That we may be the body for the world. That we may be instruments of serving and reconciling.	Assurance that Christ's promise in the signs will be fulfilled.	That the meal may be holy, the church one. That we may love and that we may be encouraged.

PART II

Analysis of the New Eucharistic Prayers

ALAN F. DETSCHER

7

Preface, Sanctus, Post-Sanctus

In a concrete way the contemporary eucharistic prayers of the Roman, Episcopal, Lutheran, Methodist, and Presbyterian Churches manifest the growing theological and liturgical consensus on the nature and function of the anaphora. The convergence evidenced by the prayers is visible especially in those portions of the anaphora that precede the institution narrative: the preface with its introductory dialog, the sanctus, and the post-sanctus.

I. Preface

From an early date the eucharistic prayers of the western Churches have shown a great deal of variety in the preface (*inlatio, contestatio, immolatio*). In the Spanish, Gallican, and Ambrosian rites the preface was variable to the extent that most Masses had their own proper prefaces;[1] the Roman rite was somewhat less exuberant in this regard.[2] The Anglican and Lutheran Churches as well as those Protestant Churches that retained a traditional form of eucharistic prayer continued to provide variable prefaces, though in a lesser number than the Roman Church.[3]

The eastern Churches, however, have operated on the basis of a different principle. They have seen the eucharistic prayer as a unit that does not admit to variation. The need for variety in the celebration was and is met by providing alternative anaphoras, rather than by providing alternatives for the different portions of the prayer.[4] This is most evident in the Syrian family of Churches where vast numbers of eucharistic prayers still abound.[5]

We see two forms of preface in the east and the west: the invariable prayer contained in the eastern anaphora is a hymn of praise to God, especially as Creator, and the variable preface of the western eucharistic prayer which is most often Christological and focuses on one of the mysteries of redemption in Christ. Modern revisions of the eucharistic prayer exhibit both the eastern and the western forms of the preface. Each of the Churches provides one or more anaphoras that use a variable preface while, at the same time, providing anaphoras that can be used only with a fixed or invariable preface.

The summary of Chart 7.1 which follows indicates how each Church has handled the preface in relation to the whole anaphora.

Roman Catholic Church (The Sacramentary)[6]

There are four eucharistic prayers that allow for variable prefaces: Eucharistic Prayers I (Roman Canon), II, III. (Note: Canon II may also be used with an invariable preface.)

Six eucharistic prayers have invariable prefaces: Eucharistic Prayer IV, Eucharistic Prayers I and II for Reconciliation, Eucharistic Prayers I, II, and III for Masses with Children. (Note: Eucharistic Prayer III for Children does allow for an Easter variation in the preface.)

The present *Sacramentary* contains a collection of eighty-four variable prefaces.

Episcopal Church (Book of Common Prayer, 1979)[7]

The Prayer Book has eucharistic prayers that allow for variable prefaces: Great Thanksgiving A and B, Rite I; Great Thanksgiving A and B, Rite II; Great Thanksgiving Form I and Form II, An Order for Celebrating the Holy Eucharist. (Note: in these last two prayers the celebrant may use his own words or one of the prefaces.)

In addition, there are two eucharistic prayers with fixed prefaces: Great Thanksgiving C and D, Rite II.

There are twenty-three variable prefaces in both traditional and contemporary language for use with the eucharistic prayers.

Lutheran Churches (Lutheran Book of Worship)[8]

The *Lutheran Book of Worship* (Minister's edition) has five eucharistic prayers that allow for variable prefaces. (Note: one of these is based on a Swedish prayer and consists of preface, sanctus, post-sanctus and institution narrative. This prayer is not numbered in the LBW.)[9]

Or the minister may follow the classic Lutheran practice of using a variable preface, the sanctus, and the institution narrative.

There are thirteen variable prefaces.

Methodist Church (At the Lord's Table)[10]

The collection contains one eucharistic prayer that allows for the use of variable prefaces: Great Thanksgiving No. 2.

There are twenty eucharistic prayers with fixed prefaces: Great Thanksgiving Nos. 1, 3–8, 10–22.

There is also one eucharistic prayer without a sanctus which makes no clear distinction between the preface and post sanctus: Great Thanksgiving No. 9.

At the Lord's Table contains four variable prefaces.

Presbyterian Church (The Service for the Lord's Day)[11]

This new service book has four eucharistic prayers that allow for variable prefaces: Great Prayer of Thanksgiving A, B, C, F. (Note: prayers B and C may be used with a fixed preface.)

There is one eucharistic prayer without the sanctus (Hippolytus): Thanksgiving D, and one eucharistic prayer without sanctus or institution narrative: Thanksgiving H.

Finally, there are two eucharistic prayers with invariable prefaces: Thanksgiving E, G.

The book includes a collection of thirty-one variable prefaces.

The Variable Preface

An examination of the variable prefaces of these liturgical books discloses certain features which are held in common. The preface is always addressed to the first person of the Trinity. The title most often used is "Father." In some of the prefaces, especially the Presbyterian ones, the title "God" alone is used, but from the context it is clear that the reference is to God the Father.

The preface offers thanks and praise to God in one of two ways: either it praises God for what he has done, or God is praised through Jesus Christ our Lord. The Christologically centered preface (through Jesus Christ) is the most common form of the preface and is the basic form of the Western Church. These prefaces are usually seasonal in nature and focus on one aspect of the mystery of redemption in Christ

Chart 7.1
Prefaces

	Variable Preface	Invariable Preface
Episcopal		
1	x	
2	x	
A	x	
B	x	
C		x
D		x
Form 1	x	
Form 2	x	
Presbyterian		
A	x	
B	x	
C	x	
D		x
E		x
F	x	
G		x
H		x
Lutheran		
I	x	
II	x	
III	x	
Swedish	x	
IV	x	
Methodist		
1		x
2	x	
3		x
4		x
5		x
6		x
7		x
8		x
9		x
10		x
11		x
12		x
13		x
14		x
15		x
16		x

Chart 7.1
Prefaces (Continued)

	Variable Preface	Invariable Preface
17		x
18		x
19		x
20		x
21		x
22		x
Roman		
I	x	
II	x	
III	x	
IV		x
RI		x
RII		x
CI		x
CII		x
CIII		x

which is being celebrated on the particular feast or during the present season.

Fixed or Invariable Preface

The invariable prefaces generally have creation as their theme: the creation of light, the whole universe, the world, or humanity. Some of the prefaces speak of both creation and redemption in Christ, that is, the creation of the human race, its fall and God's plan for redemption manifested in the person of his Son, Jesus Christ. We might call this a mixed preface as it incorporates both the creation theme (so common in the eastern form of the preface) as well as the Christological dimension most common in the Western variable prefaces.

The Roman Eucharistic Prayer for Children I is unique among all the prefaces in that it concludes with intercessions, somewhat in the manner of the Alexandrian anaphoral tradition.

Introduction and Conclusion of the Preface

All the contemporary prefaces are introduced by the traditional dialog: The Lord be with you . . . Lift up your hearts . . . Let us give thanks to the Lord our God. The use of the greeting, "The Lord be with you," is a restoration of the ancient traditional form of the dialog. It had been dropped from most of the reformation liturgies.

The ICET version of the dialog is used in all the prayers in contemporary language. It might be noted that the Roman form of the dialog includes an earlier form of the ICET text in the response to the second acclamation: Lift up your hearts. We lift them *up* to the Lord. The word "up" is not found in the later ICET versions of the dialog. The dialog has a two-fold function: it is both an invitation to participate in the prayer (Lift up your hearts) and a formal approval of the congregation for the one who presides to proceed with the thanksgiving (Let us give thanks . . . It is right and just).

The preface concludes by uniting the praise of the Church with that of the angels and saints. The Episcopal and Lutheran prefaces have a set conclusion which is used with all the prefaces. The Roman, Methodist, and Presbyterian prefaces exhibit a greater variety of conclusions. The conclusion has the basic function of uniting the praise of the preface with the sanctus of the whole company of heaven. At times the conclusion seems to be merely tacked on to the end of the preface and does not form a smooth transition to the sanctus . . .

II. Sanctus

The sanctus is a congregational hymn based on Isaiah 6:3 and Psalm 118:26. It is found in all but five of the eucharistic prayers we are studying. The Episcopal Order for Celebrating the Holy Communion, Forms 1 and 2, Presbyterian eucharistic prayers D and H, and the Methodist eucharistic prayer 9 do not have the sanctus. It thus seems that the sanctus is to remain an integral part of the anaphora even though it may be omitted on occasion. Lutheran Great Thanksgiving IV is a translation of the Anaphora of St. Hippolytus, and therefore does not include the sanctus.

All the contemporary language anaphoras include the full ICET version of the sanctus with the *Benedictus:*

> Blessed is he who comes in the name of the Lord.
> Hosanna in the highest.

The English reformers had dropped the *Benedictus* because they thought that it supported the Roman theory of transubstantiation and a view of the real presence which they rejected. Luther, on the other hand, retained the *Benedictus* in his *Formula Missae* and even suggested that it be accompanied by the elevation.

An interesting use of the sanctus is found in the Roman Eucharistic Prayers for children 1 and 2, where portions of the sanctus are used as a refrain throughout the preface—for example, in the Eucharistic Prayer for Masses with Children II: "Glory to God in the highest" or "Hosanna in the highest." Eucharistic Prayer for Masses with Children I uses the first half of the sanctus (through "Hosanna in the highest") for the first half of the preface and the *Benedictus* for the second half of the preface. In the second prayer the *Benedictus* is carried over into the post-sanctus as an acclamation which ties together the preface, sanctus, and post-sanctus. The Episcopal Great Thanksgiving C also uses congregational responses throughout the preface. The refrains, in order, are:

1. Glory to you for ever and ever.
2. By your will they were created and have their being.
3. Have mercy, Lord, for we are sinners in your sight.
4. By his blood, he reconciled us.
   By his wounds, we are healed.
5. Holy, holy, holy Lord, etc.

III. Post-Sanctus

The portion of the eucharistic prayer that follows the sanctus is known as the post-sanctus (*Vere Sanctus*) and in the Spanish, Gallican, and ancient Ambrosian rites was a variable part of the anaphora. The post-sanctus for Holy Saturday of the Ambrosian rite has been used as the basis of a new eucharistic prayer in the revised *Missale Ambrosianum* (Eucharistic Prayer VI).[12]

The post-sanctus is linked to the sanctus by its first words which usually pick up one of the words or themes of the sanctus, e.g., "holy," "glory," "praise," "blessed," "blessing," although this is not always the case. In many of the prayers the introductory phrases of the prayer refer in a general way back to the preface and take up the theme of thanksgiving.

In those prayers which follow the Roman pattern of an *epiclesis* before the words of institution, the post-sanctus leads into the first epiclesis. Those anaphoras which are based on the Antiochene type of eucharistic prayer have a post-sanctus prayer which leads directly into the institution narrative.

The prayers which follow the Roman pattern are: all nine Roman eucharistic prayers, Episcopal Great Thanksgiving C and Form I of the Order for Celebrating the Holy Eucharist, Lutheran brief prayer

(Swedish form), and the Methodist Great Thanksgiving 2. An examination of the post-sanctus prayers of the various anaphoras reveals four basic types of prayers:

1. Salvation History in the Old Testament and in Christ

In this form of the prayer God's intervention in history is recounted: creation, the covenant and the law, the prophets of the Old Testament and the salvific works of Christ which lead into the account of the Last Supper. This form of the post-sanctus is found in Episcopal prayers B and D; Presbyterian prayers E and F; Methodist prayers 4, 5, 6, 14: Roman prayers 3 and 4 and Reconciliation I.

2. Salvation History in Christ

This form of the post-sanctus recounts the saving work of Christ. The prayer is Christological in theme, although it is addressed to the Father. When this type of prayer is used in an anaphora having a fixed preface, containing the theme of creation, the anaphora takes on a trinitarian structure: preface—the work of the Father in creation; post-sanctus—the work of the Son in redemption (this theme is continued in the institution narrative and anamnesis); epiclesis—the work of the Spirit in the Church. This second type of post-sanctus is the most common form used in the new eucharistic prayers.

This form is found in Roman eucharistic prayer for Reconciliation I, and Children III; Episcopal Great Thanksgiving 1, 2, A, B, Form I and II; Lutheran 1, 2, 3, Brief Swedish prayer, 4; Methodist Great Thanksgiving: All texts; Presbyterian prayers A, B, C, E.

3. The Father

This type of post-sanctus is usually very brief and speaks of the Father alone. The second Roman eucharistic prayer is an example of this type of post-sanctus: "Lord, you are holy indeed, the fountain of all holiness." A variant of this type of prayer is found in the United Methodist prayers and briefly mentions both the Father and the Son: "Truly holy are you, and blessed is your Son Jesus Christ."

4. Trinitarian

This form of the prayer mentions each of the persons of the Trinity. Its classic form is seen in the various versions of Basil[13] which are in use in all the Churches but the Lutheran. Although the prayer speaks of the work of each of the persons of the Trinity it is nevertheless ad-

Chart 7.2.
Post-Sanctus

	Addressed to:		Themes:		Work of:	
	Father	God	Creation	Old Testament	Son	Holy Spirit
Episcopal						
1	x				x	
2	x				x	
A	x				x	
B		x	x	x	x	
C	x					x
D		x	x	x	x	x
Form 1		x			x	
Form 2		x			x	
Presbyterian						
A		x			x	
B		x			x	
C	x				x	
D						
E		x	x	x	x	
F		x	x	x	x	
G						
H						
Lutheran						
I		x	x	x	x	
II		x		x	x	
III		x			x	
Swedish		x				
IV	x				x	
Methodist						
1		x			x	
2	x				x	
3	x				x	
4		x	x	x	x	
5		x	x		x	
6		x	x	x	x	
7		x			x (name only)	
8		x			x	
9						
10		x			x	
11		x			x (name only)	
12	x				x	
13		x			x (name only)	
14		x	x		x	
15		x			x	
16		x			x (name only)	

Chart 7.2.
Post-Sanctus (Continued)

| | Addressed to: | | Themes: | | Work of: | |
	Father	God	Creation	Old Testament	Son	Holy Spirit
17		x			x (name only)	
18		x			x (name only)	
19	x				x	
20		x			x	
21		x			x	
22		x			x	
Roman						
I	x					
II		x				
III	x		x		x	x
IV		x	x	x	x	x
RI	x			x		
RII	x				x	
CI	x					
CII	x				x	x
CII		x			x	

dressed to the Father. The post-sanctus of the third Roman eucharistic prayer takes this form.

Function of the Post-Sanctus

The post-sanctus continues the anamnetic praise of God begun in the preface. It focuses most commonly on the redemptive work of the Son, although this does not exclude the mention of the whole Trinity. The recounting of the salvific actions of Christ leads into the institution narrative.

When there is a fixed or invariable preface and the anaphora is seasonal or thematic, the post-sanctus is often the place where the particular theme is developed in greater detail.

In some of the prayers that have a variable preface the creation-Old Testament themes are found in the post-sanctus. This, however, gives the impression of starting over when the variable preface has already spoken of the redemptive work of Christ.[14]

IV. Problems and Questions

1. The Western tradition uses a variable preface for the anaphora which can express the theme of the feast or season. A difficulty arises

with this usage when a variable preface does not praise God for his creative action, but only for the works of the Son. This lacuna is compounded when the post-sanctus focuses only on the redemptive work of Christ.

Some of the anaphoras have attempted to resolve this difficulty by having a longer fixed portion of the preface which speaks of the work of the Father in creation and in the Old Testament and at its end provides for a variable insert for the feast of season (e.g., the Church of England).[15]

2. Another problem arises when the post-sanctus does not logically flow from what has been said in the preface, and most especially when the post-sanctus starts all over again with creation; this is again related to the problem of the variable preface.

3. In some cases the sanctus seems to interrupt the prayer. Should it be moved to another position as suggested by Ratcliff (to the end of the anaphora) or simply be omitted?[16]

4. Should there be more congregational acclamations throughout the preface and post-sanctus as in the Roman Eucharistic Prayer for Children and the Episcopal Great Thanksgiving C?

5. Might not the post-sanctus be seen as the place for variable inserts rather than the preface? This would allow for a fixed preface as in the Eastern anaphoras with a creation theme, yet also respond to the need to particularize the anaphora in keeping with the theme of the celebration.

NOTES

1. See J.M. Neale, *The Ancient Liturgies of the Gallican Church* (New York: AMS Press, 1970).

2. For example, the *Leonine (Verona) Sacramentary* had two hundred and sixty-seven prefaces and the pre-Vatican II Missal had fifteen prefaces.

3. The 1662 edition of the Book of Common Prayer, for example, had six prefaces.

4. The Byzantine Churches routinely use the anaphoras of St. John Chrysostom and St. Basil.

5. The West-Syrian family of Churches has a corpus of approximately one hundred anaphoras. The Syriac Maronite Catholic Church in the United States of America has thirteen anaphoras that are in actual use.

6. *Sacramentary*, 2nd ed. (New York: Catholic Book Publishing Co., 1985).

7. *Book of Common Prayer* (New York: Church Hymnal Corporation and Seabury Press, 1979).

8. *Lutheran Book of Worship,* Ministers Edition (Minneapolis: Augsburg Publishing House, 1978).

9. See the Swedish eucharistic prayer, *ibid.,* no. 3, pp. 224–25.

10. *At the Lord's Table,* Supplemental Resources 9 (Nashville: Abingdon). See also *The Book of Services* (Nashville: United Methodist Publishing House, 1985).

11. *The Service for the Lord's Day,* Supplemental Liturgical Resource I (Philadelphia: Westminster Press, 1984).

12. *Messale ambrosiano festivo* (Torino: Marietti, 1983), pp. 667–69.

13. Eucharistic Prayer IV (Roman), Eucharistic Prayer D (Episcopal), Great Thanksgiving G (Methodist), Great Prayer of Thanksgiving E (Presbyterian).

14. See, for example, Presbyterian Great Prayer of Thanksgiving F and Lutheran Great Thanksgiving I.

15. See First and Third Eucharistic Prayers, Rite A in *The Alternative Service Book,* 1980 (Oxford: Oxford University Press and A. R. Mowbray, 1980), pp. 130–31 and 136. These prayers tend to be Christological and only allude to creation in reference to Christ.

16. See E. C. Ratcliff, *Liturgical Studies,* ed. by A. H. Couratin and D. H. Tripp (London: S.P.C.K., 1976), pp. 18–40.

GORDON W. LATHROP

8

The Institution Narrative

The liturgical use of the narrative of the institution of the Eucharist has classically developed in such a way as to be influenced freely by the various biblical accounts of the Supper but to be determined finally by none of them. This fact may reflect the long tradition of improvisation in Eucharistic praying as well as the diversity in the oral tradition which lay behind the gospels and to some extent continued after they were written, perhaps especially in such a tradition-bearing locus as the Eucharist. Or it may arise from the later liturgical tendency toward a certain free harmonization of the gospel and Pauline accounts, as the liturgy sought to present the one Christ in the midst of the four witnesses. As yet later reflection might have it, the continuing freedom of the text of the institution narrative may demonstrate the conviction that in the sacramental action the church is face to face with the One who is prior to both sacrament and scripture and encountered as living in both. Still, even if there are two sources for the knowledge of Christ, the Eucharist will always be the eating and drinking of the same mystery to which the scripture bears witness—thus the free text of the institution narrative will always encounter the scriptural texts as a rule and canon of orthodoxy.

In any case, a survey of the forms of the *verba institutionis* in the oldest witnesses—in Paul, in the synoptics, perhaps we may add the early third century text which is the first example preserved of the use

of the narrative in a prayer—is useful as a touchstone against which
to measure the continuing diversity of the institution narrative in contemporary American Eucharistic praying. Several points of comparison might be chosen, as Chart 8.1 will indicate:

These texts may be for us a witness to the primitive freedom and
diversity of Eucharistic proclamation come also among us. But as these
texts are held next to each other and next to the biblical texts it may be
that several editorial comments suggest themselves. It is not that we
are in quest of the single perfect American English text. But mutual
critique, certainly mutual awareness of the characteristics of diversity,
may help us toward an authenticity in local proclamation which is
fully aware of the surrounding horizon of the whole catholic church.
What follows is a contribution to such a critique and awareness:

1. Many of the changes in or differences from biblical language
found here are strong and clear and useful: Language which inserts
the narrative into the context of Trinitarian prayer can be helpful, as
in "gave you thanks." "All people" is a good contemporary alternative
for what biblical scholars think may be the technical term "the many."
And, if the developing tendency of the New Testament language were
to be taken as norm, one specific difference from that norm should be
noted in these texts: the movement toward making the bread-word
and the cup-word parallel in structure and meaning, a movement
present in the New Testament itself if one takes 1 Corinthians as the
earliest text, need not be continued. It is good, even deeply valuable,
to say, "this is my body . . . this cup is the new covenant in my blood,"
to let the bread and the cup words have their own structure and life
in speaking to us the mystery of Christ. In general the tendency of
these prayers to move away from the parallelism is to be lauded.

2. On the other hand, for the sake of faithfulness to the biblical mystery itself, these texts might have moved in some specific ways toward
a *greater* freedom from the letter of the biblical texts. The precise in-
dication of those to whom the bread and cup are given—disciples,
"friends," them—need not be stated, especially if "take and eat" is
included in the bread-word. In fact, the absence of such named objects
of the gift may make the gift mysteriously available to us all, now,
without requiring us to imagine ourselves as "disciples," then. Both
Paul and Hippolytus have a deep *liturgical* sense here. Such a sense
about the mystery proclaimed in the present time might also raise the
question as to whether it is good that every one of these contemporary
prayers includes in the cup-word some form of the Matthean "forgiveness of sins." It is not that this note of eucharistic meaning should
be forgotten, but simply that the Western tradition has so overem-

Chart 8.1

	Matthew 26:26–29	Mark 14:22–25	Luke 22:15–20	Paul 1 Cor 11:23–26	Hippolytus Ap. Trad. 4 (Latin Text)
time indication	as they were eating	as they were eating	(first cup and vow of abstention)	on the night when he was betrayed	(handed over to a death he freely accepted, in order to destroy death.
words for bread prayer	blessed	blessed	when he had given thanks	when he had given thanks	giving thanks to you
bread given to:	the disciples	them (the 12)	them (the apostles)	—	—
bread-word	"Take, eat; this is my body."	"Take; this is my body."	"This is my body which is given for you. Do this in remembrance of me."	"This is my body which is for you. Do this in remembrance of me."	"Take, eat, this is my body which will be broken for you."
words for cup prayer	when he had given thanks	when he had given thanks	likewise the cup after supper	in the same way also the cup, after supper	in the same way also the cup
cup given to:	them	them, and they all drank of it	—	—	—
cup-word	"Drink of it, all of you; for this is my blood of the covenant, which is poured out for many for the forgiveness of sins." vow of abstention	"This is my blood of the covenant, which is poured out for many." vow of abstention	"This cup which is poured out for you is the new covenant in my blood." word on betrayal	"This cup is the new covenant in my blood. Do this, as often as you drink it, in remembrance of me." For as often as you	"This is my blood poured out for you when you do this, do it for the remembrance of me.

Chart 8.2

	Lutheran Book of Worship (1978) Prayers I, II	Roman Sacramentary Prayer I (Canon)	Roman Sacramentary Prayer II	Book of Common Prayer (1979) Rite II Prayer C	Presbyterian Supplemental Liturgical Resource (1984) Prayer A	Methodist At the Lord's Table (1981) Prayer 1
time indication	in the night in which he was betrayed	the day before he suffered	before he was given up to death	on the night he was betrayed	on the night before he died	on the night in which he gave himself up for us
words for bread prayer	gave thanks	looking up to heaven, to you his almighty Father, he gave you thanks and praise	gave you thanks	said the blessing	gave thanks to you	after giving you thanks
bread given to:	disciples	disciples	disciples	friends	disciples	disciples
bread-word	"Take and eat; this is my body, given for you. Do this for the remembrance of me."	"Take this, all of you, and eat it: this is my body which will be given up for you."	"Take this, all of you, and eat it: this is my body which will be given up for you."	"Take, eat: This is my Body, which is given for you. Do this for the remembrance of me."	"Take, eat. This is my body, given for you. Do this for the remembrance of me."	"Take, eat; this is my body which is given for you."

Chart 8.2 (continued)

	Lutheran Book of Worship (1978) Prayers, I,II	Roman Sacramentary Prayer I (Canon)	Roman Sacramentary Prayer II	Book of Common Prayer (1979) Rite II Prayer C	Presbyterian Supplemental Liturgical Resource (1984) Prayer A	Methodist At the Lord's Table (1981) Prayer 1
words for cup prayer	gave thanks	again he gave you thanks and praise	again he gave you thanks and praise	gave thanks	in the same way	again he returned thanks to you
cup given to:	for all to drink	disciples	disciples		—	disciples
cup-word	"This cup is the new covenant in my blood, shed for you and for all people for the forgiveness of sin. Do this for the remembrance of me."	"Take this, all of you, and drink from it: this is the cup of my blood, the blood of the new and everlasting covenant. It will be shed for you and for all, so that sins may be forgiven. Do this in memory of me."		"Drink this, all of you: This is my Blood of the new Covenant, which is shed for you and for many for the forgiveness of sins. Whenever you drink it, do this for the remembrance of me."	"This cup is the new covenant sealed in my blood, shed for you for the forgiveness of sins. Do this for the remembrance of me."	"Drink from this, all of you, this is the cup of the new covenant in my blood, poured out for you and many, for the forgiveness of sins."

phasized and, to some extent, trivialized and privatized it as to leave
the contemporary hearer in need of the correction available in the
other rich biblical metaphors. (It is to be noted that certain confessional
characteristics come to expression precisely here: Lutherans forgive
sin; Roman Catholics set up a future economy of forgiveness—"so that
sins may be forgiven"—presumably in the church.) If the institution
narrative in the liturgy is not just a harmony and pastiche of all four
biblical texts, then this phrase need not always be included. "The new
covenant in my blood" or "my blood of the covenant, poured out for
the many" stands strongly and beautifully on its own.

3. Still, I am not calling for cavalier freedom from the biblical witness. For the sake of the very mystery at the heart of both scripture
and sacrament, one could have wished for a greater faithfulness to biblical language in some specific instances in these contemporary texts:
Certainly excessive additions or elaborations should be avoided, even
if they are traditional, if they reduce clarity and simplicity or become,
to our ears, melodramatic or false. "Lifted eyes," "friends," and "new
and everlasting covenant" probably fall into these categories. Good
oral proclamation today, however, does not necessarily need short
lines for the sake of clarity. Longer and more elegant English sentences, echoing the syntax of the biblical languages, could have been
more recovered than generally is the case in these texts. And most especially: The Latin use of the future tense ("will be given up," "will
be shed") should be avoided, in spite of its antiquity, in favor of the
strong and mysterious present passive of biblical and Greek liturgical
use. The words are proclaimed now, as the gift of the present crucified
and risen Christ ("my body given for you . . . my blood shed for
you"), not as an historical drama in which we put ourselves in the up-
per room, imagining a future crucifixion with a distant goal ("so that
sins may be forgiven"). It may in fact be a kind of a-liturgical histori-
cization which is the source of this Latin future tense (the Latin and
Ethiopic translations of the Apostolic Tradition have it for the bread-
word; the Apostolic Constitution VIII does not). Here the biblical texts
can help us toward liturgical meaning.

4. Other examples of biblical speech might be considered as possible improvements. The command to "do this" is perhaps best repeated, in Pauline manner, after each word. The distinction between
"blessing" and "giving thanks" (found in Mark and Matthew), the latter seeming to indicate the longer prayer at the end of the meal, might
be maintained. But these matters carry no urgency for liturgical meaning.

The fascinating thing remains that the institution narrative—which some regard as the very essence of the scripture, as the summary of the gospel of Jesus Christ, as his "last testament," and, in any case, as his clearest interpretation of himself—continues to be, also in these texts, a richly important test case on the relationship of scripture and liturgy. The question which must continue to have our attention is this: How do the proclaimed texts serve the mystery of Christ in the midst of the assembly?

DAVID N. POWER, O.M.I.

9

The Anamnesis: Remembering, We Offer

I. What Is Remembered

The common interest in the anamnesis section of eucharistic prayers is that of expressing the object of memorial in an extended and amplified way. Many of the controversies about the Eucharist or Lord's Supper in western Christianity had to do with the ways in which the sacrament related to the sacrifice of Christ's death. The Reformation traditions emphasized that the Lord's Supper is sacrament and testament of the forgiveness of sins, the proclamation and promise of mercy to those who profess to live by the gospel. The Reformers attacked the Catholic practices and theologies of eucharistic sacrifice, finding in them a blasphemy against the sufficiency of the sacrifice of Christ's atoning death. Catholic teaching, on the other hand, as formulated in the Council of Trent, underlined the sacrificial nature of the Mass, but related it to the death of Christ as memorial and representation, and as an efficacious application of the merits and satisfactions of Christ's once and for all sacrifice. Recent dialogues between the churches have largely resolved this problem by use of the biblical image of *anamnesis* or memorial, and by a rediscovery of the great prayer of thanksgiving as a memorial proclamation of the salvific works of God. It can then be understood that the eucharist has reality only as a sacrament and memorial of Christ's work, and that whatever is said of the eucharist as sacrifice is said within this context, and not by way of adding anything to the sacrifice of Jesus Christ.

Much of the past controversy, however, centered around the explanation of Christ's death as a sacrifice for sin, since medieval redemption theories spoke in this way. The return to a biblical and patristic tradition of memorial, and the new interest in the study of ancient eucharistic prayers, alerted the churches to the fact that the death of Christ could not be considered alone, but that its meaning belonged within the totality of the deeds and mysteries of Christ's flesh and in the anticipation of his second coming. The images of Christ's redemption evoked in the biblical and liturgical tradition of the pre-medieval churches are more ample than those which relate only to sacrifice and especially to sacrifice as a satisfaction offered for sin. They are comprehensive of the incarnation, of the preaching and ministry of Jesus, of the passion and death, and of the resurrection and ascension, and are incomplete without images which express the anticipation of God's kingdom and of the second coming of Christ. In composing the *anamnesis* section of new eucharistic prayers, therefore, the challenge was to move from a narrow focus on the sacrifice of Christ's death to a more comprehensive commemoration of the total saving work of the mysteries of his flesh. The Faith and Order statement on Eucharist promulgated as the Lima document[1] gives evidence of this change of mentality in the contrast that is there found between no. 5 and no. 6 of the paper.

Par. 5 reads:

The eucharist is the memorial of the crucified and risen Christ, i.e. the living and effective sign of his sacrifice, accomplished once and for all on the cross and still operative on behalf of all humankind.

Par. 6 is more ample:

Christ himself with all he has accomplished for us and for all creation (in his incarnation, servanthood, ministry, teaching, suffering, sacrifice, resurrection, ascension and sending of the Spirit) is present in this *anamnesis*, granting us communion with himself. The eucharist is also the foretaste of his *parousia* and of the final kingdom.

It is par. 6 which is more in keeping with the church's prayer tradition and which is reflected in the anamnesis section of the new prayers of the USA churches. The old Roman Canon, still in use in the Roman liturgy as Prayer I, recalls Christ's "passion, his resurrection from the dead, and his ascension into glory."[2] Eucharistic Prayer IV is the most ample of the eight prayers of the sacramentary, for in it "we recall Christ's death, his descent among the dead, his resurrection, and his ascension to (God's) right hand," and we also look forward "to his coming in glory."[3]

Among the four eucharistic prayers of the *Lutheran Book of Worship* the most extensive expression of memorial in the anamnesis is found in Prayer II:

> . . . we remember the incarnation of your Son: his human birth and the covenant he made with us. We remember the sacrifice of his life: his eating with outcasts and sinners, and his acceptance of death. But chiefly we remember his rising from the tomb, his ascension to the seat of power, and his sending of the holy and life-giving Spirit.

The note of anticipation is also expressed in this prayer, which continues:

> We cry out for the resurrection of our lives, when Christ will come again in beauty and power to share with us the great and promised feast.[4]

In the Episcopal *Book of Common Prayer*, among the four new prayers of Rite II Prayer D corresponds here to Eucharistic Prayer IV of the Roman sacramentary, for they are both reworkings of the Egyptian Anaphora of Basil. The other prayers of Rite II, as well as the two prayers of Rite I, recall more simply the death and resurrection, or the death, resurrection and ascension, expressing as well the expectation of Christ's coming in glory, with the exception of Prayer I of Rite I and of Prayer A of Rite II.[5]

In the collection of twenty-two prayers of the United Methodist Church, *At the Lord's Table*, the phrase "in remembrance of all your mighty acts in Jesus Christ" runs through the anamnesis of most of the prayers.[6] It is then amplified according to the celebration of the liturgical seasons or feasts. In prayers 10, 12, 16, 17, and 20, this anamnesis is preceded by a memorial recital, proper to the season or occasion. Here, by way of example, is that for Advent:

> By the baptism of his suffering, death and resurrection you gave birth to your Church, delivered us from captivity to sin and death, and made with us a new covenant.[7]

In prayers 12, 14, 15, 19 and 20, the anamnesis is itself extended. For example, the Great Thanksgiving 19, celebrating the Gift of Food, reads:

> Therefore, recalling your Son's death and resurrection, his ascension and his abiding presence through your Holy Spirit, we ask you, etc.[8]

In these Methodist prayers, the expectation of Christ's second coming is transposed to the section which contains the epiclesis, and is therefore missing from the anamnesis, except in *A Common Eucharistic Prayer*, which the Methodist Church shares with other churches.

In the *Service for the Lord's Day* of the United Presbyterian Churches,[8a] most of the texts for the Great Thanksgiving Prayer do not extend the remembrance very much in the anamnesis. Prayers A and B simply recall "your mighty acts in Jesus Christ," Prayer F "the redemption won for us in Jesus Christ," Prayer H the "death and resurrection," and Prayer G the "resurrection and glory." The one lengthy anamnesis is that of Prayer C, which recalls "his incarnation and holy life, his death and glorious resurrection, his ascension and continued intercession," and also includes the expectation of Christ's second coming.

Many of these prayers associate a people's acclamation with the anamnesis. The Roman Sacramentary has introduced it into all eucharistic prayers, placing it immediately after the supper narrative, in response to the presider's invitation to proclaim the mystery of faith. The *Lutheran Book of Worship* uses the acclamation in the first two prayers, also placing it after the supper narrative. Needless to say, this procedure focuses attention on the words of Christ and interjects a proclamatory phrase between the narrative and the thanksgiving of the anamnesis.

Prayers A and B of the *Book of Common Prayer* place the people's acclamation at the same spot. A Common Prayer, which is Prayer D in the BCP, Prayer E in *The Service for the Lord's Day*, and Prayer 6 in *At the Lord's Table*, includes a congregational acclamational after the anamnesis, which is a thanksgiving rather than a proclamation:

> We praise you, we bless you,
> we give thanks to you,
> and we pray to you, Lord our God.

Prayers 4 and 5 of the Methodist eucharist place the proclamation after the anamnesis, while Prayer 1 has it after the narrative. Four of the prayers of the Presbyterian service place it after the anamnesis (A,C,F,G), while one (B) has it after the narrative.

When the people's acclamation comes after the anamnesis, it is more integrally a part of it and occurs between this summation of thanksgiving and the intercession for the Holy Spirit and the gifts of redemption. When placed after the narrative, it is something of an interruption in the prayer and accentuates the words of Christ in the supper narrative, or the proclamatory understanding of the eucharistic sacrament, rather than the thanksgiving nature of the prayer as a whole.

II. Confessional Concerns: The Presence of Christ

Because of the place at which it is situated in the eucharistic prayer, namely after the supper narrative, the anamnesis is prone to be subjected in its composition to confessional interests, which relate back to sixteenth century controversies and divisions. In particular, one sees in this section of the prayer how the churches wish to deal with the issues of Christ's presence and of eucharistic sacrifice. We shall look first to the question of presence.

The new prayers of the Roman sacramentary quite obviously continue to give consecratory power to the repetition of Christ's words over the bread and wine. Though they have introduced an epiclesis, this is in the form of the double epiclesis, over the gifts before the narrative and for the congregation after the narrative. While this question is treated in another essay in this collection, what is of interest here is how this affects the anamnesis. In all the prayers, one finds that the elements are spoken of in such a way as to designate them as Christ's body and blood, the transformation by implication being attributed to the words of the narrative. Eucharistic Prayer IV refers to the elements directly as Christ's body and blood, Eucharistic Prayer II, by a mutilation of the text of the *Apostolic Tradition*, as "living bread" and "saving cup."[9] The second prayer for Masses with children says: "He put himself into our hands to be the sacrifice we offer you."[10]

In *The Book of Common Prayer*, Rite II, Prayer C omits any reference to the elements in the anamnesis, but prayers A, B and D refer to them as "gifts," "bread and wine," and "this bread and this cup" respectively. The two more traditionally Anglican prayers of Rite I refer to them as "holy gifts."[11] The Lutheran prayers use similar terms. There is little reference to the gifts in the anamnesis of the prayers of the United Methodist Church, but Great Thanksgiving I, which dates back to an earlier composition, expresses a sense of Christ's presence in the memorial which tries to overcome confessional problems with theologies of real presence. The text reads:

> We experience anew, most merciful God, the suffering and death, the resurrection and ascension of your Son. . . . [12]

This needs to be taken in conjunction with the way that the prayer renders the memorial command of the supper narrative:

> When we eat this bread and drink this cup, we experience anew the presence of the Lord Jesus Christ and look forward to his coming in final victory.

The idiosyncratic phrase for presence is "we experience anew." On the one hand, this seems to be intended to express a sacramental rather than a physical presence of Christ, and it avoids any similarity to more catholic expressions of real presence, such as those which designate the gifts as the body and blood. On the other hand, it is clearly a way of expressing the notion that Christ's presence in the memorial is to be understood in the context of the representation of his saving acts, so that the presence and the acts are both together experienced anew.

III. Confessional Concerns: The Eucharistic Sacrifice

The question of Christ's presence is closely allied to the question of offering and sacrifice, and the way in which these prayers favor the language of offering or sacrifice parallels the way in which they refer to the gifts or elements. It is at this point of the anamnesis-offering that confessional divergence shows up most sharply in the new eucharistic compositions, and that the prayers are still haunted by the ancient controversies over the doctrine and practice of the Lord's Supper or Mass.

It will be remembered that the Reformers repudiated the notion that offering or sacrifice belonged to the essence of the sacrament of the Lord's Supper, especially if this was to be understood as propitiatory, or an offering for sins. Since the dominant Roman Catholic interpretation of the Roman Canon at the time of the Reformation was that, either in the consecration, or after it, the priest in Christ's name offered the body and blood of Christ to God, the Reformers could have nothing to do with this prayer. On the other hand, they did leave room within their different liturgies for an offering of the "sacrifice of praise and thanksgiving," or for the offering of themselves by the faithful to God, in union with Christ. Both the sacrifice of thanksgiving and the self-offering of the faithful were, however, seen more as the fruit of communion than as acts that belonged to the essence of the remembrance of Christ's death or sacrifice. In some respects, this paralleled the common contemporary catholic piety, but catholic doctrine and practice held to the notion that the eucharist was in its essence a sacrifice, and that done in representation of Christ's sacrifice it could be offered by the minister for the forgiveness of sins. What eluded those on both sides of the controversy was the connection between the sacrifice of thanksgiving and the self-offering of the faithful on the one hand, and the efficacious representation of Christ's sacrifice on the other.

What has now become clear, from studies of early eucharistic traditions, is that the efficacious memorial of Christ's mysteries, and in particular of his death, took place within, or in close connection with, a prayer of memorial thanksgiving. It appears to be still unclear whether in some traditions the supper narrative was proclaimed at a point of the celebration other than within the prayer, and how much the proclamatory nature of the narrative was considered an essential complement to the prayer's proclamation by way of praise and thanksgiving, or how necessary it was considered to repeat Christ's words over the bread and wine. These problems apart, however, in their prayer-book revisions the churches in the USA relate the efficacious memorial to the sacrifice of praise and thanksgiving, as either means or context of this memorial, rather than as accompaniment or fruit. Within this general convergence, however, confessional differences persevere.

The greatest problem is whether or not it is proper to use language that allows the church to offer Christ himself, or Christ's body and blood, to God. The Roman Catholic Church is so convinced of the purpose of this usage that its new prayers actually represent a eucharistic innovation in this respect. Eucharistic Prayer IV says quite flatly that "we offer you his body and blood, the acceptable sacrifice which brings salvation to the whole world."[13] Eucharistic Prayer III extends its offering of the holy and living sacrifice into the epiclesis, where it becomes clear that this means an offering of Christ as Victim (the traditional Latin *hostia* being apparently intended that way in this prayer).[14] The composers of Eucharistic Prayer IV have not been loath to change the bread and wine of the Anaphora of Basil, on which they draw, into the "body and blood," in order to express unambiguously the doctrine that the church offers Christ, just as those responsible for the transposition of the prayer of the *Apostolic Tradition* used the term "living bread and saving cup" to express the object of offering.

The result of this use of language is to attenuate the connection between the memorial sacrifice of thanksgiving and the essential offering of the Mass for the forgiveness of sins. It cannot really be said that the eucharistic offering proper is done by means of the thanksgiving offering, i.e., that memorial of Christ's mysteries that is efficacious for sin and redemption. Rather, this efficacious remembrance comes about by means of an offering of the consecrated body and blood that takes place within the larger context of thanksgiving. The Roman Catholic party to the dialogue with the World Lutheran Federation chose to uphold this kind of language as a proper interpretation of the teaching of the Council of Trent.[15] Whereas, however, the Council of Trent wished to affirm that the priest offers the victim for the forgiveness of sins, the dialogue participants, taking a lead from the USA Lutheran/RC dialogue, proffered the unique explanation that by offering the body and blood the Church expresses its total reliance on Christ and on his offering to the Father and at the same time expresses its own self-offering, in communion with Christ.[16] The effect of this, however, is to relate the self-offering of the church with a distinct act of offering the body and blood made present by the consecratory words of the narrative, rather than with the memorial act of thanksgiving, whereby the mysteries of Christ are remembered and represented in doxology. In brief, then, as far as the Roman Catholic prayers are concerned, consecration of the bread and wine and the efficacious renewal of Christ's sacrifice, wherein the church joins with Christ in self-surrender and whereby it obtains the forgiveness of sins, seem to be distinguished from the act of memorial thanksgiving, even though this is the context into which they are inserted.

The Lutheran partners to the world dialogue expressed their reservations about this kind of language, preferring not to speak at all of the "sacrifice of the Mass," lest this point to a propitiatory value that distinguishes sacrifice from sacrament. This concern is quite evident in the new eucharistic prayers of the American *Lutheran Book of Worship*. Not only do these prayers not allow the church to offer Christ, but in the anamnesis they do not even offer bread and wine, departing also in this from traditional expressions. Prayers I and II affirm that "with this bread and cup we remember" the Lord's deeds, thus accentuating the efficacy of what is remembered rather than an act of the church.[17] Prayers III and IV make it clear that the only sacrifice which the church offers is one of praise and thanksgiving,[18] but this book also makes a change in the prayer of the Apostolic Tradition, which is used as Prayer IV, by saying "we lift this bread and cup," rather than "we offer." There seems to have been some odd allusion in this to the fact that Luther retained the elevation of the gifts after the institution narrative.[19] The problem, therefore, extends not only to the offering of Christ by the church, but to the traditional language of offering bread and wine, within a prayer of praise and thanksgiving, done in Christ's remembrance.

The four eucharistic prayers of Rite II of *The Book of Common Prayer* speak very clearly of the memorial of Christ's work as a sacrifice of thanksgiving, or of praise and thanksgiving, and the anamnesis includes the offering of the bread and wine. This is true also of the more traditionally expressed prayers of Rite I, which also, after the anamnesis and the epiclesis, include ample expression of the community's self-offering, in union with Christ. In the anamnesis itself, however, none of the six prayers mentions either offering Christ or the self-offering of the church. In other words, while the making of memorial is very clearly linked with the sacrifice of praise and thanksgiving, the self-offering of the church could be read as an appendage to this, and nothing in the prayer interprets the offering as an offering of Christ's body and blood.

When from these prayers one turns to the *Final Report* of the Anglican/Roman Catholic dialogue, one finds that the participants appear to have had some difficulty in sorting out the respective roles of the body of the church and of the ordained minister. The section of the report on the naming of the eucharist as sacrifice states that in making memorial of Christ "the Church in celebrating the eucharist gives thanks for the gift of Christ's sacrifice and identifies itself with the will of Christ who has offered himself to the Father on behalf of all mankind (sic)."[20] In the section of the report on ordained ministry, however, the role of the church as a whole and the role of the priest are distinguished:

> At the eucharist Christ's people do what he commanded in memory of himself and Christ unites them sacramentally with himself in his self-offering. But in this action it is only the ordained minister who presides at the eucharist, in which, in the name of Christ and on behalf of his Church, he recites the narrative of the institution of the Last Supper, and invokes the Holy Spirit upon the gifts.[21]

This could lead to the impression that the essence of the eucharist is that which is done by the priest, and that the self-offering of the people is done in conjunction with that, but not as essential to it. Pope John Paul II in writing on the eucharist has expressed himself in this way.[22] The same very firm distinction between the essential action of the Eucharist and the self-offering of the church is certainly not found in the BCP prayers, but they do leave themselves open to an interpretation of this sort in the separation of the self-offering from the anamnesis. As we have seen, Catholic apologists in the Lutheran/Roman Catholic dialogue include this self-offering in the offering of Christ's body and blood, though this is nowhere expressed in the RC eucharistic prayers. Since the Episcopal prayers avoid mention of offering Christ, clearly there can be no resort in their regard to this type of explanation.

It is the collection of Methodist prayers which, in the anamnesis, successfully unites the different aspects of the memorial sacrifice. In the form that is the common basis of all the prayers, it is said:

> Therefore, in remembrance of all your mighty acts in Jesus Christ, we ask you to accept this our sacrifice of praise and thanksgiving, which we offer in union with Christ's sacrifice for us, as a living and holy surrender of ourselves.[23]

In this way of praying, it is clear that the memorial and representation of Christ's sacrifice is done through a prayer that is a sacrifice of praise and thanksgiving. It is likewise clear that this act is an act of the church's self-surrender, and that such self-surrender is a communion in Christ's own sacrifice. The memorial action, however, is not presented as an offering of Christ by the Church. It is a memorial sacrifice, which allows the church to be one with the sacrifice that is commemorated. What the Methodist prayers omit, however, is any mention of the offering of bread and wine.

The Presbyterian prayers in *The Service for the Lord's Day* include no reference to an offering of Christ's body and blood. This apart, they offer a variety of options, as far as sacrificial language is concerned. Prayer A, in its anamnesis, has no mention of offering, but states that in remembrance "we take this bread and cup and give you praise and thanksgiving." Prayer H speaks of the eucharist as a sacrifice of praise but has no further mention of offering or sacrifice. Prayers B and F at this point accentuate the self-offering of the faithful that takes place in the eucharistic thanksgiving. Prayer B reads: "With praise and thanksgiving we offer ourselves to you to be a living sacrifice, dedicated to your service," and Prayer F is similar. On the other hand, Prayers C and G are concerned with how the church at prayer relates to Christ's own sacrifices. Thus in Prayer C, the church claims Christ's eternal sacrifice and celebrates the memorial which he commanded.[24] The anamnesis of Prayer G is not easily distinguishable from the direct recall of the eucharistic institution. Instead of a supper narrative, followed by an anamnesis, we read:

God of mercy, in thanks we remember how Jesus invites us to his table,
imprinting on our hearts his sacrifice on the cross.

The rest of the paragraph makes no further mention of offering or of
sacrifice, and concludes with the memorial proclamation of the people.

A distinctive note of the prayer peculiar to the Presbyterian service
is that the Great Prayer of Thanksgiving includes the institution or gift
of the eucharist to the church among the deeds for which memorial
thanksgiving is made in the first part of the prayer. This means that
the anamnesis forms the transition from memorial thanksgiving to
supplication, leading from the last gift remembered, which is the eucharist itself, to the prayer for the Spirit. This would appear to relate
closely to the function of the anamnesis in early Christian eucharists,
as will be explained further on in this essay. It should further be noted
that prayers G and H mention the institution, but do not give the narrative.

The difference between the Roman Catholic tradition and other
confessional traditions in the use of the language of offering and sacrifice shows up quite succinctly in a comparison between Eucharistic
Prayer IV of the Roman Sacramentary and A Common Eucharistic
Prayer, which is Prayer D in the BCP, Prayer 6 in *At the Lord's Table*,
and Prayer D in *The Service of the Lord's Day*. EP IV served as the basis
for the Common Prayer. It draws on the Egyptian Anaphora of Basil,
the Liturgy of James and the Apostolic Constitutions. The Roman text
has introduced an epiclesis before the supper narrative, which does
not occur in the original sources and which has not been used in A
Common Prayer. EP IV has also changed the terms of the sources
which it uses for the anamnesis-oblatio into an offering of Christ's
body and blood, whereas the Common Prayer, as it appears in the
other current books of worship, keeps the wording of an offering of
bread and cup. The usage of EP IV is in substance the same usage as
is found in the other Roman prayers. What the other churches do with
the language of offering and sacrifice in their more distinctive prayers
has been seen. By and large, one could say that the axiom *lex orandi
lex credendi* has been used in the composition of the anamnesis in such
a way as to accommodate the prayer to one's own doctrinal position
on this score. The one prayer that is free of any mention of sacrifice or
offering is Prayer A of *The Service for the Lord's Day*. It is thus the only
one to remind us of a tradition wherein offering is not a part of the
prayer's anamnesis. By that same token, it may remind us that a better
grasp of the *lex orandi* could help us to get beyond confessional concerns in this part of the eucharistic prayer.

IV. The Anamnesis in Early Prayers

In examining early eucharists, two questions need to be asked about the anamnesis: (a) What place does it have in the prayer as a whole and why is it linked to the supper narrative? (b) Why does it contain oblation formulas and what do they mean?

Whatever the fine points of the discussion over the eucharistic nature of the prayers in *Didache* X[25] and *Apostolic Constitutions* VII, these texts suggest that there were prayers that did not have the supper narrative. This would be corroborated were one to find in favor of its absence in the prayer of *Addai and Mari,* and also were one to accept the prayer of the *Acts of Thomas* as an alternative tradition to what might be called the prayer of mainstream orthodoxy.[26] Taking the *Apostolic Tradition* and the *Liturgy of James*[27] as examples of prayers in which it does occur, one finds that the narrative is in the thanksgiving section of the eucharist rather than in the supplicatory section. The flow of the prayer places the Lord's Supper at the end of those blessings which are commemorated and for which thanks is rendered. It is the final gift that Christ left to the church, the gift whereby he remains ever present among the disciples.

In the *Liturgy of James,* this leads to an expression of anamnesis proclamation and thanksgiving, which sums up, in what the Romance languages would call a *reprise,* the entire flow of the church's thanksgiving and remembrance. This structurally leads into the intercessions, the burden of which is that those who participate in these mysteries and in the table of the Lord's body and blood may be filled with the eschatological Spirit. In other words, the anamnesis is the bridge between the memorial thanksgiving and the intercessions. Since the eucharist is the gift whereby Christ remains present in the church, it has the eschatological significance of fulfillment, and its remembrance, which is also its celebration, is the natural pledge of the Spirit and the basis for intercession.

The place of the anamnesis in the *Apostolic Tradition* could be interpreted in the same way, but its position is not as clear. The text given here is a prayer to be proclaimed by a bishop on the occasion of his ordination. Since it contains the phrase "giving you thanks because you have held us worthy to stand before you and minister to you," the anamnesis reads like a final item in the list of those salvific deeds for which God is thanked. The deeds remembered are creation, incarnation, death and descent into hell, and the gifts given to the church, which are the eucharist and the episcopal ministry. The thanksgiving for the episcopal ministry, however, since it relates immediately to the

eucharist, over which the bishop presides, is the occasion to recapi-
tulate the eucharistic act as a remembrance of Christ's death and resurrection. It then flows naturally into the invocation for the gift of the
Holy Spirit, of which the eucharist and its episcopal ministry are the
guarantee.

In the Roman Canon, the supper narrative, with the anamnesis, occurs in the supplicatory rather than in the thanksgiving section of the
prayer. It cannot therefore be said to be one of the divine deeds for
which memorial thanksgiving is rendered. It appears instead as the
basis for confident hope and intercession, or the "charter story"[28]
which is the foundation for the church's liturgical remembrance and
by the same token for its confident supplication. If, in obedience to
God's command, the church keeps memorial, then it can be assured
of the gifts of divine grace. In the Latin Canon, whether in its Roman
or in its Ambrosian version, the supper narrative is placed in the context of suppliant offering. The anamnesis phrase recapitulates what
has been done in rendering thanksgiving according to Christ's command, and thus reintroduces a more ardent supplication for the acceptance of the church's offering and the sanctification of those who
offer.

Whether or not *Addai and Mari* originally contained a supper narrative, the reference to the form or ordinance leads to the anamnesis
and the anamnesis leads to the invocation for the descent of the Spirit
upon the offering, so that through it the eschatological gifts which the
people await may be assured. In the original text, there may have been
no epiclesis and the prayer would have gone from the anamnesis to
the petition for eschatological graces.

Both Louis Ligier and Cesare Giraudo[28a] explain the presence of the
supper narrative in the eucharistic prayer as an insertion or embolism,
comparable to embolisms in Jewish blessings that are inserted to mark
special days, occasions or feasts. Ligier compares Christian eucharist
and Jewish table prayer. Giraudo compares Christian eucharist and
the *todah* prayer tradition. In either case, the embolism is inserted into
a prayer as specific recall of the origin or commandment according to
which a festive day is kept or a blessing is made. To the recall of the
charter story or divine ordinance, a short benediction is added. An example of such an embolism is this insertion into the synagogue prayer
or into the table prayer on the sabbath:

> Blessed art thou, O YHWH our God, King of the universe, who hast sanc-
> tified us by thy commandments and taken pleasure in us. And thy holy
> Sabbath thou hast given us in love as an inheritance, a memorial of the

creation; for this day is the commencement of the holy convocations, a
remembrance of the departure from Egypt. For thou hast chosen us, and
thou hast sanctified us above all nations; and thy holy Sabbath hast thou
given us for an inheritance, in love and in favour. Blessed art thou, O
YHWH, who sanctifiest the Sabbath.[28b]

It would be a mistake to try to make a linear connection between
Jewish blessing and Christian eucharist, but examples of this sort
nonetheless help us to see what part the supper narrative plays in the
eucharist, and what way the anamnesis formula is connected with it.
The move from thanksgiving to supplication would be complete without narrative or anamnesis. When inserted, however, the narrative
gives the ordinance or charter story for the blessing, and after it the
anamnesis as recapitulative blessing allows for the transition to supplication. Like Kilpatrick, one might actually combine the hypothesis
that the supper narrative serves as charter story with the hypothesis
that it is the final saving deed or gift for which thanks is rendered.

There are indeed differences in the placement of the supper narrative in these different prayers, and therefore of the anamnesis which
is adjoined to the recall of the supper and its memorial command. In
every case, however, the anamnesis serves as a recapitulation of
thanksgiving and focuses it particularly on the death and resurrection,
and in some cases on eschatological expectation. It therefore serves
structurally, even if an embolism, as a connection between memorial
thanksgiving and supplication, especially for the gift of the eschatological Spirit, with whom the assurance of all other graces comes. This
is the case whether the supplication has already been introduced before the narrative, or whether the supper narrative (together with the
recall of the ministry which serves it, as in Hippolytus) concludes the
remembrance of actions for which thanksgiving is due. The position
of the narrative is quite well summed up by G. Kilpatrick, when he
writes:

> In this way we can explain the presence and position of the Institution
> Narrative in the liturgy. The Eucharist is an example of the charter-ritual
> pattern where the Institution Narrative is present because it is the charter
> story. It takes its place in the Eucharistic Prayer because it appears there
> in its chronological place in the saving acts of the Lord.[29]

To this it would have to be added that the anamnesis formula then
recapitulates the church's remembrance and thus leads into the prayer
for the Spirit. As Kilpatrick remarks, such an understanding of the inclusion of the narrative undercuts the doctrine "that these words are

present as constituting the factor of consecration."[30] This would also
mean that the *anamnesis* formula cannot relate to the narrative as if it
did contain the power of consecration, but must rather be placed in
relation to the entire prayer as a unit. It is the *anamnesis* or memorial
of the prayer as a whole which represents the mysteries of Christ and
which represents the sanctifying presence of the Spirit in the church.
The meaning of the anamnesis formula in the technical sense derives
from the entire text of the anamnesis prayer.

Though it is necessary to be cautious in drawing comparisons between Christian eucharist and Jewish prayers of blessing, whether *berakah* or *todah*, and to eschew any sense of natural evolution from one
to the other, some limited comparison bears out the transitional role
of the anamnesis formula. In his book already cited, Cesare Giraudo
points to the transition in Jewish blessings from proclamatory remembrance to supplication by way of a quick and succinct recall of what
has been commemorated. This is what he refers to as a move from *Memores* to *Memento*, or from the fidelity of the people in keeping remembrance, as God commands, to the prayer that God will remember, in
virtue of the divine pledge given in past deeds of salvation that are
now remembered.[31] As on the sabbath, as quoted above, this can be
very readily connected with a recall of a divine ordinance stipulating
the way in which the people are to keep memorial. There is no unique
and constant way in which the transition is made from thanksgiving
recital to supplication, so it would be wrong to think of a set form that
could have served as a model for Christian prayer. However, institution or covenant oracles, or short commemorative or recapitulatory
blessings, function in a variety of ways to make this transition. A further example can be quoted here, namely that of the *Birkat Hammāzôn*
in the Italian recension, as given by Giraudo on pp. 240f. Therein, a
thanksgiving recital of the deeds worked by God for the people during
the exodus from Egypt concludes with a quotation from Deuteronomy
8:10: "And you shall eat and be full, and you shall bless the Lord
your God for the good land he has given you." There immediately
follows the acclamation: "Blessed are you, Lord, for the land and for
food," and thus the transition is made to supplication for Jerusalem
and the temple and the kingdom of David, that is to say, for the eschatological blessings which are prefigured in the exodus events and
covenant. Without drawing anyone to one connection between a
Jewish prayer and a Christian one, or without setting down any in-
violable formula, this kind of comparison does help us to see the role
played in Christian eucharist by the supper narrative and by the anamnesis formula.

V. Anamnesis Offering

The recapitulative role of the anamnesis formula serves as a good introduction to its use of words of offering and sacrifice. Historically, a number of questions remain unanswered on this count. Did the anamnesis formula always include an offering? Did an accent on offering come into the prayer with the supper narrative and the anamnesis formula? Does the use of sacrificial imagery depend on Jewish influence or does it have a specifically Christian origin, arising perhaps from reasons peculiar to a Gentile environment?

If the text of the *Didache* and of *Apostolic Constitutions* VII are to be taken as eucharistic prayers, quite clearly the prayer did not have a sacrificial tone in the beginning. In the prayer of Hippolytus, this is still quite low-key and occurs in the anamnesis formula. The commemoration of Christ's death and resurrection is done through an offering of bread and cup, with thanksgiving. One can either say that the bread and wine are offered because thanksgiving is recited over them, or that the offering is the thanksgiving made over the bread and wine. In any case, the offering of thanksgiving and the offering of bread and wine belong together. There is a readiness here on the part of the church to refer to its own actions as an offering, but this is done in strict dependence on the representation of Christ's death and resurrection through memorial recital and through the gift of the Spirit. In some way, however, the offering of bread and wine is included in the action. It is not only the prayer itself, or the sacrifice of praise and thanksgiving, which constitutes the church's offering and the sacrament of Christ's death and resurrection. The sacramental action includes the offering of bread and wine, however this may be said to be done. This is also true of that other source of current prayers, the Anaphora of Basil of Caeserea, wherein we read:

> We also, remembering his holy sufferings, and his resurrection from the dead, and his return to heaven, and his session at the right hand of the Father, and his glorious and fearful coming, have set forth before you your own from your own gifts, this bread and this cup.[31]

There is no warrant in these prayers for offering bread and wine independently of the thanksgiving over them, but that an offering of them is done as an integral part of the thanksgiving prayer is evident enough, as it is also evident that this is not to be confused with an offering of the body and blood of Christ. Opinions on the original form of the prayer of *Addai and Mari* are varied, but if one follows the views of Botte and Bouyer, it contained no mention at all of offering, just as it contained no invocation of the Holy Spirit,[32] but made a transition from a post-narrative anamnesis to a prayer for the forgiveness of sins and the hope of the resurrection. This would allow the anamnesis the simple but purposeful role of summarizing the church's commemorative blessing and founding its confident supplication.

The sacrificial aspect of the Roman Canon and the Alexandrian liturgy is much more prominent. In the Middle Ages and at Trent, the Roman Canon's anamnesis was misunderstood to mean purely and simply an offering of Christ's body and blood. To understood what is being offered in this formula, one has to go back to the offering and the supplication which is made prior to the supper narrative. The sacrifice which the church is offering and which it asks to be made acceptable is the sacrifice of praise and thanksgiving, but this includes an offering of the elements of bread and wine. The prayer for the acceptance of that praise, in which the prophecy of Malachi is fulfilled, includes within itself a prayer for the acceptance and sanctification of the elements.[33] As Bouyer states it, the eucharist or memorial thanksgiving of the church is materialized in the elements of bread and wine, which are then called "holy and spotless" by way of reference to the eucharist by which they are offered.[34] This is as true for their offering in the anamnesis formula as it is for their offering in the prayer which precedes the institution narrative. After the narrative, however, the obedient memorial of the church is recapitulated and the prayer for acceptance can be urged more forcefully. The sacrificial interpretation of the act is strengthened by the appeal to the typological offerings of Abraham, Abel and Melchisedech.

In the Alexandrian anaphora of Basil, the offering in the anamnesis formula is stated in the past tense. What this may include is perhaps known from a comparison with the Alexandrian liturgy of Mark. There is a lengthy and inclusive offering section in that anaphora, well before the introduction of the supper narrative. It includes not only the bread and wine, but all the offerings of the faithful, which are given along with and expressed in the offering of bread and wine:

> Receive, o God, the thank-offerings of those who offer the sacrifices, at your holy and heavenly and intellectual altar in the vastnesses of heaven by the ministry of your archangels; of those who offered much and little, secretly and openly, willingly but unable, and those who offered the offerings today. . . .[35]

To sum up what has been said, one can discern several meanings in the offering clauses of the anamnesis formula, when that is taken in the context of the whole prayer. The primary sense is that the praise and thanksgiving which is made to God for the death and resurrection of Christ is a sacrifice of praise and thanksgiving. It is through this act that the salvific mysteries of Christ are represented and rendered efficacious, in the power of the Holy Spirit. In a secondary sense, the offering includes the bread and wine over which the thanksgiving is made. In a further sense, it includes all that the faithful have offered in conjunction with the eucharistic celebration, for the needs of the liturgy and the needs of the community, of which the offering of bread and wine is a ritual expression. By this third meaning, we are reminded of what Irenaeus wrote of the bread and wine as the first-fruits of creation and the gifts of those who have been set free,[36] and of what Augustine wrote in *The City of God* of the eucharist as the expression of all the acts of the faithful that are done to lead to communion with God, that is of the spiritual sacrifices which they perform as members of Christ's body in pursuance of their desire for God.[37]

Not only in the Roman and Alexandrian liturgies, but in other traditions also of east and west the sacrificial tone of the eucharistic prayer became quite pronounced. How do we account for this, in relation to the early mellow tones of the prayers of Hippolytus and *Addai and Mari,* to say nothing of the *Didache?*

Henri Cazelles explained the connection between eucharistic meal, thanksgiving prayer and sacrifice, by relating them to the peace offering, or *"todah* sacrifice," of Leviticus 7:11–14. If the peace offering is made for thanksgiving, according to that text, with the thank offering the person will also offer "unleavened cakes mixed with oil, unleavened wafers spread with oil, and cakes of fine flour well mixed with oil." A *todah* prayer, a sacrificial offering, and a cereal offering are joined together. From a reading of this text, Cazelles concluded to a sacrificial reading of *todah* prayers, as well as to a sacrificial reading of later Judaic practices which retained the offering of cereal foods and thanksgiving prayer, without the offering of animal sacrifices. It was but one step further to find in such practices a precedent for the Christian eucharist and a basis for the sacrificial tone of the Christian eucharistic prayer.[38] This sacrificial reading of the *todah* tradition, and its connection with the offering of food, was supported by Jean Laporte in a study of Philo of Alexandria.[39]

Giraudo, however, distances himself from such interpretations. According to his study, it would appear that thanksgiving or *todah* prayers did indeed often accompany the offering of sacrifices in the

temple, but this cannot be taken as a foundation for a sacrificial interpretation of the *todah* prayer tradition as such. Such prayers are to be
found in many other circumstances, where there is no link to sacrifice.
By way of example, he cites Isaiah 51:3, Jeremiah 30:19, Psalm 42:5,
and Psalm 50:14,23.[40] He also finds that the ritual intended in Leviticus
7:11–14 is so little known that one cannot base sound theories on that
text.

There would then seem to be little foundation in the Hebrew scriptures or in traditions of Jewish prayer for the introduction of a sacrificial note into the Christian eucharistic prayer. It is quite likely that
early Christian churches did not see the prayer in such light, and that
they did not have any intention of offering bread and wine when they
blessed them. While Christian writers looked to Malachi 1:11 when
they spoke of the eucharist as a sacrifice of praise and thanksgiving,
this way of looking at Christian prayer and ritual does not seem to
have had specifically semitic roots. It may have arisen in a Gentile
world wherein the offering of sacrifices was taken to be the fundamental act of religion. While Christians did not take part in the common sacrifices of their neighbors, they claimed to have their own
worship or sacrifice in their eucharistic prayer and ritual, as they
claimed that a life regenerated in baptism was in itself a sacrifice worthy of God. This is not the place, however, to go into the origin and
development of Christian sacrificial ideas.[41] The point to be made is
simply that a sacrificial reading of the prayer and ritual of the Lord's
Supper was appended to an earlier understanding of it as a memorial
representation of and participation in the saving death and resurrection of Jesus Christ.

The current interest in sacrificial language in ecumenical dialogues
and in the composition of eucharistic prayers seems to take it for
granted that sacrifice and offering are primary categories in which to
explain the meaning of Christ's death, as well as the meaning of the
eucharistic memorial action. The issue is then to sort out and inter-
connect the various referents of this language, which are the death of
Christ, the eucharistic prayer, the deeds or gifts of the faithful, and
the bread and wine, according to the particular confessional modality
of each church. What seems to be hardly noticed is that in early anaphoras Christ's saving mysteries are rarely referred to as a sacrifice, so
that the whole question of explaining the memorial sacrifice of the eucharist by way of reference to the sacrifice which it commemorates is
turned on its head. Other images of redemption found in Christian
prayer, such as ransom and purchase, the harrowing of hell, the restoration of immortality through the incarnation of the Word, have at

least equal prominence. In current prayers, the amplification of the object of memorial to include incarnation, resurrection, ascension and the sitting at the right hand of God, might well have led to less preoccupation with the language of offering and of sacrifice in the anamnesis formula, and allowed for a clearer view of what the nature and role of that formula really is.

VI. Conclusion

The composition of the anamnesis formula in contemporary eucharistic prayers of the churches in the USA is haunted by a preoccupation with the consecratory nature of the institution narrative and with sacrificial language. Were its role in the prayer tradition better observed, this problem need not arise and the prayer would benefit. The anamnesis is in essence a short and recapitulative acclamation of praise or blessing, which either makes the transition from thanksgiving to intercession, or indicates that the ground for intercession is found in the memorial thanksgiving. In Giraudo's pithy phrase, it marks the passage from *Memores* to *Memento*. It has an eschatological character, not only because it may include an anticipation of the second coming but more importantly because it points to the eucharist itself as the fulfillment and presence of the divine blessings given to humanity in Jesus Christ who is remembered and who is the ever present Lord of the church and of humanity. It is therefore the proper foundation for the invocation of the eschatological Spirit, who holds the church in the unity of the one Body of Christ and of the one hope of mercy and immortality. This upholds rather than contradicts the perception that the memorial is kept in the power of the Spirit, and that the church convenes only by that grace. The anamnesis formula is usually preceded by the supper narrative, but there is reason to suggest that this need not necessarily be the case. However, the connection between the two does indicate that eucharist is kept in virtue of Christ's memorial command and in continuity with the Last Supper, where Christ first gathered his disciples at the table of his body and blood. Lastly, the anamnesis formula does not necessarily have to incorporate sacrificial language or the offering of bread and wine, even though it often does so. Were some contemporary prayers to drop this language, in favor of a clearer expression of recapitulative thanksgiving and a smoother transition to epiclesis, that might serve to bring out the point that the eucharist is primarily the participation in Christ's pasch through memorial thanksgiving, eschatological prayer, and table participation in the blessed gift of Christ's body and blood. Sacrifice is not a necessary category for the interpretation of Christ's death, for an interpretation of the life of the Christian reborn in the Spirit, or for an interpretation of the eucharistic action, however rooted it may be in the religious imagination. But that is another story. The intention in this essay has been merely to dislodge that image somewhat by comparing contemporary compositions with an earlier tradition. Christ and the Spirit are present and active in the church by that prayer and ritual whereby it keeps memorial and glorifies God. Keeping memory and expressing faith in the promises given in Christ are the purpose of the eucharistic action, and these are expressed primarily in making thanksgiving and in responding to the invitation to eat and drink Christ's body and blood. Within such a rite there is place for offering bread and wine and for self-surrender, but these should not be allowed to take a primary place in the explanation of, or in the prayer of, the Supper. When such language is used, it has to be understood totally as *one* expression of the meaning of the prayer of memorial thanksgiving. It is hard to find any solid justification for saying that the church offers Christ to God. As the Lutheran/Roman Catholic agreed statement shows, such an expression has to die the death of a thousand qualifications in order to avoid putting the church's own offering on a par with Christ's offering. Finally, when the eucharistic prayer is called a sacrifice of praise and thanksgiving, that is by way of stating that for Christian people this is the primary act of worship rendered to God, in acknowledgment of the benefits of creation and redemption. It is not because the word *sacrifice* is to be given the literal signification of making an offering. All the prayers examined from contemporary service books seem, at least in part, to have been subjected to the confusions that dominated the discussion of sacrifice in the sixteenth century and from which we are not yet thoroughly freed. The one exception is Great Thanksgiving Prayer A of the Presbyterian service, which brings us back to a stage in eucharistic tradition when sacrificial language did not occur in the prayer, and when its character as a prayer of memorial thanksgiving was consequently unencumbered by such concerns.

NOTES

1. Faith and Order Paper No. 111, *Baptism, Eucharist and Ministry* (Geneva: WCC 1982):11.

2. *Roman Sacramentary* (New York: Catholic Book Publishing Company 1985):546.

3. *Ibid.* 559.

4. *Lutheran Book of Worship*, Ministers Edition (Minneapolis: Augsburg, 1978):222f.

5. *The Book of Common Prayer* according to the use of the Episcopal Church (New York: The Church Hymnal Corporation and the Seabury Press 1979):335, 342, 363, 369, 371, 374.)

6. *At the Lord's Table: A Communion Service Book for Use by the Minister*, Supplemental Worship Resource 9 (Nashville: Abingdon, 1981).

7. *Op. cit.* 28.

8. *Op. cit.* 46.

8a. *The Service for the Lord's Day: The Worship of God*, Supplemental Liturgical Resource 1 prepared by The Joint Office of Worship for the Presbyterian Church (U.S.A.) and the Cumberland Presbyterian Church (Philadelphia: Westminster, 1984):88–118.

9. *Sacramentary* 550.

10. *Eucharistic Prayers for Masses with Children* (Washington, D.C.: ICEL 1975).

11. BCP 335,342.

12. *At the Lord's Table* 12.

13. *L.c.*

14. *L.c.*

15. Lutheran/Roman Catholic Joint Commission, *The Eucharist* (Geneva: The Lutheran World Federation 1980):20f.

16. *L.c.* For the one text where Martin Luther gives passing acknowledgment to the phrase "I offer Christ," cf. "Treatise on the New Testament, that is, The Holy Mass," in Luther's Works, vol. 35, *Word and Sacrament* 1 (Philadelphia: Fortress 1960):102.

17. LBW 222f.

18. *Op. cit.* 225f.

19. Cf. Paul V. Marshall, "The Eucharistic Rite of the Lutheran Book of Worship," *Worship* 54 (1980):254f.

20. Anglican-Roman Catholic International Commission, *The Final Report* (Cincinnati & Washington, D.C.: Forward Movement Publications & USCC 1982):20.

21. *Op. cit.* 41.

22. Pope John Paul II, "Dominicae Cenae," *Notitiae* XVI (1980):138.

23. *L.c.*

24. *L.c.*

24a. This is in line with the Reformed Tradition; cf. J.M. Barkley, "Pleading His Eternal Sacrifice in the Reformed Liturgy," in *The Sacrifice of Praise*, edited by Bryan Spinks (Rome: Ed. Liturgiche 1981):123–140.

25. For English translations, wherever possible, I use *Prayers of the Eucharist: Early and Reformed*, edited by R.C.D. Jasper and G.J. Cuming (New York: Oxford U.P., 2nd edition 1980). The text of the Didache prayer is given on p. 15.

26. On the prayer in *Apostolic Constitutions* VII, 25–26, and on the prayer in

the *Acts of Thomas*, cf. G. Rouwhorst, "Bénédiction, action de grâce, supplication: les oraisons de table dans le Judaisme et les célébrations eucharistiques des chrétiens syriaques," *Questions Liturgiques* 61 (1980):211–240, and A. Verheul, "Les prières eucharistiques dans les Constitutiones Apostolorum," *Questions Liturgiques* 61 (1980):129–143.

27. *Prayers of the Eucharist* 22f. and 62f.

28. Cf. G.D. Kilpatrick, *The Eucharist in Bible and Liturgy* (Cambridge: Cambridge U.P. 1983):69–80.

28a. L. Ligier, "The Origins of the Eucharistic Prayer," *Studia Liturgica* 9 (1973):161–185; C. Giraudo, *La Struttura Letteraria della Preghiera Eucharistica* (Rome: Biblical Institute Press 1981).

28b. *Seder R. Amran Gaon,* Part II, edited with an English translation and introduction by Tryggve Kronholm (Lund: CWK Gleerup 1974): 44f.

29. *Op. cit.* 79.

30. *L.c.*

31. *Prayers of the Eucharist* 36.

32. See the proposed reconstruction of the prayer in L. Bouyer, *Eucharist* (Notre Dame & London: University of Notre Dame Press 1968): 154ff.

33. *Prayers of the Eucharist* 120–122.

34. *Op. cit.* 238–240.

35. *Prayers of the Eucharist* 51.

36. Irenaeus, *Adversus Haereses* IV, 17–18.

37. Augustine, *De Civitate Dei* X, 6.

38. H. Cazelles, "L'anaphore et l'Ancient Testament," in *Eucharisties d'Orient et d'Occident* I (Paris: Cerf 1971):11–21.

39. J. Laporte, *La Doctrine Eucharistique chez Philon d'Alexandrie* (Paris: Beauchesne 1972). Against Giraudo, several authors support the sacrificial thesis: A. Gerhards, "Die Literarische Struktur des eucharistischen Hochgebets," *Liturgisches Jahrbuch* 33 (1983):90–104: H. B. Meyer, "Das Werden der literarischen Struktur des Hochgebets," *Zeitschrift für katholische Theologie* 105 (1983):201: T. Talley, "The Literary Structure of the Eucharistic Prayer," *Worship* 58 (1984):418f. The common reference is to H. Gese, "Die Herkunft des Herrenmahls," in *Zur biblischen Theologie. Alttestamentliche Vorträge* (Munich 1977):107–127.

40. *Op. cit.* 266f.

41. For studies on the anamnesis, cf. J.-P. Montminy, "L'Offrande Sacrificielle dans L'Anamnèse des Liturgies Anciennes," *Revue des Sciences Philosophiques et Théologiques* 50 (1966):385–406, and K. Stevenson, "Anaphoral Offering: Some Observations on Eastern Eucharistic Prayers," *Ephemerides Liturgicae* 94 (1980):209–228.

JOHN H. McKENNA, C.M.

10

The Epiclesis Revisited

With the advent of liturgical renewal, a great number of eucharistic prayers have appeared in the various Christian churches.[1] The purpose of this study is to compare the epicleses within those eucharistic prayers. A presupposition of the study is that a fully developed epiclesis generally contains three elements:

(1) an appeal for the Holy Spirit
(2) to transform or sanctify the bread and wine
(3) so that they may benefit those who partake of them worthily.[2]

I. Anglican: *The Book of Common Prayer*

The first set of eucharistic prayers to occupy our attention is that of the *Book of Common Prayer*. Eucharistic Prayer I has been retained without change from the 1928 book.[3] The text of the epiclesis reads:

> And we most humbly beseech thee, O merciful Father, to hear us; and, of thy almighty goodness, vouchsafe to bless and sanctify, with thy Word and Holy Spirit, these thy gifts and creatures of bread and wine; that we, receiving them according to thy Son our Savior Jesus Christ's holy institution, in remembrance of his death and passion, may be partakers of his most blessed Body and Blood.[4]

The First Person of the Trinity as addressee is asked to bless and sanctify "the bread and wine" with the Word and Holy Spirit. By retaining the first Standard Book's (1793) capitalization of "Word" the prayer seems to refer to the incarnate Word and not, as Cranmer had intended, to the institution narrative.[5] There is no epiclesis upon the people and no eschatological reference in the epiclesis or elsewhere.[6] The desired benefit is that those receiving might be partakers of Christ's body and blood.

The text of the epiclesis in Eucharistic Prayer II is:

> And we most humbly beseech thee, O merciful Father, to hear us, and with thy Word and Holy Spirit, to bless and sanctify these thy gifts of bread and wine, that they may be unto us the Body and Blood of thy dearly-beloved Son Jesus Christ.[7]

Once again the First Person of the Trinity is the addressee, as throughout this set of eucharistic prayers, even though the terms may vary. Again the request is to bless and sanctify the gifts that they "may be unto us" the body and blood of Jesus Christ.

Eucharistic Prayer A has some variations. It reads:

> Sanctify them by your Holy Spirit to be for your people the Body and Blood of your Son, the holy food and drink of new and unending life in him. Sanctify us also that we may faithfully receive this holy Sacrament, and serve you in unity, constancy, and peace; and at the last day bring us with all your saints into the joy of your eternal kingdom.[8]

Here we have a petition to sanctify the gifts by the Holy Spirit "to be for your people" Christ's body and blood. There is an epiclesis upon the people[9] that they might partake "faithfully" and serve in unity, constancy and peace. There is also an eschatological reference.

Eucharistic Prayer B has a lengthier epiclesis:

> We pray you, gracious God, to send your Holy Spirit upon these gifts that they may be the Sacrament of the Body of Christ and his Blood of the new Covenant. Unite us to your Son in his sacrifice, that we may be acceptable through him, being sanctified by the Holy Spirit. In the fullness of time, put all things in subjection under your Christ, and bring us to that heavenly country where, with (_____ and) all your saints, we may enter the everlasting heritage of your sons and daughters; through Jesus Christ our Lord, the firstborn of all creation, the head of the Church, and the author of our salvation.[10]

The First Person of the Trinity ("gracious God") is asked to send the Holy Spirit upon the gifts that they "may be the Sacrament" of Christ's body and blood. There is also an epiclesis on the people that they may be united to Christ's sacrifice, be acceptable and be sanctified. There is no mention of partaking but the eschatological dimension is once again prominent.

Eucharistic Prayer C is much more terse:

> And so, Father, we who have been redeemed by him, and made a new people by water and the Spirit, now bring before you these gifts. Sanctify them by your Holy Spirit to be the Body and Blood of Jesus Christ our Lord.[11]

Linking Eucharist with Baptism, it simply asks the First Person of the Trinity to sanctify the gifts "to be" Christ's body and blood. There is no epiclesis on the people, no further benefits requested and no eschatological reference.

Eucharistic Prayer D does contain some of these elements:

> Lord, we pray that in your goodness and mercy your Holy Spirit may descend upon us, and upon these gifts, sanctifying them and showing them to be the holy gifts for your holy people, the bread of life and the cup of salvation, the Body and Blood of your Son Jesus Christ.
>
> Grant that all who share this bread and cup may become one body and one spirit, a living sacrifice in Christ, to the praise of your name.[12]

The petition is for the Holy Spirit to descend upon people and gifts "sanctifying and showing" the gifts to be the body and blood of Jesus Christ. The prayer also asks that those partaking become united and "a living sacrifice of praise." It is significant that, although this eucharistic prayer is practically identical with the *Roman Missal*'s Eucharistic Prayer IV, here the epiclesis follows the institution narrative. The Roman version opts to split the epiclesis, placing the invocation over the gifts before the institution narrative.

II. *Lutheran Book of Worship*

Here we will treat the full eucharistic prayer, although other options are offered.[13] The epiclesis in Eucharistic Prayer I reads:

> Send now, we pray, your Holy Spirit, the spirit of our Lord and of his resurrection, that we who receive the Lord's body and blood may live to

the praise of your glory and receive our inheritance with all your saints
in light.[14]

The addressee is the First Person of the Trinity, as it is throughout
this set of eucharistic prayers. The request is for the sending of the
Holy Spirit. The "spirit of our Lord and of his resurrection" is deliberately ambiguous to include a sense of "the essential meaning, mood,
and disposition."[15] No mention is made of the Spirit coming upon the
gifts or upon the people, although this may be implied. The transformation of the gifts receives no attention. Rather, the focus is on the
effect of partaking in the Lord's body and blood, viz., that those who
do may live to the praise of God's glory and receive their "eschatological" inheritance.

The epiclesis text in Eucharistic Prayer II is similar:

> Send now, we pray, your Holy Spirit, that we and all who share in this
> bread and cup may be united in the fellowship of the Holy Spirit, may
> enter the fullness of the kingdom of heaven, and may receive our inher-
> itance with all your saints in light.[16]

Again there is no mention of the effect of the Spirit's sending on the
gifts but rather on the desired effect of receiving them, viz., unity, en-
tering into the heavenly kingdom and the inheritance of the saints.

Eucharistic Prayer III has a lengthier epiclesis:

> . . . . we implore you mercifully to accept our praise and thanksgiving,
> and, with your Word and Holy Spirit, to bless us, your servants, and
> these your own gifts of bread and wine; that we and all who share in the
> body and blood of your Son may be filled with heavenly peace and joy,
> and, receiving the forgiveness of sin, may be sanctified in soul and body,
> and have our portion with all your saints.[17]

This time the petition is for Word and Spirit "to bless" both gifts and
people. Once again the emphasis is not on the changing of the gifts
but the benefits for those partaking, viz., peace, joy, forgiveness, sanctified souls and bodies. The eschatological dimension again appears.

Eucharistic Prayer IV is Gordon Lathrop's translation of Hippolytus.[18] The epiclesis reads:

> Send your Spirit upon these gifts of your Church; gather into one all who
> share this bread and wine; fill us with your Holy Spirit to establish our
> faith in truth, that we may praise and glorify you through your Son Jesus
> Christ.[19]

Now the request is for the sending of the Spirit upon the gifts and the filling of the people with the same Holy Spirit. Unity, establishing of faith in truth are asked for those who share in the bread and wine that they may give praise and glory to God.

III. Methodist: *At the Lord's Table*

The epiclesis in Great Thanksgiving 1 reads:

> Send the power of your Holy Spirit on us, gathered here out of love for you, and on these gifts. May the Spirit help us know in the breaking of this bread and the drinking of this wine the presence of Christ who gave his body and blood for all. And may the Spirit make us one with Christ, one with each other, and one in service to all the world.[20]

The request is for the "power" of the Holy Spirit on gifts and people that the breaking of bread and drinking of wine may lead to knowing the presence of Christ. Unity will become another benefit.

Great Thanksgiving 2 does not really have an epiclesis as such. Rather it has a prayer that those receiving may be partakers of the divine nature. This appears before the institution narrative.[21] After the narrative there comes a prayer for the acceptance of the people's sacrifice of praise and thanksgiving, for forgiveness and other benefits of Christ's passion.[22]

Great Thanksgiving 3 has the following epiclesis:

> And we beseech thee, O merciful Father, to bless and sanctify with thy Holy Spirit both us and these thy gifts of bread and wine, that the bread which we break may be the communion of the body of Christ and the cup of blessing which we bless, the communion of his blood.[23]

The prayer asks simply that the First Person of the Trinity bless and sanctify both gifts and people with his Holy Spirit. This will have the effect that the bread and cup may be the communion of the body and blood of Christ.

Great Thanksgiving 4 is the same as Eucharistic Prayer II from *Word/ Bread/Cup* by the Consultation on Church Union.[24]

The epiclesis reads:

> Loving God, pour out your Holy Spirit upon us and upon these gifts, that they may be for us the body and blood of our Savior Jesus Christ. Grant that we may be for the world the body of Christ, redeemed through his blood, serving and reconciling all people to you.[25]

This prayer asks the pouring out of the Spirit that the gifts may be Christ's body and blood for the people and the people may be Christ's body serving and reconciling the world. No explicit mention is made of receiving nor is there an eschatological dimension. This latter trait is characteristic of the first six epicleses in this set.

The epiclesis text in Great Thanksgiving 5 is:

> Send, we pray, your Holy Spirit on us, gathered here out of love for you, and on this offering. May your Spirit make real the signs that through breaking bread and drinking wine together we may know Christ present among us. By the Spirit make us one with the goodness of Christ, as you made him one with our sinfulness, that we may be one with each other and one in service to all you have created.[26]

The sending of the Spirit has for its purpose to "make real the signs" that the partakers may know Christ present among them (cf. G.T. 1, 7) and be one in serving the world.

Great Thanksgiving 6 parallels Eucharistic Prayer D in the *Book of Common Prayer* and Eucharistic Prayer IV in the Roman Missal. The epiclesis reads:

> Lord, we pray that in your goodness and mercy your Holy Spirit may descend upon us, and upon these gifts, sanctifying them and showing them to be the holy gifts for your holy people, the bread of life and the cup of salvation, the body and blood of your Son Jesus Christ. Grant that all who share this bread and cup may become one body and one spirit, a living sacrifice in Christ to the praise of your Name.[27]

This time the descent of the Holy Spirit is requested that the Spirit sanctify the gifts and show them to be Christ's body and blood. Those partaking will hopefully be united and become a living sacrifice of praise. Despite the similarities with Eucharistic Prayer IV of the Roman Missal, the epiclesis here, as in the Anglican Eucharistic Prayer D, *follows* the institution narrative.

The epiclesis in Great Thanksgiving 7 has become the prototype for those in Great Thanksgiving 8–22, which either repeat this one exactly or make minor alterations:

> Send the power of your Holy Spirit on us and on these gifts, that in the breaking of this bread and the drinking of this wine we may know the presence of the living Christ; be one body in him, cleansed by his blood; faithfully serve him in the world; and look forward to his coming in final victory.[28]

As in Great Thanksgiving 1, the petition is for the sending of the *power* of the Holy Spirit on gifts and people. The desired effect is that in the partaking the people may know the presence of Christ, be one with him and find forgiveness. The service theme again appears and the eschatological dimension does so for the first time.

Finally, we have the Great Thanksgiving officially adopted by the General Conference of the United Methodist Church in May 1984. The epiclesis, which follows the institution narrative, reads:

> Pour out your Holy Spirit on us, gathered here, and on these gifts of bread and wine. Make them be for us the body and blood of Christ, that we may be for the world the body of Christ, redeemed by his blood.
>
> By your Spirit make us one with Christ, one with each other and one in ministry to all the world, until Christ comes in final victory and we feast at his heavenly banquet.[29]

This is perhaps the most complete of all the modern epicleses. While there is no explicit mention of partaking of the gifts, the appeal is for the pouring out of the Spirit on those gathered together and on the gifts. The transformation of the gifts is strongly stated—"Make them be for us . . . " The prayer also spells out the purpose of this transformation, viz., that the people become Christ's body and blood for the world and united in their ministry to that world. The inclusion of Christ's final coming and the heavenly banquet makes clear the eschatological dimension.

IV. Presbyterian: *The Service for the Lord's Day*

The epiclesis in Great Prayers of Thanksgiving A, B, C may be before or after the institution narrative, depending on whether or not the latter is said in relationship to the breaking of the bread.[30]

The epiclesis reads:

> Gracious God, pour out your Holy Spirit upon us, that this bread and this cup may be for us the body and blood of our Lord, and that we, and all who share this feast, may be one with Christ and he with us. Fill us with eternal life, that with joy we may be his faithful people until we feast with him in glory.[31]

The pouring out of the Holy Spirit on the *people* has for its desired effect that the bread and cup may be for them the body and blood of

the Lord. Unity, joy, faithfulness and eternal life are further objects of
the prayer. The eschatological dimension is also evident.

The text of the epiclesis in Great Prayer of Thanksgiving B is:

> Gracious God, pour out your Holy Spirit on us, and on these your gifts
> of bread and wine, that in eating this bread and drinking this cup, we
> may know the presence of Christ and be made one with him, and one
> with all who come to this table.
>
> In union with your church in heaven and on earth, we pray that you will
> fulfill your eternal purpose in us and in all the world.[32]

Here the pouring out of the Spirit is on both gifts and people that
the partaking may lead to recognizing the presence of Christ and to
unity. Once again an eschatological note is present.

In Great Prayer of Thanksgiving C the epiclesis is shorter:

> Merciful God, by your Holy Spirit bless and make holy both us and these
> your gifts of bread and wine, that the bread we break may be the com-
> munion of the body of Christ, and the cup we bless may be the com-
> munion of the blood of Christ.[33]

The request is simply for the Holy Spirit to bless and make holy people and gifts that the latter be "the communion of" the body and blood
of Christ.

Great Prayer of Thanksgiving D reflects Hippolytus as does the epiclesis:

> We ask you to send your Holy Spirit upon the offering of the holy church,
> gathering into one all who share these holy mysteries, filling us with the
> Holy Spirit and confirming our faith in the truth, that together we may
> praise you and give you glory, through your Servant, Jesus Christ.[34]

The sending of the Spirit upon the offerings and the filling of the
people with that same Holy Spirit has unity, confirmation of faith in
truth and God's glory and praise as its object.

Great Prayer of Thanksgiving E parallels the Roman Catholic Eucharistic Prayer IV, the Methodist Great Thanksgiving 6 and the Anglican Eucharistic Prayer D. Here the epiclesis is *after* the institution
narrative and reads:

> Lord, we pray that in your goodness and mercy your Holy Spirit may
> descend upon us, and upon these gifts, sanctifying them and showing

them to be holy gifts for your holy people, the bread of life and the cup of salvation, the body and blood of your Son Jesus Christ.

Grant that all who share this bread and cup may become one body and one spirit, a living sacrifice in Christ, to the praise of your name.[35]

Here the descent of the Holy Spirit upon gifts and people is to sanctify the gifts and show them to be the body and blood of Jesus Christ.

Great Prayer of Thanksgiving F has its parallel in the Methodist Great Thanksgiving 5 which is based on the Consultation on Church Union's Eucharistic Prayer II. The epiclesis reads:

Loving God, pour out your Holy Spirit upon us and upon these gifts, that they may be for us the body and blood of our Savior Jesus Christ. Grant that we may be for the world the body of Christ, redeemed through his blood serving and reconciling all people to you.[36]

As mentioned above, the desired effect of the outpouring of the Spirit on gifts and people is that the former "may be for us" Christ's body and blood while the latter may be Christ's body for the world. The service and reconciliation themes again emerge.

The epiclesis in Great Prayer of Thanksgiving G and H *precedes* the institution narrative which is said in relationship to the breaking of the bread.[37] The epiclesis is terse:

Almighty God, pour out your Holy Spirit upon us, that as we receive bread and wine we may be assured that Christ's promise in these signs will be fulfilled.[38]

The request is simply that, through the outpouring of the Spirit upon the people, those receiving the bread and wine be assured of the fulfillment of Christ's promise in these signs. No mention is made of any transformation (although this may be implied) or of any further themes often connected with epicleses.

Finally, the epiclesis in Great Prayer of Thanksgiving H is as follows:

Send to us your Holy Spirit that this meal may be holy and your people may become one. Unite us in faith, inspire us to love, encourage us with hope, that we may receive Christ as he comes to us in this holy banquet.[39]

The request is for the sending of the Spirit that the "meal may be holy." The desired effects are unity, faith, hope, love and receiving Christ as he comes in this meal.

V. Roman Catholic Eucharistic Prayers

The final set of Eucharistic prayers for consideration are those contained in the *Roman Missal*, including the eucharistic prayers for Masses with Children and for Masses of Reconciliation.

Eucharistic Prayer I is really a translation, with slight modifications, of the old Roman Canon. There is no epiclesis, as we have defined it, since there is no mention of the Holy Spirit. There are, however, two prayers for acceptance, one before the institution narrative and one following it. The first reads:

> Bless and approve our offering;
> make it acceptable to you,
> an offering in spirit and in truth.
> Let it become for us
> the body and blood of Jesus Christ,
> your only Son, our Lord.[40]

This does contain a typical epiclesis element, viz., a prayer that the offering become for us Christ's body and blood. The appeal to bless, approve, make acceptable is also similar to appeals found in other fully developed epicleses.

The second prayer for acceptance reads:

> Almighty God,
> we pray that your angel may take this sacrifice
> to your altar in heaven.
> Then, as we receive from this altar
> the sacred body and blood of your Son,
> let us be filled with every grace and blessing.[41]

The image in this prayer is somewhat unique. Instead of involving a descent it calls for an ascent to the heavenly altar at the hand of God's angel. The benefits for those receiving are sweeping—every grace and blessing.

The remaining eucharistic prayers also contain a relatively unique element, viz., a "split epiclesis." Only in the ancient Alexandrian type[42] and more recently in the Liturgy of Lima[43] does one, to my knowledge, find this phenomenon. The laconic character of these epicleses is also striking. The epiclesis (or epicleses) in Eucharistic Prayer II, based on Hippolytus, reads:

a) Let your Spirit come upon these gifts to make them holy,

so that they may become for us
the body and blood of our Lord, Jesus Christ.

b) May all of us who share in the body and blood of Christ
be brought together in unity by the Holy Spirit.[44]

The first part is much more explicit than the Hippolytan text[45] in asking that the gifts "become for us" Christ's body and blood. The second part is even more concise, asking only that the partakers be "brought together in unity."

The epiclesis in Eucharistic Prayer III is only slightly more developed:

a) We ask you to make them holy by the power of your Spirit,
that they may become the body and blood
of your Son, our Lord Jesus Christ,
at whose command we celebrate this eucharist.

b) Grant that we, who are nourished by his body and blood,
may be filled with his Holy Spirit,
and become one body, one spirit in Christ.[46]

It asks the Father to make the gifts holy, that they become Christ's body and blood and that those receiving them be filled with the Spirit and become one.

As we have noted above, Eucharistic Prayer IV parallels Eucharistic Prayer D (Anglican), Great Thanksgiving 6 (Methodist) and Great Prayer of Thanksgiving E (Presbyterian). Here, however, the epiclesis is "split" and reads:

a) Father, may this Holy Spirit sanctify these offerings.
Let them become the body and blood of Jesus Christ our Lord
as we celebrate the great mystery
which he left us as an everlasting covenant.[47]

b) Lord, look upon this sacrifice which you have given to your Church;
and by your Holy Spirit, gather all who share this one bread and
one cup
into one body of Christ, a living sacrifice of praise.[48]

This epiclesis basically repeats the request of those in II and III to transform the gifts and achieve unity, simply adding the notion of a "living sacrifice of praise" as the eucharistic prayers which parallel it have done. Interestingly, for the Roman Catholic tradition, the second

part of the epiclesis continues to refer to the transformed gifts as
"bread" and "cup."

The text within Eucharistic Prayer for Masses with Children I is as
follows:

a) We bring you bread and wine
   and ask you to send your Holy Spirit to make these gifts
   the body and blood of Jesus your Son.[49]

b) Father,
   because you love us,
   you invite us to come to your table.
   Fill us with the joy of the Holy Spirit
   as we receive the body and blood of your Son.[50]

Again the epiclesis is "split" and laconic. It asks simply that the
sending of the Holy Spirit make the gifts the body and blood of Jesus
that those receiving be filled with the joy of the Spirit.

The epiclesis in Eucharistic Prayer for Masses with Children II is
similar:

a) God our Father,
   we now ask you
   to send your Holy Spirit
   to change these gifts of bread and wine
   into the body and blood
   of Jesus Christ, our Lord.[51]

b) Lord our God,
   listen to our prayer.
   Send the Holy Spirit
   to all of us who share in this meal.
   May this Spirit bring us closer together
   in the family of the Church,
   with N., our pope,
   N., our bishop,
   all other bishops,
   and all who serve your people.[52]

Here the appeal is for the sending of the Spirit upon the gifts to
"change" them and upon the people sharing the meal to unite them.

Children III is slightly different:

a) Father,
   we ask you to bless these gifts of bread and wine

and make them holy.
Change them into the body and blood of
Jesus Christ, your Son.[53]

b) Father in heaven,
   you have called us
   to receive the body and blood of Christ at this table
   and to be filled with the joy of the Holy Spirit.
   Through this sacred meal
   give us strength to please you more and more.[54]

The desired effect in the first part is similar to the others (bless, make holy, change) but there is no mention of the Spirit. In the second part the request is to fill those partaking with the joy of the Holy Spirit and strengthen them to please God.

Eucharistic Prayer for Masses of Reconciliation I offers a typical Roman Catholic pattern:

a) Look with kindness on your people
   gathered here before you;
   send forth the power of your Spirit
   so that these gifts may become for us
   the body and blood of your beloved Son, Jesus the Christ,
   in whom we have become your sons and daughters.[55]

b) Father,
   look with love
   on those you have called
   to share in the one sacrifice of Christ.
   By the power of your Holy Spirit
   make them one body,
   healed of all division.[56]

The sending forth of the Spirit's power is to lead to the gifts becoming "for us" the body and blood of Christ. The sharing of one sacrifice of Christ is to lead to unity, i.e., healing of all division.

Finally, we have the most concise of all epicleses in Reconciliation II:

a) We ask you to sanctify these gifts
   by the power of your Spirit,
   as we now fulfill your Son's command.[57]

b) Fill us with his Spirit
   through our sharing in this meal.
   May he take away all that divides us.[58]

This is the only time in a Roman Catholic prayer that there is no mention of Christ's body and blood. There is simply an appeal to sanctify the gifts and to fill those sharing the meal with the Holy Spirit so that divisions disappear.

The charts following this chapter should provide a helpful summary, with the ancient epicleses serving as a basis of comparison for the modern ones.

VI. Conclusions

Having looked at the data, I now invite you to reflect on the implications. The starting point is the epiclesis in the early Christian texts. While in no way providing an inflexible norm, these texts do provide us with a basis for comparison.

Some general characteristics seem evident. One is the reference to some change in the bread and wine in the direction of Christ's body and blood. Another is the frequent appearance of the eschatological dimension and the rich variety of "other benefits." Finally, there is almost invariably a reference to partaking of the gifts.

The epicleses in the *Book of Common Prayer* seem to exhibit no significant variances from this pattern. One might simply note that had the term "word" been left as Cranmer intended it, as a reference to the institution narrative rather than the incarnate Word, we might have a compromise form which would draw us closer to the early Christian emphases. This viewed the eucharistic prayer in its entirety as "consecratory," with two highpoints—the institution narrative and the epiclesis.[59]

The Lutheran epicleses reveal a significant variation. There is no reference to a change of the bread and wine into the body and blood of Christ. This element is characteristic of most early epicleses. Is its absence due to an emphasis on the institution narrative as "consecratory" or a desire to avoid the implications of certain terms—or both? On the other hand, the Lutheran prayers show a strong sense of the eschatological dimension.

The Methodist epicleses reveal an emphasis on calling down the Spirit upon the people. The eschatological note is missing in the first six Great Thanksgivings but is present in the next sixteen—mainly because they use number seven as a prototype. The text made official in May 1984 has a strong eschatological emphasis and is probably the most complete resumé of elements traditionally associated with the epiclesis. It also forcefully underlines the transformation of the gifts as well as the assembly.

The Presbyterian prayers also show a great awareness of the calling down of the Spirit upon the people as well as the gifts. The eschatological dimension is lacking in most of the epicleses. The option to say the institution narrative with the breaking of the bread—thus placing the epiclesis before the institution narrative—is a significant variant from the ancient pattern.

The Roman Catholic pattern is perhaps the most problematic when compared to the early Christian epicleses. Here we find the stress on the unity of those partaking which is common to many of the modern epicleses and a good number of the ancient ones. The "split" epiclesis, however, is found only in the Alexandrian type of earlier prayers and is an isolated phenomenon among more modern ones. Most probably this is a vestige of the old (but *not* ancient) "moment of consecration" problem and the fear that mentioning a change in the gifts *after* the institution narrative would somehow rob the latter of its consecratory power.

Unfortunately, this pattern has several disadvantages. It neglects the stronger of the ancient traditions. It also interrupts the flow of the narration of the wonderful things God has accomplished in creation and in history. It fails to emphasize the basic helplessness or praying attitude of the assembly and thus fails to help avoid a "magical" notion of the institution narrative. Finally, this pattern could rob the epiclesis of one of its greatest strengths, viz., the ability to underline the unity between "consecration" and communion.[60] The fact that this pattern continues to be imposed on Roman Catholic eucharistic prayers[61] calls for serious reconsideration.

The changing of the gifts into Christ's body and blood finds forceful emphasis in the Roman Catholic epicleses. There is, however, no trace of an eschatological dimension (which appears in the intercessions following the epiclesis) and, besides unity, other benefits to those partaking are extremely sparse.

Obviously, the epiclesis is only one element in the eucharistic prayers and to isolate it, as we have done in this study, is to risk one-sidedness. Nevertheless, a comparison of the epiclesis in different traditions is revealing. At times, it shows contrasting mentalities, if not theological biases. At other times, it reveals the fruit of ecumenical dialogue and scholarship. One can only hope that this latter will yield further enrichment for all traditions and lead us closer to that day when Christ's final victory and the unity for which the epiclesis so often prays will become a reality.

NOTES

1. A version of this article has appeared in *Ephemerides Liturgicae* 99 (Nos. 4–5, 1985) 314–336.

2. Cf. J. H. McKenna, *Eucharist and Holy Spirit* (= Alcuin Club Collections #57) (Great Wakering: Mayhew-McCrimmon, 1975) 101–02 and "Eucharistic Epiclesis: Myopia or Microcosm?" *Theological Studies* 36 (June 1975) 265. See also J. H. McKenna, "The Eucharistic Epiclesis in Twentieth Century Theology (1900–1966)," *Ephemerides Liturgicae* 90 (1976) 289–328 and 446–482.

3. Cf. R. H. Miller, *Study Guide for the Holy Eucharist* (proposed Book of Common Prayer) (Wilton, Conn.: Morehouse-Barlow, 1977) 24.

4. *Ibid.*, 335.

5. M. J. Hatchett, *Commentary on the American Prayer Book* (New York: Seabury, 1980) 369–71.

6. Cf. *ibid.*, 307.

7. Miller, 342.

8. *Ibid.*, 363.

9. Cf. Hatchett, 371.

10. Miller, 369.

11. *Ibid.*, 371.

12. *Ibid.*, 375.

13. Cf. P. H. Pfatteicher and C. R. Messerli, *Manual on the Liturgy* (Lutheran Book of Worship) (Minneapolis, Minn.: Augsburg Publishing House, 1979) 241–43.

14. *Lutheran Book of Worship* (Ministers Desk Edition) (Minneapolis, Minn.: Augsburg Publishing House, 1978) 223. Henceforth *LBW*.

15. Cf. Pfatteicher, 238.

16. *LBW*, 223.

17. *LBW*, 225.

18. Pfatteicher, 241.

19. *LBW*, 226.

20. *At the Lord's Table* (A Communion Service Book for Use by the Minister) (Nashville: Abingdon, 1981) 12–13.

21. *Ibid.*, 14.

22. *Ibid.*, 15.

23. *Ibid.*, 17.

24. *Word/Bread/Cup* (Consultation on Church Union) (Cincinnati, Ohio: Forward Movement Publications, 1978) 25–27.

25. *At the Lord's Table*, 19.

26. *Ibid.*, 21.

27. *Ibid.*, 23.

28. *Ibid.*, 24–25.

29. Cf. *The Book of Services: Containing the General Services of the Church Adopted by the 1984 General Conference* (Nashville: The United Methodist Publishing House, 1985) 24–25. This, together with the "prayer of consecration"

in the old liturgies of the former Methodist and Evangelical United Brethren churches which united in 1968 to form the United Methodist Church, has official status. Other eucharistic prayers, such as those in *At the Lord's Table*, may be used but they are unofficial.

30. *The Service for the Lord's Day: The Worship of God* (Supplemental Liturgical Resource 1) (Philadelphia: Westminster Press, 1984) 96.

31. *Ibid.*, 97.

32. *Ibid.*, 100.

33. *Ibid.*, 105.

34. *Ibid.*, 107.

35. *Ibid.*, 110.

36. *Ibid.*, 114.

37. *Ibid.*, 117–18.

38. *Ibid.*, 117.

39. *Ibid.*, 118.

40. *The Roman Missal: The Sacramentary* (English Translation prepared by the International Commission on English in the Liturgy) (New York: Catholic Book Publishing Company, 1985) 544.

41. *Ibid.*, 546.

42. Cf. McKenna, *Eucharist and Holy Spirit*, 23–29, 46.

43. M. Thurian and G. Wainwright (eds.), *Baptism and Eucharist* (Ecumenical Convergence in Celebration) (Grand Rapids: Wm. B. Eerdmans, 1983) 253. One wonders if this is an ecumenical gesture toward Rome.

44. *The Roman Missal*, 549 and 550.

45. Cf. *Eucharistic Prayer of Hippolytus* (Text for Consultation) (Washington, D.C.: International Commission on English in the Liturgy, 1983) 9.

46. *The Roman Missal*, 552 and 554.

47. *Ibid.*, 558.

48. *Ibid.*, 559. Note that the second edition (1985) has changed "this bread and wine" to "this one bread and one cup." This is to bring out more clearly the link with 1 Corinthians 10:17 and the role of the eucharist as sign and cause of unity. Cf. Bishops' Committee on the Liturgy's *Newsletter* 21 (January 1985) 1.

49. *The Roman Missal*, 1104.

50. *Ibid.*, 1106.

51. *Ibid.*, 1110.

52. *Ibid.*, 1112.

53. *Ibid.*, 1116.

54. *Ibid.*, 1118.

55. *Ibid.*, 1123.

56. *Ibid.*, 1126.

57. *Ibid.*, 1129.

58. *Ibid.*, 1131.

59. Cf. McKenna, *Eucharist and Holy Spirit*, 48–71, especially 69–71.

60. *Ibid.*, 206–207.

61. Cf. *An Original Eucharistic Prayer: Text 1* (Washington, D.C.: International Committee on English in the Liturgy, 1984), 11 and 13–14. An earlier version read: "May the Spirit of holiness move among us always inspiring our vision and guiding our hearts in union with **N.**, our pope, **N.**, our bishop, and all who preach the gospel of peace to the poor." This second petition, perhaps in an effort toward brevity, seems to have been swallowed up in the prayers which preceded and followed it.

Chart 10.1.
The Epiclesis in the Ancient Anaphoras and Contemporary Eucharistic Prayers.

Anaphora	After instit. narrative	Father as Addressee	asked	For Holy Spirit	upon us	upon elements	so that bread, wine → Body, Blood	so that partakers benefit			
								unity	forgiveness	resurr. &/or eternal life (eschatological)	other benefits
Apost. Trad.	x	x	(mittas)	x	—	oblationem s. ecclesiae		x	—	—	filled w. H. Spirit, confirm in faith
Test. of O. Lord[1]	x	x	(mitte)	x	—	potum, escam		—	x	x	" " + spiritual health strength, not judgment & condemnation
Ap. Const.	x	x	χαταπέμψης	x	—	Θυσίαν	ἵνα ἀποδήνη	—	x	x	fullness of H. Spirit defense against Sata reconciliation
Alexandrian Type											
Gr. Mark (1)	before	x	πλήρωσον	your blessing through the visitation of H. Sp.	—	Θυσίαν		—	—	—	—
(II)	x	x	ἔπιδ ἐφ᾽ἡμᾶς ἐξαπόστειλον	x	—	ἄρτους, ποτήρια	ἵνα ἁγιάση τελειώση ποιήση	—	x	x	various virtues, renewal of body & soul & spirit
Der Balyzeh (I)	before	x	πλήρωσον ἤθεας-χαταπέμψαι	x	—	χτίσματα	χαί ποίησον	x (?)	—	(?)	—

[1]acc. to Botte's reconstruction

Chart 10.1.
The Epiclesis in the Ancient Anaphoras and Contemporary Eucharistic Prayers (Continued)

Anaphora	After instit. narrative	Father as Addressee	asked	For Holy Spirit	upon us	upon elements	so that bread, wine → Body, Blood	so that partakers benefit			other benefits
								unity	forgiveness	resurr. &/or eternal life (eschatological)	
(II)	x	x (?)		(?)	(?)	(?)	(?)	(?)	(?)	(?)	(?) power of H. Sp. strengthening, increasing, of faith, hope, eternal life (?)
Serapion (I)	before	x	πλήρωσον	your power & participation	—	θυσίαν	—	—	—	—	—
(II) Antiochean Tipe[2]	x	x	ἐπιδημησάτω	Logos	—	ἄρτον, ποτήριον	ἵνα γένηται	—	—	—	healing, strength not condemnation
Chrysostom	x	x	χατάπεμψον	x	x	προχείμενα δῶρα	χαὶ ποίησον ...μεταβαλών	x	x	—	sobriety, fullness of kingdom, not condemnation (eschat.?)
Basil (Byz.)	x	x	ἐλθεῖν	x	x	″	χαὶ εὐλογῆσαι ἁγιάσαι ἀναδεῖξαι	x	—	x	
Basil (Alex.)	x	x	descendat	x	x	dona proposita	et sanctificet et ostendantur[3]	x	—	x	sanctification of soul and body
Gr. James	x	x	ἐξαπόστειλον χατάπεμψον	x	x	προχείμενα ἅγία δῶρα	ἵνα ἁγιάση ποιήση	—	x	x	health of body & soul, good works, strength of Church against threats

Syr. James	x	x	mitte	x	oblationes propositae	x	ut...faciat	—	x	" "
Twelve Ap.	x	x	mittas	x	oblationes propositae	—	et ostendas	—	x	health of soul & body, enlightened understanding
East Syrian Type										
Addai-Mari	x	x (?)	veniat quiescat	x	— oblationem	—	et †benedicat...sanctificet[3]	—	x	—
Theodore	x	x	veniat illabitur inhabitat	grace of H. Sp.	x panem, calicem	grace of H. Sp.	et benedicat et sanctificet et obsignet in nomine Patris, Filii, Sp. Sancti...et fiat	—	x	health of body & soul
Nestorius	x	x	veniat quiescat	grace of H. Sp.	— oblationem	grace of H. Sp.	et benedicat, sanctificet, et faciat... transmutante	—	x	purification of mind and body, enlightened understanding
Later W. Tradition										
Roman Canon "Quam oblationem"	before	x	facere benedictam, ascriptam, ratam rationabilem, acceptabilemque	—	—	—	et fiat nobis	—	—	
"Supplices"	x	x	jube haec perferri...in conspectu...tuae	—	—	—	—	—	—	filled with every heavenly grace and blessing
Gallican-Mozarabic										(The number and variety of the *post-secreta* and *post-pridie* prayers seem to preclude presenting any as really "typical")

[2]to this group belong Testament of Our Lord, Apost. Const. as well
[3]no mention made of body and blood
[4]there is no institution narrative in the present text

Chart 10.1.
The Epiclesis in the Ancient Anaphoras and Contemporary Eucharistic Prayers (Continued)

Anaphora	After instit. narrative	Father as Addressee	asked	For Holy Spirit	upon us	upon elements	so that bread, wine → Body, Blood	so that partakers benefit			other benefits
								unity	forgiveness	resurr. &/or eternal life (eschatological)	
Bk. of Common Prayer (E.P. I)	x	x	bless sanctify	w/Word & H. Sp.	—	x	—	—	—	—	partake of Body & Blood
Alternate Forms											
E.P. II	x	x	bless sanctify	w/Word & H. Sp.	—	x	"...may be unto us"	—	—	—	—
E.P. A	x	x	sanctify by H. Sp.	x	x	x	"to be for your people."	x	—	x	constancy peace
E.P. B	x	x	send H. Sp.	x	x	x	"...may be Sacrament of"	x w/ Xst	—	x	acceptable, sanctified
E.P. C	before (?)	x	sanctify by H. Sp.	x	—	x	"...to be..."	—	—	—	—
E.P. D	x	x	H. Sp. descend	x	x	x	sanctify, showing to be holy gift...body & blood...	x	—	—	living sacrifice of praise
Lutheran Bk. of Worship											
E.P. I	x	x	send H. Sp.	x	—	—	—	—	—	x	may live to praise your glory
E.P. II	x	x	send H. Sp.	x	—	—	—	—	x	x	—

	C1	C2	C3	C4	C5	C6	C7	C8	C9	C10	C11
E.P. III	x	x	bless		x	x	—	—	x	x	peace, joy, soul & body sanctified
E.P. IV	x	x	send H. Sp., fill us w/H. sp.	w/Word & H. Sp.	x	x	—	x	—	—	establish faith truth, that praise glorify you
At the Lord's Table (Methodist)											
G.T. 1	x	x	send power of H. Sp.	power of H.Sp.	x	x	—	x	—	—	know presence of Christ
G.T. 2 (a)	before	x	hear us, grant	—	—	—	—	—	—	—	partakers of divine nature
(b)	x	x	accept, grant	—	—	—	—	—	x	—	all other benefits of passion
G.T. 3	x	x	bless & sanctify	x	x	x	"may be… communion of body, blood"	—	—	—	—
G.T. 4	x	x	pour out your Spirit	x	x	x	"may be for us body & blood"	—	—	—	we body of Christ, serving, reconciling
G.T. 5	x	x	send H. Sp.	x	x	x	"make real the signs"	x	—	—	may know Christ presence
G.T. 6	x	x	H. Sp. descend	x	x	x	"sanctifying, showing them to be…"	x	—	—	living sacrifice of praise
G.T. 7**	x	x	send power of H. Sp.	power of H. Sp.	x	x	—	x	x	x	may know presence Christ faithfully serve
G.T. (1984)	x	x	pour out H. Sp.	x	x	x	"make them be for us"	x	—	x	we Body of Christ; ministering

**prototype for #'s 8-22

Chart 10.1.
The Epiclesis in the Ancient Anaphoras and Contemporary Eucharistic Prayers (Continued)

Anaphora	After instit. narrative	Father as Addressee	asked	For Holy Spirit	upon us	upon elements	so that bread, wine → Body, Blood	so that partakers benefit			
								unity	forgiveness	resurr. &/or eternal life (eschatological)	other benefits
Service for the Lord's Day (Presbyterian)											
G.P.T. A	x or before*	x	pour out H. Sp.	x	x	—	"may be for us"	x	—	x	eternal life, joy, be faithful people
G.P.T. B	x or before*	x	pour out H. Sp.	x	x	x	—	x	—	x	may know Christ's presence
G.P.T. C	x or before*	x	H. Sp. bless make holy	x	x	x	"may be communion of body, blood"	—	—	—	—
G.P.T. D	x	x	send H. Sp.	x	x	x		x	—	—	confirm faith in truth; fill us w/H. Sp.; we praise, give glory
G.P.T. E	x	x	H. Sp. descend	x	x	x	"sanctifying, showing them to be..."	—	—	—	—
G.P.T. F	x	x	pour out H. Sp.	x	x	x	"may be for us"	—	—	—	we body of Christ, serving reconciling
G.P.T. G	before***	x	pour out H. Sp.	x	x	—	—	—	—	—	assured Christ promises in these fulfilled

G.P.T H	before***	x	send to us H. Sp.	x	x	—	"may be holy"	x	—	—	faith, hope, love; receive Christ in m
Roman Catholic											
E.P. I											
(a)	before	x	bless, approve, make acceptable	x	—	—	"become for us"	x	—	—	—
(b)	x	x	take sacrifice to heaven	—	—	—	—	—	—	—	filled with every grace & blessing
E.P. II											
(a)	before	x	Spirit come upon	x	x	x	"may become us"	x	—	—	—
(b)	x	—	—	—	—	—	—	—	—	—	—
E.P. III											
(a)	before	x	make holy by power of H. Sp.	x	x	—	"may become…"	x	—	—	filled with H. Sp.
(b)	x	x	—	—	—	—	—	—	—	—	—
E.P. IV											
(a)	before	x	H. Sp. sanctify	x	x	—	"become…"	x	—	—	—
(b)	x	x	look up & by your H. Sp.	x	x	—	—	—	—	—	living sacrifice of praise
Children I											
(a)	before	x	send your H. Sp.	x	x	—	"make these gifts…"	x	—	—	fill with joy of H. Sp.
(b)	x	—	—	—	—	—	—	—	—	—	—
Children II											
(a)	before	x	send your H. Sp.	x	x	—	"change…into"	x	—	—	—
(b)	x	x	listen to our prayer, send H. Sp.	x	x	—	—	—	x	—	—

*option to say institution narrative with breaking of bread
***institution narrative said with breaking of bread

Children III								
(a)	before	x	bless these gifts	—	x	make holy, change them for us	x	—
(b)	x	x	—	x	—	—	—	fill w/joy of H. Sp. give strength to please
Reconciliation I								
(a)	before	x	look with kindness, send...power of H. Sp.	power of H. Sp.	x	become for us	x	—
(b)	x	x	look with love	x	—	—	—	healed of all division
Reconciliation II								
(a)	before	x	sanctify gifts by power of H. Sp.	power of H. Sp.	x	—	x	—
(b)	x	x	fill us with his Spirit	x	x	—	x	—

From J. H. McKenna, "The Eucharistic Epiclesis in twentieth century theology," *Ephemerides Liturgicae* 99 (Nos. 4–5, 1985), 329–334.

FRANK C. SENN

11

Intercessions and Commemorations in the Anaphora

I. Intercessions and Commemorations in the Eucharistic Traditions

Intercession was already an element in the Jewish table prayers known as *Birkat ha-mazon,* which are commonly regarded as a model for Christian eucharistic prayers. The third petition, the blessing for Jerusalem, is a supplication asking God to remember his people, his city, his sanctuary, and beseeching him to restore the kingdom of the house of David.

The comparable petition in the table prayers in *Didache* 10 asks God to remember the church, to deliver it from all evil, and bring it together from the ends of the earth into his kingdom.

The East Syrian Anaphora of Addai and Mari is a bipartite prayer of thanksgiving and supplication. The supplicatory section begins by asking God to "be graciously mindful of all the pious and righteous fathers who were pleasing in your sight . . . And grant us your tranquility and your peace for all the days of this age, that all the inhabitants of the earth may know you . . . ."[1]

The anaphora in *The Apostolic Tradition* of Hippolytus has an epiclesis which petitions the fruits of the communion, but no commemorations or intercessions on behalf of someone or something other than a thanksgiving for the ministry of the newly consecrated bishop who is presumably presiding at this ordination eucharist. The lack of intercession and commemoration can be regarded as a departure from tradition at this point; but the special occasion of which this anaphora was a part argues against regarding it as archetypal.

The element of intercession is very prominent in the anaphoras of the fourth and fifth centuries, and thereafter. It has been conjectured that the copious intercessions in these anaphoras reflect a possible transference of intercessions from the synaxis. But the Eastern liturgies especially have retained intercessions in the synaxis in the form of litanies. W. Jardine Grisbrooke suggests that the development of specific intercessions in the anaphora may more likely reflect the practice of reading the diptychs.[2]

The deacon read a list of names of those who had brought offerings. Later this custom was expanded to include offerings made "for" someone—including the living and the dead. The Syro-Byzantine anaphoras of St. James and St. Basil are diptychal to a marked degree. They include the following commemorations and intercessions:

St. James	*St. Basil*
1. holy places ("we offer for . . .")	1. commemoration of the saints
2. holy church ("we offer for . . .")	2. for the departed
3. the hierarchy (be mindful, O Lord, of . . ." all the following)	3. for the church
	4. for those who bring offerings
4. all cities and orthodox inhabitants	5. for those who do good
5. travelers, exiles, prisoners	6. for those who dwell in the desert (monks, hermits)
6. the sick, suffering, etc.	7. for virgins, and all who live well
7. the troubled, distressed	
8. the clergy	8. for rulers (originally emperor and empress)
9. for peace, unity, concord	9. for magistrates and those in authority
10. favorable weather and harvests	10. general intercession for all classes of people and the absent
11. those who do good	
12. offerers of this Eucharist	11. for preservation from trouble and distress
13. celebrant and deacons	12. for the hierarchy of the place
14. commemoration of the saints	13. for every orthodox bishopric
15. the faithful departed	

16. ourselves—for a Christian
    end to our lives.

14. for the celebrant
15. for all the clergy
16. concluding prayer
    beseeching a variety of gifts.
    All except the first and last
    begin, "Be mindful, O Lord . . ."
    (sometimes rendered
    "Remember").

The intercessions in the Anaphora of St. John Chrysostom represent an abbreviation of this tradition, as follows:

1. commemoration of the saints
2. for the departed
3. for every orthodox bishopric and all the clergy
4. for the world, the church, God's people, Christian princes, the sovereign (emperor) and the royal family, and for the army
5. for the hierarchy of the place
6. for this city, and every city and countryside and the faithful dwelling therein
7. for travelers, the sick, the suffering, and prisoners
8. for those who do good works (the diptychs of the living are read here).

The first and fourth petitions begin "for"; the rest, "Be mindful . . . "

In the West Syrian anaphoras the intercessions and commemorations occur after the epiclesis and petition for the fruits of communion and before the concluding doxology. The whole Antiochene anaphora structure has enamored drafters of recent eucharistic prayers, but it is important to note that this represents only *one* ancient Christian eucharistic pattern. Other patterns are quite different.

In the Alexandrian liturgies the intercessions were placed in the course of the introductory part of the eucharistic prayer. In the Liturgy of St. Mark they are quite copious, and they occur before the sanctus.

In the Gallican-Mozarabic liturgies the diptychs were read after the offering, and concluded with the prayer called *post nomina*, which in the Roman rite is called *super oblatio* or *secreta*. In other words, the intercessions occur as a part of the offertory and do not appear in the eucharistic prayer as such.

In the Roman Canon the intercessions comprise five sections after the sanctus, three of which—*Te igitur* (for the church and the hierarchy), the *Memento* of the living, and the *Communicantes* (commemoration of the saints)—occur before the institution narrative, and two of which—the *Memento* of the dead and a second commemoration of the saints in the *Nobis quoque peccatoribus*—occur between the institution narrative and the concluding doxology. The *Hanc igitur* is probably a relic of a former second or alternative diptych of the living since a number of variable *Hanc igiturs* are found in the so-called Leonine or Verona Sacramentary.

These intercessions and commemorations seem scattered throughout the Canon and not logically arranged. But they fall into place if the whole Roman Anaphora is regarded as having a bipartite structure such as we see in the East Syrian anaphoras rather than a tripartite structure such as we see in the West Syrian anaphoras. That is, instead of being divided into the neat Nicene distinctions of the praise of the Father, the remembrance of the Son, and the supplication of the Holy Spirit, the Roman Canon is divided according to a more ancient pattern of *praise* of the Father through the Son and *supplication* or petition for the benefits of the new life in Christ. The demarcation between the two sections is the sanctus. If this is granted the post-sanctus section is quite logical. The intercessions for the whole church (*Te igitur*), for particular persons (*Memento Domine*), in union with all the saints (*Communicantes*), and for special needs (*Hanc igitur*) are offered with the bread and wine (*Quam oblationem*), because Christ commanded it (*Qui pridie*). The offering is made in remembrance of Christ's passion and death (*Unde et memores*), on the basis of which the Church implores the Father to accept its oblation as he once accepted the offerings of the Old Testament patriarchs (*Supra quae*), to be pleased with it and make it beneficial to those who receive the sacrament (*Supplices te*), in spite of our unworthiness (*Nobis quoque*). (Omitted from this scheme is the *Memento* of the dead, which does not appear in the Gelasian Sacramentary *Codex Reginensis* 316, and may therefore be regarded as a later interpolation.)

Some early Reformation eucharistic prayers, which still followed the pattern of the Roman Canon, retained intercessions. The post-sanctus section in the Canon of the German Mass prepared by Diebold Schwartz for Strassbourg (1524–25) included prayers for those in authority and the congregation, before petitioning the fruits of Communion which led to the institution narrative.

In the Mark Brandenburg Church Order (1540) the minister quietly offers four German prayers while the choir sings the sanctus in Latin: for the emperor and rulers, for the clergy, for Christian unity, and for the forgiveness of sins—this last being a petition for the benefits of Communion just before the singing of the institution narrative.

The post-sanctus section in the eucharistic prayer in the first Prayer Book of King Edward VI (1549) beseeches God on behalf of the universal church; the king of England, his councillors and magistrates; all bishops, pastors and curates; and all who are in any trouble, sorrow, need, sickness or any other adversity. This is followed by praise and thanksgiving "for the wonderful grace and virtue declared in thy saints," which leads to a commendation of the faithful departed.

In the second Prayer Book of King Edward VI (1552) all of these intercessions are removed from the Canon and form the Prayer for the Church Militant in the offertory-section of the liturgy; there are no intercessions or commemorations of the saints in the eucharistic prayer. The same pattern pertained in other Protestant liturgies. In some German territories Lutheran Church Orders specified that if there were no communicants the litany might be sung after the sermon, followed by collects and the benediction—thus presaging the restoration of the general intercessions to the Liturgy of the Word.

II. Critique and Retrieval of Anaphoral Intercessions

Since many of the contemporary eucharistic prayers we shall be analyzing are products of the Reformation Churches, it would be well to inquire concerning the reformers' objections to intercession in the Eucharist. We find that these center on the *solus Christus* emphasis of their teachings. Martin Luther's sermon, *The Abomination of the Secret Mass*, a polemical commentary on the Canon of the Mass, may be taken as illustrative of their objections. Luther ridicules the offering of the bread and wine in the *Te igitur* on behalf of the holy catholic Church, asking whether God should "have any regard for the gifts and the sacrifice, which are nothing but yet unconsecrated bread and wine?"[3] Luther's concern here is that the unconsecrated elements cannot reconcile us to God (although reception of the body and blood of Christ *is* for forgiveness and reconciliation). But after the consecration (at the words of institution) it is a blasphemous reversal of the object of the sacrament to offer to God what he is giving to his people. Commenting on the *Unde et memores* Luther says, "See, here the canon comes again to the offering, for now the bread has become the body of Christ . . . The priest offers up once again the Lord Christ, who offered himself only once . . ."[4] Perhaps the *solus Christus* theme is most clearly articulated in Luther's commentary on the *Communicantes*.

Christ instituted his body and blood as a remembrance of him, and for our fellowship who live here upon earth. But this fool of a canon makes of it a remembrance and fellowship of the departed saints, and sets them up as intercessors and mediators precisely at the very moment and in the very function when it is dealing and should be dealing with the sole mediator, Christ; thus it leads us from Christ to the saints.[5]

Commenting on the commemoration of the dead, Luther said: "This part is worth money, so that they do not say Mass in vain."[6] It cannot be forgotten that the most often said Mass in the Western Middle Ages was the votive Mass, and that this provided a lucrative source of stipends. The catalogue of the fruits of the Mass grew endless, and Masses for the dead were closely associated with this. This in turn depended on the doctrine of purgatory and the teaching that a series of votive Masses resulted in the liberation of souls from the pain of punishment.[7] These issues were addressed in no uncertain terms in The Smalcald Articles of 1536, which were drafted by Luther and his colleagues in response to the call of Pope Paul III for a general council. The article on the Mass in Part II asserts that the Mass "has been the supreme and most precious of the papal idolatries, for it is held that this sacrifice or work of the Mass (even when it is offered by an evil scoundrel) delivers men from their sins, both here in this life and yonder in purgatory, although in reality this can and must be done by the Lamb of God alone . . . ."[8] The article further rejects the use of the Mass for private purposes. "Nor is it right (even if everything else is in order) for anyone to use the sacrament, which is the common possession of the Church, to meet his own private need and thus trifle with it according to his own pleasure apart from the fellowship of the Church."[9] This would seem to categorically reject votive Masses other than those celebrated for common purposes. It would further suggest that even weddings and funerals could be celebrated in the context of the Eucharist only as long as it was a eucharistic celebration of the congregation, with Communion available to all who are eligible to receive. Yet even here caution must be observed, because the very concept of a votive Mass can foster works-righteousness—i.e. the attempt to attain a blessing from God apart from faith in his word of promise. This is why the article on the Mass in the Smalcald Articles is confronted with "the first and chief article . . . that Jesus Christ, our God and Lord, 'was put to death for our trespasses and raised again for our justification' (Rom. 4:25)."[10]

The doctrine of justification by grace through faith stands as a corrective to any works-righteous piety. But it should be recognized that it is essentially a *false piety* which the doctrine of justification corrects. So gross were the distortions which the reformers confronted that those who adhere to their teachings have been wary ever since of any return to those practices which involve even the *possibility* of human influence on God. It was on this basis that Oliver K. Olson objected to "cultic elements" in the eucharistic prayer. He used the word "cult" "in a special way to designate the attempt to manipulate God."[11]

> The cultic elements of the "eucharistic prayer," as we have defined them, are the *anamnesis* (because of its being informed by the platonic *anamnesis* doctrine and hence "efficacious" in a Pelagian manner) and the *epiclesis* (for a number of reasons including its blurring the Christocentric nature of the sacrament). In addition we could name the intercessions, which are cultic because of the view that the closer to the *verba*, or the consecration, they are, the more effective.[12]

There can be no question of the church's intercession being "more effective," in a theological sense, at one time or another. The Reformation was not opposed to intercessory prayer; if anything, reformed liturgies restored a good deal of intercessory prayer by including it in the office of prone, in the Liturgy of the Word, and in morning and evening prayer. But all intercession is offered in the power and by virtue of the sacrifice of Christ, which is specifically recalled and represented before the Father in the Eucharist. The inclusion of names of the living and the dead in the eucharistic prayer also strengthens the sense of the eucharistic fellowship. And, finally, it reminds the Church of the "not yet" dimension of Christian life in this world at the very moment in which the eschatological "now" of the real presence of Christ is celebrated and experienced. For these reasons there may be a desire even in the Reformation traditions to restore intercessions and commemorations in the Eucharist.

This is not to suggest that intercessory prayers elsewhere in the Liturgy of Word and Eucharistic Meal are not ultimately related to the Eucharist, or that there shouldn't be intercessions and commemorations elsewhere. The question that really needs to be asked and addressed is: why should there be intercessions as a part of the eucharistic prayer? Alexander Schmemann has given an admirable answer:

> . . . . it is the very joy of the Kingdom that makes us *remember* the world and pray for it. It is the very communion with the Holy Spirit that enables us to love the world with the love of Christ. The Eucharist is the sacrament of unity and the *moment of truth*: here we see the world in Christ,

as it really is, and not from our particular and therefore limited and partial points of view. Intercession begins here, in the glory of the messianic banquet, and this is the only true beginning for the Church's mission. It is when, having "put aside all earthly care," we seem to have left *this world*, that we, in fact, recover it in all its reality.

> Intercession constitutes, thus, the only real preparation for communion. For in and through communion not only do we become one body and one spirit, but we are restored to that solidarity and love which the world has lost.[13]

The church lives a precarious and ambivalent existence betwixt and between "this world" and "the life of the world to come." It is a community which lives "in but not of the world." The church cannot come to the Lord's Supper with a world-escaping religiosity and forget the concerns which occupy it as it pursues the mission it has been given. Nor can it forget that the trials and tribulations of life in this world are not permanent, for Christ the first fruits of the kingdom has already been raised from the dead. Intercessions and commemorations are made, therefore, in relation to the anticipated, if not yet realized, victory of Christ and his kingdom. At the very threshold of participating in Christ and his kingdom, at least proleptically, the members of the eucharistic assembly remember all with whom they share the vision and mission of the kingdom, and ask God to remember them too.

III. Analysis of New Eucharistic Prayers

Given the Reformation concerns we have delineated, it is not surprising that new Lutheran eucharistic prayers lack specific intercessions and commemorations. The closest they come is the penultimate paragraph in Great Thanksgivings I and II in the *Lutheran Book of Worship: Ministers Edition*, which is the same in both prayers:

> Join our prayers
> with those of your servants
> of every time and every place,
> and unite them
> with the ceaseless petitions
> of our great high priest
> until he comes
> as victorious Lord of all.[14]

It is a *hint* that classical eucharistic prayers included intercessions and commemorations as a way of expanding the praying community's consciousness of the wider fellowship of the church militant and triumphant.

There is the possibility of commemoration of the faithful departed and the saints in Eucharistic Prayer B in Holy Eucharist II in *The Book of Common Prayer* of The Episcopal Church. After the epiclesis the prayer injects an eschatological plea:

> In the fullness of time, put all things in subjection under your Christ, and bring us to that heavenly country where, with [_____ and] all your saints, we may enter the everlasting heritage of your sons and daughters . . .[15]

The *BCP* includes, as Eucharistic Prayer D in Holy Eucharist II, a prayer based on the Anaphora of St. Basil which was prepared by an ecumenical group of liturgical scholars. This ecumenical prayer is also included in the United Methodist publication, *At the Lord's Table*, and the Presbyterian resource, *The Service for the Lord's Day*. It had been included, without the specific intercessions and commemorations, in the Inter-Lutheran Commission on Worship publication, *The Great Thanksgiving*, and was used therefore with some sense of ecclesiastical approval even though it was not included in the *LBW*.

This prayer has a general intercession for the church, and then includes in brackets specific intercessions for "all who minister in your Church" (with specific mention of specific ministers), "all your people, and those who seek your truth," a blank remembrance to be filled in by the presiding minister, and "all who have died in the peace of Christ." The last intercession leads to a concluding commemoration: "And grant that we may find our inheritance with [the Blessed Virgin Mary, with patriarchs, prophets, apostles, and martyrs, with _____ and] all the saints who have found favor with you in ages past."[16]

At the Lord's Table has, apart from this ecumenical prayer (No. 6), several eucharistic prayers which include elements of intercession and commemoration. Great Thanksgiving 4: From *Word/Bread/Cup* includes an intercession for the church and remembrance of the saints and the faithful departed. This prayer was produced by the Commission on Worship of the Consultation on Church Union, and its revised text (184) also appears in *The Service for the Lord's Day* as Great Thanksgiving F. The relevant text is:

> Remember your Church,
> scattered upon the face of the earth;
> gather it in unity
> and preserve it in truth.

Remember the saints
who have gone before us
[especially _____ and _____
(here may occur special names)].
In communion with them
and with all creation,
we worship and glorify you always . . .

Several other prayers in *ALT* may be noted. No. 17 for Pentecost includes an intercession for the church based on *Didache* 10, which combined the eschatological thrust with a sense of mission associated with baptism, as follows:

Remember, Lord, your Church.
Guard it from all evil,
and preserve it by your love.
Gather it from the four winds
into your kingdom.
By the baptism of water
and your Holy Spirit
send us as your witnesses
into all the world,
in the name of Jesus Christ our Lord,
until he comes in final victory.[17]

No. 18 for All Saints and memorial occasions includes a commemoration of "those whom we name before you . . . [in our hearts]."[18]
No. 20 for Christ the King or civic occasions includes the petition,

Hasten the day
when the prophets' dream
shall come to pass,
when justice shall roll down like waters
and righteousness
like an ever-flowing stream,
when nation shall not lift up sword
against nation,
neither shall they learn war any more.[19]

No. 21 for Christian Marriage includes a petition for the bride and groom. And No. 22 for Funerals and Memorial Services includes the petition,

Renew our communion with all your saints,
especially (name)
and all those most dear to us.
May we run with perseverance
the race that is set before us,
and with them
receive the unfading crown of glory,
through your Son Jesus Christ.[20]

Apart from the ecumenical prayer (Great Thanksgiving E) and the COCU prayer (Great Thanksgiving F), *SLD* has a remarkable series of intercessions and commemorations in a prayer written specifically for this resource book: Great Thanksgiving B. These are optional, but they include intercessions for the church, "the world of nations," "our family and friends," "the sick and the suffering, the aged and the dying," as well as a remembrance of the faithful departed.[21] This constitutes the most copious section of intercession in a eucharistic prayer written by a denominational commission among the Protestant resources at which we have looked.

When we turn to the Roman Catholic tradition, we are not surprised to find a significant role for intercession and commemoration in the eucharistic prayers now authorized for official or provisional use. The Roman Catholic prayers always include intercession for the Pope, the bishop of the diocese, other clergy, the whole Church, the faithful departed (especially when the prayer is used for Masses for the dead), as well as commemoration of the saints.

Eucharistic Prayer I is the classical Roman Canon. As we have seen, this prayer includes intercession for the Church, a commemoration of the living, and a commemoration of the saints in the post-sanctus section, as well as a commemoration of the dead and a second commemoration of the saints in the post-narrative section just before the concluding doxology. What is noteworthy is that in all the new eucharistic prayers, except one among those included for Masses with children, the intercessions and commemorations are located toward the end of the prayer.

Eucharistic Prayer II is based on the Anaphora of Hippolytus. The intercessions flow quite naturally from the petition for the unity of the Church in the (second) epiclesis.

Eucharistic Prayer III is based on the Gallican-Hispanic tradition, which, let us recall, was originally without intercessions in the anaphora. Here the petitions for God's acceptance of the Church's offering and the gift of unity in the reception of the sacrament lead to the commemorations. The intercessions follow, concluding with the same theme of unity. At this point the remembrance of the dead may be inserted. There is then a petition for all the faithful departed and a concluding eschatological note: "We hope to enjoy for ever the vision of your glory . . . "

Eucharistic Prayer IV is based on the Anaphora of St. Basil, and its intercessions are diptychal in nature: "Lord, remember . . . " The commemorations follow the intercessions and lead us back to the eschatological vision: "Then, in your kingdom, freed from the corruption of sin and death, we shall sing your glory with every creature through Christ our Lord, through whom you give us everything that is good."

The inclusion of an eschatological vision just before the concluding doxology is a remarkable feature of the new Roman Catholic eucharistic prayers. It is especially poignant in Eucharistic Prayer for Masses of Reconciliation II:

> In that new world where the fullness of your peace will be revealed,
> gather people of every race, language, and way of life
> to share in the one eternal banquet.[22]

The only noteworthy feature in Eucharistic Prayer for Masses of Reconciliation I is the paucity of the element of intercession and commemoration; one would have expected the opposite.

Eucharistic Prayer for Children I is of interest because it includes, in Alexandrian style, specific names and a general commemoration in the introductory part of the prayer before the sanctus. Leaving aside questions of content, or even the whole question of writing eucharistic prayers for children (it opens the door to prayers for other special interest groups; and one could argue that children should simply grow into the Christian community in its fullness, like everyone else), the progression of ideas in Prayer II is especially satisfactory. There is a natural flow from invocation of the Spirit, petition for the unity of the Church, remembrance of those (presumably) not present (families and friends, those who have died), to commemoration of the faithful departed and eschatological plea.[23]

IV. Possibilities for Anaphoral Intercessions

This leads to a concluding thought about what should be included in eucharistic intercessions. Obviously the restoration of specific intercessions in the prayers at the end of the synaxis is a development to be welcomed. Care should be taken, therefore, that the eucharistic intercessions complement and not unduly duplicate the synaxis intercessions. This can best be done, it seems to me, if the eucharistic intercessions concentrate on the dimensions of the eucharistic fellowship which need articulation. This could include remembrance of the churches with whom the local church is in fellowship; those who are a part of the local eucharistic assembly, but are absent from it (especially the sick, the homebound, the imprisoned, etc., who might be included in the extended distribution of the sacrament after the Liturgy); and those who have been a part of the eucharistic fellowship on earth, but now rest from their labors (former members of the parish or diocese as well as the saints listed in calendars of commemoration). This leaves plenty of other persons and concerns for which to pray in the synaxis intercessions.

It also needs to be asked whether the probable diptychal origin of the eucharistic intercessions suggests that the practice of reading the diptychs should be restored. There is no doubt that it can lead to mischief (people on an ego-trip reveling in opportunities to have their names publicly recited—a nuisance and potential mine-field for every pastor), to false piety (works-righteousness), and even to pious corruptions (the traffic in Mass-stipends). Yet the offering of material gifts has proven to be a way of relating liturgy to daily life, worship to culture. *Someone* is going to offer bread and wine, and other gifts as well. It might be possible to read the names of such offerers at the time of the presentation of the gifts (as in Gallican rite), but this would make the offertory more elaborate and further obscure the fact that the eucharistic prayer itself should articulate the meanings and purposes of the celebration—including the offering. So, with some hesitation, I conclude with the suggestion that some limited reading of diptychs be included in the eucharistic intercessions as a way of focusing the offering of the Church in its relationship to the mission of God: bread, wine, and other gifts are presented for God's use, as are the lives of the offerers. I believe this practice could be especially significant at ritual occasions such as baptisms and weddings, and also on occasions of thanksgiving for childbirth, restoration to health, anniversaries, etc. A diptychal intercession might be framed as follows:

Remember, Lord, **names** who rejoice in **cause or event,** and from the many gifts you have given **them** offer with thanksgiving these gifts of **bread and wine or other gifts.**

As you use these gifts in your grace for the benefit of your people, so graciously bless *their* service in your name and dedication to your kingdom.

Such diptychs, combined with the oblationary petition in the eucharistic prayer, might eliminate the need for any offertory prayer at all at the time of the presentation of the gifts.

Finally, if the Church cannot leave the world behind when it comes to Holy Communion, but also sees all things restored to communion with God in the perspective of the sacrament, the intercessions and commemorations should conclude with a plea for eschatological fulfillment. The Church's supreme plea for all for whom it intercedes is the kingdom of God and its righteousness; and it is only equipped with a vision of that kingdom and its righteousness that the Church can return to the world to proclaim and enact it.

NOTES

1. *Prayers of the Eucharist: Early and Reformed*, ed. by R. C. D. Jasper and G. J. Cuming, 2nd ed. (New York: Oxford University Press, 1980), p. 27.

2. W. Jardine Grisbrooke, "Intercession at the Eucharist," *Studia Liturgica* 4 (1965), 129–55; *ibid.* 5 (1966), 20–44, 87–103.

3. *Luther's Works*, American Edition, Vol. 36 (Philadelphia: Fortress Press, 1959), 315.

4. *Ibid.*, 320.

5. *Ibid.*, 317.

6. *Ibid.*, 322.

7. See John P. Dolan, *History of the Reformation* (Mentor-Omega Books, 1965), pp. 197ff.

8. *The Book of Concord*, trans. and ed. by Theodore G. Tappert in collaboration with Robert H. Fischer, Jaroslav Pelikan, and Arthur C. Piepkorn (Philadelphia: Fortress, 1959), p. 293.

9. *Ibid.*, p. 294.

10. *Ibid.*, p. 292.

11. Oliver K. Olson, "Contemporary Trends in Liturgy Viewed from the Perspective of Classical Lutheran Theology," *Lutheran Quarterly* 26 (1974), 124.

12. *Ibid.*, 144.

13. Alexander Schmemann, *For the Life of the World* (St. Vladimir's Seminary Press, 1973), pp. 44–45.

14. *Lutheran Book of Worship: Ministers Edition* (Minneapolis: Augsburg Publishing House and Philadelphia: Board of Publications of the Lutheran Church in America, 1978), p. 223.

15. *The Book of Common Prayer. . . According to the use of The Episcopal Church* (The Church Hymnal Corporation and Seabury Press, 1977), p. 369.

16. *Ibid.*, p. 375.

17. *At the Lord's Table. A Communion Service Book for Use by the Minister.* Supplemental Worship Resources 9 (Nashville: Abingdon, 1981), p. 43.

18. *Ibid.*, p. 45.

19. *Ibid.*, p. 49.

20. *Ibid.*, pp. 52–53.

21. *The Service for the Lord's Day,* Supplemental Liturgical Resource 1 (Philadelphia: The Westminster Press, 1984), pp. 100–01.

22. *Eucharistic Prayers for Masses with Children and for Masses of Reconciliation,* Provisional Text (Washington, D.C.: Bishops' Committee on the Liturgy, National Conference of Catholic Bishops, 1975), p. 44.

23. *Ibid.*, p. 22.

GAIL RAMSHAW-SCHMIDT

12

Our Final Praise: The Concluding Doxology

Historically Christians have concluded their eucharistic prayers with a trinitarian doxology. Contemporary eucharistic prayers continue this tradition. The prayers examined in this study—the Roman, Episcopal, Lutheran, Presbyterian, and Methodist, as well as the Lima prayer, the Taizé prayer, an ICEL original, and the COCU prayer—use one of three types of concluding doxology. Not only does the type of doxology used raise several questions of grammatical form and liturgical practice, but as well the wording of the doxology poses a central issue of contemporary theology: What is God's name?

A majority of the eucharistic prayers published in the last decade by the mainline churches use a variant of the Roman Canon's doxology. More prayers than not use this form:

> Through him, with him, and in him,
> in the unity of the Holy Spirit,
> all honor and glory is yours,
> almighty Father,
> forever and ever.

Half as many prayers use a variant of the Hippolytan doxology with its characteristic line "in your holy Church." These prayers have a doxology similar to the following:

> Through your Son Jesus Christ
> with your Holy Spirit
> in your holy Church
> all glory and honor is yours,
> almighty Father,
> now and forever.

A small number of prayers, perhaps inspired by John Chrysostom, conclude in praise to the whole Trinity. The prepositions equate rather than subordinate the three persons of the Trinity, as in the following:

> All honor and glory are yours,
> O God,
> Father, Son, and Holy Spirit,
> in your holy Church,
> now and forever.

Some of the differences between the prayers pertain to grammatical choices. For example, in attempting to downplay the masculine overtones of "through him, with him, and in him," some prayers replace the "him" with "Christ" or "whom." The triple repetition of "Christ" sounds ungainly. It appears that this valid concern should be met by using "whom" in such a construction. Another grammatical matter is the choice between a singular or a plural verb: all honor and glory is, or all honor and glory are? Here one should choose for euphony: "is yours" does not sound as good as does "are yours." Another matter of euphony is the choice of "honor and glory" or "glory and honor." Most prayers list honor first. However, "all honor" is difficult to articulate, making "all glory" the happier choice. Of the various ways to indicate the time of doxology—now and forever, forever and ever, world without end—"now and forever" suggests fuller time by including both the concrete present as well as the time into eternity, and is thus the best choice.

There is also the matter of verbal style. The choice for succinct court address as the rhetoric of prayer in the west was compounded in recent decades by a nearly universal decision to cast contemporary English prayers in the terse style and simple vocabulary of freshmen compositions. Increasingly liturgists are dissatisfied—perhaps also bored—with this concise style of corporate prayer. After all, twentieth century literature has given us not only Hemingway, but also Virginia Woolf. It could in fact be argued that the passion of prayer requires evocative images and embellished phrases, that complex sentences need not be obscure, and that the brevity of prayers does not necessarily lead to better comprehension. In the interests, then, of grand rhetoric, the double phrase "with your Holy Spirit, in your holy Church" is preferable to "in the unity of the Holy Spirit."

The eastern style of doxology with its address to the whole Trinity raises the question Joseph Jungmann attempted to resolve.[1] Jungmann demonstrated that while popular prayer and hymnody (as a liturgical concession to the people) addressed Christ, the Spirit, or the Trinity in praise, at its liturgical best the west addressed its corporate prayer to the Father, through the Son, in the Spirit. Presumably if the prayer begins with address to the Father, it should conclude in the same way. But this is merely to say that the west has been more logically consistent in its prayers than the east, which is not necessarily in every case a virtue. Perhaps less rigidity about the rule of praying to the Father would help diversify our prayers away from their excessively masculine-sounding cast.

Finally we come to the main question: What is the name of our God? More doxologies than not call God "almighty Father." Even when the prayers do not call Jesus Son, the first person is called Father. This practice, unchallenged until recently, finds its defense from many fronts, from the liturgical history of Jungmann to the contemporary systematics of Robert W. Jenson.[2] In that the eucharistic prayer, above all places in the liturgy, praises God because of the death of Christ, it is logical that the prayer's structure accord with its theology and that the wording makes clear that our prayers are acceptable by God because of our baptism into Jesus. It could thus be argued that the eucharistic prayer, especially the doxology, is the one place where address to God justifiably requires use of Father, Son, and Spirit language.

Yet some eucharistic prayers, attempting to minimize father language, avoid it in the doxology. If Mary Collins is right,[3] the name of God has always been and remains mystery; and while Trinity imagery has priority in Christian speech, "Father" is not the Christian's proper name for God. To the extent that the Church accepts this critique by feminist Christians, we are able to pray rightly to the biblical God without requiring repeated use of the word "Father." One can without denying the Christological center of the faith search for other metaphors, aware that human language is always inadequate in its naming of God. At least the prayer can be worded so that "Father" is not construed as the sole name for God or synonymous with divinity.

While there is no need for us all, or even for a single worshiping community, to agree on one doxology and use it exclusively, we could at least consider a doxology which takes into account the above concerns. Such a doxology would be similar to the following:

> Through whom, with whom, and in whom,
> with your Holy Spirit
> in your holy Church
> all glory and honor, praise and adoration are yours,
> almighty God,
> now and forever.

NOTES

1. Joseph Jungmann, *The Place of Christ in Liturgical Prayer* (Staten Island, N.Y.: Alba House, 1965), p. 192.

2. Robert W. Jenson, *The Triune Identity* (Philadelphia: Fortress Press, 1982).

3. Mary Collins, "Naming God in Public Prayer," *Worship* 59 (July 1985), 299.

R. KEVIN SEASOLTZ, O.S.B.

13

Non-Verbal Symbols and the Eucharistic Prayer

Christianity is often described as a religion of the Word. Likewise the history of Western Christianity is often read as the progressive formulation of doctrinal concepts; in fact the history of Christian doctrine is often set out as an effective way to study the history of Western Christianity. This preoccupation with doctrinal formulas is reflected in the fact that the great majority of contemporary studies of the eucharistic prayer have been restricted to an analysis of the origin, development, verbal expression and doctrinal content of the prayer. New eucharistic prayers formulated in the last twenty years also reflect an almost exclusive concern with doctrine; the printed texts, especially those formulated by Protestant churches, give little attention to the non-verbal symbols such as the postures and gestures of either the presider or the larger assembly.[1] A preoccupation with doctrinal content is especially evident in the eucharistic liturgy which Max Thurian developed for the plenary session of the Faith and Order Commission meeting in Lima, Peru, in January 1982.[2] That eucharistic prayer reads more like a doctrinal treatise than a ritual prayer to be proclaimed and celebrated. Religion, however, including Christianity, regularly expresses itself and is constituted not only in terms of doctrine but also in ritual and organizational terms as well. In fact the doctrinal, ritual and organizational aspects of religion regularly interact and affect one another either explicitly or implicitly.[3]

214

The celebration of liturgy is meant to be an essentially symbolic experience.[4] That experience is readily frustrated if liturgists attend almost exclusively to the doctrinal precision and accuracy of liturgical texts. Such a preoccupation appeals to and in fact reinforces the flat-minded literalism characteristic of so many contemporary people. The role of liturgical symbols is not primarily to convey doctrinal information but rather to engage Christian communities and persons in relationships with God and one another. It should be noted, however, that the doctrinal content of the liturgy is important because it provides the celebrating communities with a distinctive sense of identity and with important criteria by which they can evaluate their relationships with God and one another.

In recent years the ritual character of Christian liturgy has been the subject of extensive research on the part of liturgical scholars, but as already noted, little attention has been given to the ritual character of the eucharistic prayer itself, even though it is the most important prayer form in the liturgical books. Although the quality and role of music in the liturgy has been a major concern of most Western Christian churches in the last twenty years, few serious musicians have attempted to set the eucharistic prayer to music. Musical settings which have been composed have not always reflected a clear understanding of the essential constitutive elements of the eucharistic prayer and the role it plays in the eucharistic celebration as a whole. The settings themselves have generally been dull. In almost all celebrations the prayer is simply recited, not sung. Since some excellent settings have been composed for the eucharistic acclamations, the impression is given that the acclamations constitute the peak experiences of the prayer viewed from the standpoint of interest and community participation, whereas the basic content of the prayer itself is secondary and unengaging.

Serious concern for the visual environment of the liturgy has been reflected in various studies of the eucharistic space in general.[5] Particular attention has been given to the design and material of the altar as well as the eucharistic vessels. Special emphasis has been placed on the importance of eucharistic bread that looks and tastes like bread and on fidelity to the words and example of Jesus in providing communion from the cup for all who take part in the celebration of the eucharist.[6] Efforts have been made to assure an ordered choreography in the distribution of communion.[7] In the last twenty years, however, little attention has been given to the postures and gestures of either the liturgical presider or the celebrating community, especially with the goal of discerning whether these postures reinforce the text proclaimed or whether they contradict the basic claim that the eucharistic prayer is in fact the liturgical action of the whole assembly rather than the prayer of the presider simply exercising a mediatorial role on behalf of the larger assembly.

What is becoming increasingly clear is that the sonic, visual and motor components of environments in general interact with each other either to the enhancement or detriment of the quality of human experience within a specific environment. In fact each component is conditioned by the quality of the other two. For example, music is heard differently in the intimacy of the Philadelphia Academy of Music than it is in the sprawling environment of the Barbican Hall in London. It is also heard differently in the pastel environment of Davies Symphony Hall in San Francisco than it is in the brilliantly appointed opera house at the Kennedy Center in Washington, D.C. Likewise one experiences a painting such as Renoir's "Boating Party" differently when it hangs in its customary place in the warm atmosphere of the Phillips Gallery in Washington than one does when it is on loan in the formal setting of the Mellon National Gallery. People behave differently when they process past the mysterious reflecting wall of the Vietnam War memorial than they do when they saunter through the lovely gardens at Dunbarton Oaks in the spring. Gregorian chant is experienced as most appropriate in a Romanesque or Gothic church where the sound can reverberate and soar to the heights. In the same way the music of Monteverdi and Gabrieli seems most at home in Baroque salons whereas the dissonant sounds of Stockhausen and Schoenberg find a more congenial setting in a concert hall such as the Philharmonie in Berlin, designed by Hans Scharoun who was especially sensitive to the fact that the character of the place and the meaning of the actions have a reciprocal relationship.[8] To some degree at least people are learning to see the sounds, hear the colors, smell the textures, touch the smells and feel the taste of their environments.[9] Since the sonic, visual and motor components of human experience are correlative, they must be orchestrated in such a way that they are consonant with one another, else the experience is apt to be disjunctive, and conflicting signals are prone to be received by individual persons and communities.

The preceding papers in this volume have dealt almost exclusively with the text of the eucharistic prayer in its various forms. In the pages that follow an attempt will be made to reflect on some of the visual and motor aspects of the prayer as it is celebrated by worshiping communities, to highlight some of the problems that are raised by a general insensitivity to the non-verbal aspects of the prayer and to indicate some alternatives and possible directions for the future.

I. Eucharistic Prayer: Prayer of the Whole Assembly

The manner of celebrating the eucharistic prayer is not something that is accessory or secondary to the recitation of the text. In the liturgy, as in poetry, form and content can be distinguished but they cannot really be separated, for the whole environmental medium is part of the message; the whole celebration is the medium through which meaning is communicated. As already noted, attention to the celebration of the eucharistic prayer remains undeveloped in comparison with the attention that has been given to the celebration of other aspects of the liturgy, including other aspects of the eucharist. As a result most worshiping assemblies presume that the eucharistic prayer is a lengthy discursive monologue, uttered by the liturgical presider and interrupted occasionally by brief acclamations sung or recited by either a choir or the whole assembly. They often feel that they are being subjected to a barrage of irrelevant or incomprehensible words. Some liturgists have tried to eliminate this boredom by developing a multiplicity of eucharistic prayers which they hope will be attractive to the creative imaginations of the worshipers; however, the simple multiplication of optional texts has not resolved the problem. The problem can be solved only by attending to the non-verbal as well as the verbal aspects of the celebration and by grounding constructive efforts in a clear grasp of the eucharistic prayer as collective symbolic behavior.[10]

The history of the eucharistic prayer shows that there are various models which might well be explored today in our efforts to reconstitute the eucharistic prayer as the prayer of the whole community. Unfortunately, most of the prayers developed in the last twenty years have been modeled on one type, the unified monologue, with the result that the prayer has not been properly appropriated by the whole community but continues to be experienced as the almost exclusive preserve of the presider. History in fact indicates that other models were probably more widely used than the one with which we are so familiar in our churches today.[11]

1. Responsorial Model

The earliest extant examples of a eucharistic type of prayer are found in the Didache, a work generally considered to be contemporary with the later writings of the New Testament.[12] Whether or not the prayers were meant for actual eucharistic celebrations or simply as table prayers for a feast is really not important for our purposes; what is important is the eucharistic content of the prayers and their structure. The document sets out two prayers, one in chapter 9 indicating how the prayer of thanksgiving (*eucharistia*) is to be offered, and one in chapter 10 indicating how thanks should be given after a meal has been eaten. The form of the two prayers is actually the same. Each contains three sections, most likely proclaimed by the presider, and each ends with an acclamation presumably executed by the assembly. The first two sections are expressions of praise, the third is an intercession. The structure is clearly set out in the prayer from chapter 9. In that prayer the first section is praise for the chalice, the second is praise for the broken bread:

Confession of Praise

1. Presider: We thank you, our Father, for the holy vine of David your servant, which you have revealed to us through Jesus your servant.

Response: Glory be yours through all ages.

2. Presider: We thank you, our Father, for the life and knowledge you have revealed to us through Jesus your servant.

Response: Glory be yours through all ages.

Intercession

3. Presider: Just as the bread broken was first scattered on the hills, then was gathered and became one, so let your Church be gathered from the ends of the earth into your kingdom.

Response: For yours is glory and power through Jesus Christ for all ages.

The style of this text would have lent itself to effective proclamation and would have naturally elicited responses from the assembly. The responses, two short ones that are identical and a concluding one that is an elaboration on the short one, are derived from sources that would have been familiar to the people. Since from the beginning the eucharistic prayer was understood as the prayer of the whole assembly, it would have been normal for the whole assembly to participate vocally in the prayer. That would have been facilitated by structuring the prayer in what we would call today a responsorial form.[13]

2. Series of Individual Prayers

It is possible that the form of the eucharistic prayers found in the Didache developed from a more basic Jewish prayer model which consisted of a series of individual prayers.[14] Thomas Talley and others have noted the importance of the Jewish Birkat ha-mazon for the development of the Christian eucharistic prayer.[15] It consisted of three prayers and a final acclamation which was possibly recited by the whole assembly. The first prayer was a blessing to God who nourishes the universe; the second a prayer of thanksgiving for the gift of the promised land; and the third an intercession for the people of Israel and Jerusalem. This threefold pattern influenced the structure of many of the Christian eucharistic prayers which moved from praise to God through thanksgiving for salvation to intercession for the Church. The structure is reflected in the hypothetical restoration of the third-century Syrian anaphora of Addai and Mari.[16] Joseph Gelineau wonders whether the Roman canon was not originally of this type; if so, the Amens concluding each prayer would not have been later additions.[17]

Certainly the basic characteristic of this model would have been its simplicity. The presider would have improvised to the best of his ability a series of prayers which cumulatively would have formed the eucharistic prayer. The assembly would have easily participated in each of the prayers by an Amen or a longer acclamation.[18]

3. Unified Monologue

The earliest example of a eucharistic prayer in the form of a unified monologue would be the anaphora of the Apostolic Tradition.[19] Between the initial dialogue of the presider and the assembly and the final Amen proclaimed by the worshiping community, the presider would have improvised an uninterrupted discourse addressed to God and combining the confession/memorial of the first part of the prayer with the offertory/epiclesis of the second part. This model would have presumed a highly developed oratorical skill on the part of the presider. Likewise its effectiveness from a participatory point of view would have depended on the assembly's ability to listen attentively to formal theological discourse.[20] Certainly most of the eucharistic prayers developed in the past twenty years have followed this model, with the result that greater emphasis has been placed on the presider than on the whole celebrating assembly.

4. Mixed Models

Historically the unified monologue model of the eucharistic prayer gave way to various mixed models. This resulted partly from the desire on the part of the assembly for sung participation during the eucharistic prayer. In the East acclamations and troparia were gradually introduced, including the sanctus, acclamations of praise and anamnesis, and Amens after the texts of institution.[21] The same phenomenon occurred in the Roman canon with the protracted singing of the sanctus and Benedictus.[22]

In areas such as North Africa, Egypt and Ethiopia, where the assembly's active participation in the liturgy was a normal cultural phenomenon, the eucharistic prayer was structured in such a way that it was a continual dialogue between the presider, the assembly, the deacon and the choir. For example, in the Coptic liturgy of St Basil there developed as many as seventeen interventions of the people in the text of institution alone.[23] In these instances the participation of the assembly would not have interrupted the movement and direction of the prayer. The interventions would have been naturally incorporated into the prayer, so that it would be experienced as an integrated act of praise, confession, offering and intercession on the part of the whole community.[24]

Naturally a thorough study of the eucharistic prayer in the early centuries would call for an analysis and evaluation not only of the texts and their literary structure but also of the diversity of roles, the rhythms of the utterances, the music, the gestures and the environment in which the celebrations took place. Obviously this cannot be done because of lack of evidence. However what is clear is that the early Church communities made eucharist together. They created a variety of models to involve the whole assembly so that the eucharist was not simply the prayer of the presider but of the whole community. It was above all a eucharistic action.[25]

II. Development of Western Practices during the Eucharistic Prayer

It was originally the custom in Rome for the presider to proclaim the eucharistic prayer in a loud voice as a simple recitation without any melody. Once the Roman liturgy was taken to Frankish territory, various new customs developed. The *Ordo Romanus Primus* gives an important rubric indicating a basic change in the understanding of the eucharistic prayer. After mentioning the singing of the Sanctus, the rubric continues: "Quem dum expleverit, surgit pontifex solus et intrat in canone."[26] The priest enters the sanctuary of the canon alone. The canon is looked upon as the priest's prayer and is spoken in a low voice so that the bystanders can scarcely hear it. This is evident in a Frankish revision of the Roman ordo of John the Archchanter, dating from about the middle of the eighth century, where the rubric reads: "Et incipit canere dissimili voce et melodia, ita ut a circumstantibus altare tantum audiatur."[27] The priest begins to sing in a different voice and melody so that he may be heard only by those standing around the altar. By the end of the eighth century, the canon was rendered in absolute silence as is indicated in the second Roman ordo, which was a late Carolingian revision of the first Roman ordo: "Surgit solus pontifex et tacite intrat in canonem."[28]

The people had customarily thronged about the priest and joined in the music that was properly theirs, but by the ninth century a sacred silence reigned after the sanctus. It was thought to be an appropriate preparation for the approach of God in and through the canon. Like the high priest in the Hebrew Scriptures who once a year entered the Holy of Holies to offer the blood of a sacrificial animal to Yahweh, the Christian priest separated himself from the people and approached the all-holy God to offer sacrifice on behalf of the faithful. The assembly knelt at this time, or when such a posture was forbidden on Sunday and feast days, they bowed.[29]

At more solemn celebrations, a procession of clerics carrying lighted tapers came into the sanctuary after the sanctus and ranged themselves symmetrically before the altar. In some places clerics bearing swinging censers knelt to the left and right of the altar. During less solemn functions, two additional tapers were lighted after the preface. In the late Middle Ages, the custom developed whereby the so-called sanctus candle was lighted at every Mass. These rites were meant to foster a sense of reverence and mystery, above all during the recitation of the text of institution which came to be thought of as the precise moment when the bread and wine were changed into the body and blood of Christ. The people no longer followed the priest's prayers; in fact the prayers were no longer supposed to be accessible to lay people. The only aspect of the eucharistic prayer that was open to the people was the visual image of the priest extending his arms, bowing, kissing the altar, making signs of the cross over the gifts, and eventually elevating the sacred species and genuflecting before them.[30]

The basic gesture of the presider during the canon was the traditional stance of the *orans*. Praying with hands raised and outstretched, a natural posture expressing one's openness to help from a transcendent presence, was a gesture common among ancient Jews. When the posture was adopted by the Christians, they related it to Christ praying with outstretched arms on the cross.[31] Tertullian, for example, wrote: "We not only raise our hands, we also stretch them out, and copying thus the suffering of the Lord in prayer, we too confess to Christ."[32] The numerous *orantes* portrayed in the catacombs are visual witnesses to the primitive gesture. Praying with outstretched arms was a universal practice in Christian antiquity and one that was com-

mon down through the Middle Ages. During the eucharistic prayer
the gesture was originally assumed by the surrounding clergy and
most probably by the lay people until bowing became their common
gesture.[33]

The reverential bow assumed by the surrounding clergy was originally shared by the presider at the sanctus, but subsequently he was
directed to bow during various prayers of the canon, including the text
of institution. Likewise he was directed to make numerous signs of the
cross over the gifts. First evidence for such signs, to be made shortly
after the sanctus, is found at the beginning of the eighth century.[34] The
significance of the signs was, from the tenth century, a major theme
in medieval commentaries on the Mass.[35] The obvious meaning was
that the sign of the cross pointed to the sacrifice of the cross sacra-
mentalized on the altar. The gesture also took on the significance of
blessing. For the first ten centuries, an imposition of hands was the
general form used for blessing, but it was superseded more and more
by the sign of the cross, especially in Gallican territories.[36] In some instances the signs of the cross during the canon accompanied words
such as "benedictam" and "benedicis," leaving no doubt that the
signs signified a blessing.[37]

It has also been suggested that the sign of the cross was intended to
underline certain important words in the canon. The solemn prose
style that characterized the Roman canon promoted a type of speech
that would have been accompanied by oratorical gestures, at least in
certain schools of rhetoric in the Roman empire. Hence an oratorical
phrase that alluded to an object in view of the listener would have elicited a gesture drawing attention to that object. It has been suggested
that from the eighth century these gestures were stylized into signs of
the cross. In the Roman canon almost every time the gifts were mentioned a sign of the cross was indicated. The conclusion that one might
draw is that the original gesture within the canon was a demonstrative
gesture, and as such was not originally noted in the liturgical text.[38]

Since the priest was concerned with the offering up of gifts that
could not be given to an invisible God except by means of interpre-
tative words and gestures, the pointing gesture would also be a gesture of offering whenever it accompanied a petition for acceptance by
God, as in the words "petitimus uti accepta habeas; offerimus prae-
clarae maiestati tuae." Extending his hands over the gifts would have
embodied the same petition for acceptance. Hippolytus explicitly prescribed that the bishop should recite the eucharistic prayer with hands
extended over the gifts.[39] This gesture, however, never became a traditional gesture accompanying the whole eucharistic prayer but was

generally employed, as it is today in the Roman canon, during the recitation of the "Hanc igitur."[40]

The recitation of the text of institution took on its own distinctive gestures. As the priest mentioned the Lord's actions at the Last Supper, he adapted his own actions to the words in a dramatic fashion; in fact he more or less mimed the gestures that Christ presumably performed. He took the bread into his hands and lifted up his eyes toward heaven; he made the sign of the cross over the bread and then pronounced the words which were presumed to be Christ's own words at the Last Supper. He repeated the same gestures with the cup in his hand. In some areas, the priest cracked the host at the word "fregit," but he did not separate the parts. The act of giving the bread and wine to the disciples was realized only in the communion rite. With these realistic gestures, the opinion grew that it was precisely at the text of institution that Christ identified himself in a special way with the priest. It was affirmed that it was Christ himself who was active at that time and in virtue of his power the gifts were transformed into his body and blood.[41]

Various other usages strengthened this view. In some places, during an otherwise silent canon the words "take and eat; this is my body," and the corresponding words over the cup, were proclaimed in a loud voice or chanted to a solemn melody. The people affirmed the consecration with the singing of one or even several Amens at the end of each text of institution.[42] This emphasis on the text of institution overshadowed the other constitutive elements of the eucharistic prayer.

In the eleventh century there appeared a marked change in attitude toward the gifts following the text of institution, indicating a belief in the transformation of the bread and wine. According to a Cluniac customary written about 1068, at the consecration the priest should hold the host "quattuor primis digitis ad hoc ipsum ablutis."[43] Following the consecration, even when praying with outstretched arms, priests began to hold these fingers pressed together for they were believed to have touched the physical body of the Lord.

The emphasis on the text of institution also influenced the attitude of the faithful. Although the people rarely received communion at Mass during the Middle Ages, they concentrated on looking at the species and so the practice of so-called "ocular communion" developed.[44] To prevent the people from reverencing the bread before the consecration, the bishop of Paris in 1210 ordered that the priest should hold the host chest-high before the consecration and then only after the consecration should he elevate it high enough to be seen by all the faithful. That practice spread rapidly. The people's longing to see the elevated host was satisfied by the priest in his willingness to linger while elevating the host or to turn to the right and the left while doing so. In some places a dark curtain was drawn behind the altar in order to allow the white host to stand out against the background. Likewise a consecration candle was sometimes lighted and held aloft by the deacon or server when the church was too dark for the people to see the host. In monastic churches the doors of the choir, which were normally kept closed, were opened at the consecration so the people gathered in the nave could see the elevation. A small bell was also rung to signal the moment of consecration. The first evidence of its use comes from Cologne in the early thirteenth century.[45] The bell was used not only to direct the attention of the people to the moment of the showing of the sacred species but also to summon the people to the church in order to worship the sacrament. Consequently by the end of the thirteenth century the ringing of the small bell was augmented by the ringing of the large church bell, so that those who were absent from the church could pause, turn toward the church, and adore the Lord present in the Blessed Sacrament.[46]

A similar elevation of the chalice developed only gradually. The Roman missals printed in the early sixteenth century made no mention of it. There was the danger of spilling the contents of the chalice; there was also the practice of covering the chalice with the back part of the corporal folded up over it to keep the content from being contaminated by insects or dust. Furthermore an elevation of the chalice seemed incongruous because the faithful could not in fact see the precious blood in the cup. It was not until the missal of Pius V (1570) that a rubric prescribed a similar elevation of the chalice corresponding to the elevation of the host.[47]

Worship of the eucharist was also manifested by the kneeling position assumed by both the clergy and the faithful. This was often accompanied by a bow of the head. These practices naturally curbed the custom of looking at the host. The priest who was celebrating the Mass also gradually expressed his adoration of the sacrament by genuflecting before and after the elevation of the species. These acts were prescribed by the missal of Pius V.[48] When the priest genuflected, the server grasped the edge of the chasuble so that the celebrant would not be impeded in genuflecting and so that the full vestment would not be pulled away by his raised arms.[49]

Since the people did not participate actively in the prayers of the canon recited by the celebrant, they were advised to say their own prayers quietly. To express their petition for forgiveness, for a contrite reception of the last sacraments and for eternal beatitude, they were instructed to strike their breasts and sign themselves with the sign of the cross. What were originally private prayers developed by the end of the Middle Ages into common prayers and songs.[50] This emphasis on the real presence of Christ on the altar certainly obliterated the people's understanding of the Mass as an action.

The Roman canon concluded with two formulas which served as a summary and an ending of the text. The penultimate prayer suggested that all of God's gifts have come down from heaven through the mediatorship of Christ, whereas the final prayer affirmed that all honor, glory and praise are given to God only through his Son Jesus Christ. In the early centuries of the Roman canon, the conclusion of the canon was the place for blessing various natural products such as milk, honey, cheese, bread and grapes. The insertion of these blessings linked natural creation with heaven and also united the church in its act of blessing with Christ who hallows all earthly things because he is the mediator between heaven and earth. But when the actual presence of the food disappeared, the people's lives were further removed from the celebration of the eucharist and the link between heaven and earth appeared more tenuous.[51]

All good things come from God through Christ; likewise they return to God through Christ. This was shown through the final doxology. It was an old rule governing public prayer that it should generally close with praise of God, thus expressing the creature's submission to the Creator. The concluding doxology of the Roman canon not only praised God but affirmed that this praise is rendered through Christ. The accompanying gesture has traditionally supported the text, but it is a rite with a complex history. In Rome during the seventh century, the assisting archdeacon, at the words "Per ipsum," grasped the chalice with hands covered with a linen cloth and raised it up while the Pope picked up two consecrated breads, raised them to the height of the chalice brim, touched the chalice with the breads and then finished the doxology. Gradually the rite was obscured by the introduction of signs of the cross which became increasingly prominent. At first, there were two signs of the cross, then three, later four, and finally five. Both the origin and the meaning of these crosses remain obscure. What is certain is that they overwhelmed the simple strength of the elevation which accompanied the doxology.[52]

Only the final words of the doxology, "per omnia saecula saeculorum," were said aloud. The elevation was originally combined with the recitation of these words which were answered by the traditional "Amen" of the faithful. Later, however, the elevation was joined to the words "omnis honor et gloria" and the final words "per omnia saecula saeculorum" were not pronounced until the chalice and host had been replaced on the corporal. The elevation of the gifts accompanied the high point of the doxology, but the final words were not joined to the rite. In fact, they were incongruously separated from it by the action of replacing the chalice and host on the altar and also by a genuflection which seems to have been added in the late fifteenth century. Curiously the final words of the doxology, "per omnia . . . " appeared to be part of the introduction to the "Pater noster" which followed.[53]

This brief survey of the development of the Roman canon has shown that in the West the model for the eucharistic prayer was initially that of a series of prayers which were gradually brought together into a unified discourse. Although the prayer was originally thought of as an expression of the worship of the whole assembly, as the centuries passed the canon became almost exclusively the priest's prayer. Acting "in persona Christi," he represented Christ before the people and the people before Christ. Although primary emphasis was placed on the text of the prayer, the canon was gradually rendered in silence. The priest vested in traditional Mass vestments and he executed complex gestures. On his part special attention was given to the motor aspects of the rite. He assumed a standing position throughout most of the canon and held his arms outstretched in the orans position. In many churches he celebrated the Mass with his back to the assembly. The people were kept at a distance from the priest; they generally assumed a kneeling position. When the Mass was not celebrated facing the people, they would have followed only those gestures of the priest which could be seen from the back. Apart from the singing of the sanctus and Benedictus, they would have heard little of what was being said at the altar.

III. Protestant and Catholic Reforms

The Protestant and Catholic reforms of the sixteenth century brought fundamental changes in the worship of Western European Christians, especially in the celebration of the eucharist. At the beginning of the century, all church and secular leaders who were to inaugurate religious, social and political reforms were practicing Catholics whose education and theology were thoroughly consistent with late medieval content and method. A survey of the history of the Roman canon through the Middle Ages has shown that vision provided the faithful with their main access to the prayer. The liturgy was for most participants a minimally verbal experience. Auditory participation was almost non-existent as the priest's words became inaudible. But even if the canon were audible, its recitation in Latin would have inhibited understanding on the part of most of the faithful, since the majority of lay people did not know the language.

The imbalance between engagement of the visual and auditory senses of the worshipers became a focus of attention for both Roman Catholic and Protestant reformers. Both recognized the need to improve the auditory aspects of worship, but the problem of underverbalized liturgy, and of worshipers neither trained nor expected to use their ears and discursive intellects but only their eyes and their emotions, led to different responses on the part of Protestant and Catholic reformers.[54] Meister Eckhart, the German Dominican theologian and preacher, questioned the primacy given by his contemporaries to visual symbols in the liturgy.[55] The association of seeing with activity and hearing with passivity was traditional in the late Middle Ages, but Eckhart and others after him asserted the importance of hearing and the value of language to instruct, to clarify and to affect both the intellect and the emotions. One of the fundamental claims of Martin Luther and the other leaders of the Protestant reformation was that Christians must be passive in worship in the sense that they must be totally dependent on God to save them. They stressed the activity of God's word on passive worshipers. This emphasis on language and its power to intensify love and piety served as a corrective to the traditional claim that visual images best promoted Christian devotion.[56]

Auditory participation in worship represented not only a new relationship to liturgical language but also an affirmation of the spiritual equality of all believers before God. The word of God proclaimed in the assembly cut across boundaries of class and education. As a result the focal point of liturgical celebrations in Protestant reformed churches became the preaching of the word. It was the spoken word, the word read aloud and preached, that bore the greatest potential for confronting, exposing and justifying the hearer. Likewise, it was the word listened to by both minister and the rest of the faithful that was the great unifying force in the assembly. In the presence of the word, each worshiper was at the same time both saint and sinner without distinction. Congregational singing, associated with reforming movements since the fourteenth century, further enhanced the unity of the community.[57]

Luther himself was not opposed to the presence of visual images in worship; he simply thought they were generally ineffectual.[58] His tolerance, however, was not shared by Karlstadt and others.[59] Eventually

the altars in many Protestant churches were stripped and finally removed. It was felt that like the images and statues in the churches, the
elaborately carved, draped and decorated altars distracted worshipers
from attending to the language of the service. Bare communion tables
were placed in the churches, thus permitting the celebrant to face the
congregation, a posture not possible when the traditional retable altars
were placed against the wall. The result was extreme visual simplicity
which gave Protestant churches the appearance of lecture halls. In
many of the Protestant churches, the liturgy of the word was so
strongly emphasized that the liturgy of the table was often neglected or
at best celebrated as a simple communion service. Likewise the emphasis on the basic equality of all in the assembly resulted in the elimination
of traditional vestments worn by the minister.[60] Although there has
been considerable variety among the different Protestant churches
over the past four hundred years, in general the emphasis has been almost exclusively placed on verbal symbols in the liturgy with little or no
stress on the non-verbal symbols and specifically on the visual and motor dimensions of the celebrations. Congregational singing, however,
has been a strong component of the Protestant tradition.

The Roman Catholic reform inaugurated by the Council of Trent and
implemented in subsequent years also concerned itself with increas-
ing auditory participation in the liturgy as well as in preaching and
religious instruction. Anxiety over lavish church decoration occasionally resulted in iconoclastic attitudes found in the writings of a few
Catholic reformers, but in general Roman Catholics were not deprived
of visual images in their worship nor was the traditional emphasis on
the role of seeing in stimulating Christian piety displaced.[61] In fact the
churches that were built or renovated by Roman Catholics in the second half of the sixteenth century were designed in such a way that the
worshipers were concentrated in a large central nave where they could
both see and hear what took place in the sanctuary; hence the people
were brought into more immediate contact with the altar. Account was
taken of the importance of hearing the word of God by placing the
pulpit in the nave rather than in the sanctuary; however, the word was
effectively proclaimed mainly in the sermon since the rest of the liturgy continued to be celebrated in Latin. Likewise the priest continued
to execute the canon silently while facing the wall. Hence both his
words and many of his gestures were not available to the faithful.[62] In
practice the eucharist, and especially the canon, was not a rite in which
ordinary Roman Catholics participated either actively or intelligently.
Their religious piety was generally nourished by devotions rather than
by liturgical rites.

In churches renovated or constructed under Jesuit auspices, special effort was made not to miss any opportunity, auditory or visual, to engage the senses of the worshipers during the celebration of the liturgy. Their churches were generally dazzling in their appointments with the walls and ceilings adorned with paintings of saints, angels and various scriptural figures. The altars looked more like pedestals to support elaborate thrones for exposition of the reserved sacrament than tables for the celebration of a ritual sacrificial meal. However the emphasis on language, both spoken and heard, balanced at least somewhat the potentially overwhelming visual engagement. Attention was focused on the sanctuary where the priest, whose role in the liturgy was especially emphasized, embodied, acted out and verbalized the worshipers' link with the divine.[63]

The missal of Pius V, issued in 1570, stabilized the rubrics directing how the eucharist should be celebrated by Roman Catholics following the Council of Trent. The gestures accompanying the canon were clearly specified and their implementation was ensured by the establishment of the Roman Congregation of Sacred Rites.[64] These rubrics required numerous signs of the cross during the canon, as well as genuflections. They also confirmed the special emphasis placed on the recitation of the text of institution as the precise moment when transubstantiation occurred. Detailed instructions were given to the priest concerning his behavior during the canon but mention was scarcely made of the larger worshiping community. Priests generally felt obliged, under pain of sin, to observe the prescribed rubrics; hence the celebration of the eucharist and above all the rendering of the canon were uniform among Roman Catholics. Apart from minor adjustments made in the rubrics of the missal from time to time, the celebration of the canon remained both uniform and changeless until the liturgical reforms that were introduced in the Roman Catholic Church following the Second Vatican Council.[65]

IV. Recent Reforms of the Eucharistic Prayer

Roman Catholic liturgical reforms since the Council have been in many ways both radical and extensive. The developments have generally been aimed at restoring what has been best in the tradition of celebrating the eucharist. A special concern has been the promotion of intelligent, active participation on the part of the faithful. Vernacular languages have been introduced into all aspects of the liturgy, including the canon. In addition to the Roman canon, three additional eucharistic prayers were made available through efforts of the Con-

silium. Special canons for Masses celebrated with children and two eucharistic prayers to be used when reconciliation is a major theme of
the celebration have been issued. A number of original texts submitted
by national hierarchies have also been approved. Apart from the canons for Masses with children which incorporate the use of popular acclamations throughout the text, the model which has been followed
in developing new eucharistic prayers has been that of a unified monologue. In most eucharistic celebrations the canon is proclaimed facing
the people, but because of its structure the emphasis is above all on
the role of the consecrating priest. The general introduction of con-
celebration has further clericalized the canon. Instead of emphasizing
the unity of the entire eucharistic assembly, especially during the
canon, it has accentuated the unity of the ministerial priesthood.[66] Fortunately the priest's gestures throughout the canon have been simplified; multiple crosses and genuflections have been eliminated. But
the text of institution continues to be the high point of the prayer. Its
primary importance is manifest not only because of the special way in
which it is printed in the sacramentaries but also because of the way
it is proclaimed by many presiders. During the recitation of the text,
they generally assume an attitude quite different from their bearing
during other parts of the canon. Through their eye contact and their
rapport with the assembly, they act as though they are miming
Christ's own words and gestures at the Last Supper.

In most Roman Catholic churches the laity kneel from the end of the
sanctus to the end of the great Amen. Although efforts have been
made to create new texts that are poetic in their expression, the canon
is generally experienced by the faithful not as the high point of the
celebration but rather as an extended period when a doctrinal statement is recited by the presider. The impression is given that most worshipers have scarcely begun to internalize the meanings that are
proclaimed in the prayer. In contrast to other parts of the eucharist
which have been treated seriously by musicians, the canon is rarely
rendered musically. As a result reform efforts have generally failed to
engage communities in the eucharistic prayer to the extent that they
should be engaged.

Encouraged by the Roman Catholic liturgical reform in the past
twenty years, most Protestant churches have also given serious attention to the development of eucharist prayers so they can effectively
complement the traditional celebration of the word with regular celebrations of the sacrament. Apart from the eucharistic texts printed in
the revised Book of Common Prayer, the new eucharistic prayers issued by other Protestant churches do not carry detailed rubrics in-

structing the presider how to act during the canon. In general Protestant churches have not been plagued by the same inflexible rubrical mentality which has regularly been found among Roman Catholics, nor have they had any central agency similar to the Congregation for Rites to enforce rubrics. Although several manuals have been developed by Protestant liturgists suggesting effective ways to execute the eucharistic prayer and other liturgical rites, these manuals do not have binding force on the presiders.[67] Hence Protestant presiders have been much freer than Roman Catholic priests to develop their own style of celebrating the eucharistic prayer. Since almost all of the eucharistic prayers recently composed by the Protestant churches have also been modeled on the form of a unified monologue, they are facing many of the same problems that are being raised among Roman Catholics.

V. Alternate Experiences and Possible Directions

During the past twenty years, Roman Catholic and Protestant churches have generally celebrated the eucharist by using the canons which are printed in the approved liturgical books. Practices which are complementary or alternative to the official texts have also developed. In some instances presiders have used their own original prayers thought to be better adapted to the assembly. Some have improvised the prayers, more or less following the outlines of the official texts. Others have adopted the structure and language of the official texts so as to make them more significant to contemporary assemblies. At times additional acclamations have been introduced into the official texts so as to promote further involvement of the community. Some communities have claimed their right to be involved in the eucharistic prayer by reciting the whole text along with the presider. In more creative churches, efforts have been made to develop eucharistic prayers that allow for extensive dialogue so that the presider, choir and the rest of the community share in a unified action that progresses according to dynamics that are thought to be appropriate to the eucharistic prayer. The hope here has been to achieve an overall assembly action in which the text, music, gestures and distribution of roles are integrated into a eucharistic action that is in fact the ritual prayer of the whole assembly. Probably the most pastoral and traditional practice for ordinary occasions is the sound adaptation of official prayers so that the structure and language are appropriate for particular assemblies. The ideal of course is to move toward the creation of eucharistic prayers which can be used in celebrations that are overall assembly actions.[68]

Experience has generally shown that a eucharistic prayer in which the whole community participates by singing becomes, as it should be, the high point of the whole eucharistic celebration. It is a community experience in which all express in a profound way their Christian faith. In order that such celebrations be effective, it is imperative that the text and music be consonant with each other. Certainly for the people, a simple style of music is needed. In any case the music should not be the dominant element of the action; it should rather promote the cohesiveness of the whole.

An appreciation of the unity of the whole liturgy of the eucharist and an emphasis on its dynamic character would help to counteract the exaggerated emphasis that is often placed on the text of institution. Those who place such emphasis on the text of institution as exclusively consecratory implicitly seem to base their position on a descending Christology according to which Christ descends on gifts that are thought to be profane and people who are thought to be secular until the presider pronounces the words of consecration and the transformed gifts are consumed by the community.[69] If an ascending Christology were more operative in formulating eucharistic theology generally and the theology and text of the eucharistic prayer in particular, the eucharistic action could be appreciated more as a movement in which the whole assembly is drawn more closely to God through matter which has already been redeemed and sanctified through the death and resurrection of Jesus Christ and the outpouring of the Holy Spirit on all of creation. The preparation of the gifts is not simply a setting of the table for the consecration of the bread and wine, based on a theology of a descending God and a static view of transformation. In bringing forth the bread and wine as symbols of their lives as baptized Christians, the community manifests its ongoing commitment to a conversion process which is deepened through the reception of the body and blood of Christ who both brings God's life to the community and brings the members of the community into a deeper relationship with God and one another.[70]

Of all the liturgical reforms that have taken place in the last twenty years, the integral celebration of the eucharistic prayer is still one of the most underdeveloped. It is a ritual that calls for serious attention, not only to the text of the prayer, but also to the musical setting of the text and the accompanying visual and motor rhythms of both the presider and the assembly. Likewise the research that has been done on the meaning of architectural environment and the way it conditions both activity and experience should be brought to bear on the celebration of the eucharistic prayer. Little or no attention has been drawn to the fact that the quality and color of architectural materials as well as the shape and height of the building, its lighting, and the placement of altar and assembly affect the way a community experiences the celebration of the eucharistic prayer. Christian people cannot really know what the eucharistic prayer is meant to be in their lives until they experience it as expressive and constitutive of their faith on its deepest levels. That faith of course is not simply an intellectual response to God's presence set out in doctrinal formulas such as the texts of eucharistic prayers; it is above all the response of body-persons and communities who are called back to God as the images of that God who has become incarnate for us in Jesus Christ so we all might become more and more like God.

NOTES

1. See Max Thurian and Geoffrey Wainwright (eds.), *Baptism and Eucharist: Ecumenical Convergence in Celebration* (Grand Rapids: Wm. B. Eerdmans 1983) 99–255.

2. Ibid. 241–255.

3. See Andrew M. Greeley, *Religion: A Secular Theory* (New York: The Free Press 1982) 83–138; Roland Robertson, *The Sociological Interpretation of Religion* (New York: Shocken Books 1972); Guy Swanson, "The Experience of the Supernatural," in *Sociology of Religion*, ed. by Roland Robertson (Baltimore: Penguin Books 1969); Hans J. Mol, *Identity and the Sacred* (New York: The Free Press 1976).

4. David Power, *Unsearchable Riches: The Symbolic Nature of Liturgy* (New York: Pueblo Publishing Company 1984); Louis-Marie Chauvet, *Du Symbolique au Symbole: Essai sur les Sacrements* (Paris: Cerf 1979).

5. See Hans Bernhard Meyer, *Was Kirchenbau bedeutet: Ein Führer zu Sinn, Geschichte und Gegenwart* (Freiburg: Herder 1984); Adolf Adam, *Wo sich Gottes Volk versammelt: Gestalt und Symbolik des Kirchenbaus* (Freiburg: Herder 1984); Bishops' Committee on the Liturgy, *Environment and Art in Catholic Worship* (Washington, D.C.: National Conference of Catholic Bishops 1978); The Bishops' Conference of England and Wales, *The Parish Church: Principles of Liturgical Design and Reordering* (London: Catholic Truth Society 1984); *El Lugar de la Celebration* (Barcelona: Centre de Pastoral Liturgica n.d.); J.M. Zunzunegui, *La Iglesia, casa del Pueblo de Dios. Liturgia y architectura* (San Sebastián: Idatz 1979).

6. *This Holy and Living Sacrifice: Directory for the Celebration and Reception of Communion under Both Kinds* (Washington: National Conference of Catholic Bishops 1985).

7. Melissa Kay (ed.), *It Is Your Own Mystery: A Guide to the Communion Rite* (Washington: The Liturgical Conference 1977).

8. Christian Norberg-Schulz, *Meaning in Western Architecture* (New York: Rizzoli 1980) 213–216.

9. Nelson Goodman, *The Language of Art: An Approach to a Theory of Symbols* (Indianapolis: Hackett Publishing Company 1976).

10. Joseph Gelineau, *The Eucharistic Prayer: Praise of the Whole Assembly* (Washington, D.C.: The Pastoral Press 1985) 1; Francis Sullivan, "Introduce Poetry into the Eucharistic Prayer: A Radical Proposal?" *Pastoral Music,* 10/2 (December–January 1986) 22–26.

11. Eugenio Costa, "Can the Eucharistic Prayer Ever Change?" *Pastoral Music,* 10/2 (December–January 1986) 17–21; Gelineau, ibid. 7–11.

12. Willy Rordorf, "The Didache," in *The Eucharist and the Early Christians* by Willy Rordorf and Others (New York: Pueblo Publishing Company 1978) 1–23.

13. Gelineau 7–8.

14. Ibid. 8

15. Thomas J. Talley, "From Berakah to Eucharistein: A Reopening Question," *Worship* 50 (1976) 138–158. H. Cazelles, "L'anaphore et l'ancien testament," *Eucharisties d'orient et d'occident* (Paris: Cerf 1970) 11–21; Cesare Giraudo, *La Struttura Letteraria della Preghiera Eucharistica* (Rome: Biblical Institute Press 1981) 81–177.

16. R.C.D. Jasper and G.J. Cuming, *Prayers of the Eucharist: Early and Reformed* (London: Collins 1975) 26–28; W. F. Macomber, "The Oldest Known Text of the Anaphora of the Apostles Addai and Mari," *Orientalia Christiana Periodica* 32 (1966) 335–371.

17. Gelineau, op. cit. 9.

18. Ibid.

19. Jasper and Cuming 21-15.

20. Gelineau 9.

21. Ibid. 10

22. Joseph A. Jungmann, *The Mass of the Roman Rite: Its Origins and Development,* vol. 2 (New York: Benziger Brothers, Inc. 1955) 128–138.

23. Gelineau 10.

24. Ibid.

25. Ibid.; Costa 18–19.

26. Michel Andrieu, *Les Ordines Romani du Haut Moyen Âge,* vol. 2 (Louvain: Spicilegium Sacrum Lovaniense 1948) 95. See Jungmann 138.

27. Andrieu, *Les Ordines Romani,* vol 3 (Louvain: Spicilegium Sacrum Lovaniense 1951) 103.

28. Jungmann 104.

29. Ibid. 138–139.

30. Ibid. 240.

31. Balthasar Fischer, *Signs Words and Gestures* (New York: Pueblo Publish-

ing Company 1981) 26–28; Ludwig Eisenhofer and Joseph Lechner, *The Liturgy of the Roman Rite* (New York: Herder and Herder 1953) 92.

32. *Apology,* chap. 30, verse 4: *Apologetical Works and Minucius Felix Octavus* (New York: Fathers of the Church, Inc. 1950) 86.

33. Eisenhofer and Lechner, ibid.

34. Jungmann 143.

35. Ibid.

36. Romano Guardini, *Sacred Signs* (Wilmington, Del.: Michael Glazier, Inc. 1979) 13–14; Jungmann 145–146; Eisenhofer and Lechner 93–94.

37. Jungmann 144

38. Ibid. 144–145.

39. Jasper and Cumming 22. See also Jungmann 147.

40. Jungmann, ibid.

41. Jungmann 202–203.

42. Ibid. 204.

43. Ibid. 205.

44. See Nathan Mitchell, *Cult and Controversy: The Worship of the Eucharist Outside Mass* (New York: Pueblo Publishing Company 1982) 66–198.

45. Jungmann 208–209.

46. Ibid. 210.

47. For a comparison of the rubrics of the institution narrative in the 1570 and 1970 Roman missals see Herman A.J. Wegman, "The Rubrics of the In-stitution-Narrative in the Roman Missal 1970," in *Liturgia: Opera divina et umana. Studi sulla riforma liturgica afferti a S.E. Mons. Annibale Bugnini in occa-sione del suo 70° complanno a cura di. Pierre Jounel, Reiner Kaczynski, Gollardo Pas-qualetti* (Roma: CLV Edizioni Liturgische 1982) 319–328.

48. Jungmann 212–213.

49. Ibid. 213 214.

50. Ibid. 214–216.

51. Ibid. 259–261.

52. Ibid. 268–273.

53. Ibid. 273.

54. Margaret R. Miles, *Images as Insight: Visual Understanding in Western Christianity and Secular Culture* (Boston: Beacon Press 1985) 95–99.

55. Ibid. 100–101.

56. Ibid. 101.

57. Ibid. 104–106.

58. Ibid. 101.

59. Ibid. 101–102.

60. Ibid. 105.

61. Ibid. 109.

62. See Adam 54–61; Meyer 61–67.

63. Cornelius Bouman, "The History of the Architectural Setting of the In-terior of the Church," *Participation in the Mass* (Washington, D.C.: The Litur-

gical Conference 1960) 93; J.A. Jungmann, *Pastoral Liturgy* (New York: Herder and Herder 1967) 80–89.

64. See Frederick McManus, *The Congregation of Sacred Rites* (Washington, D.C.: The Catholic University Press 1954).

65. P.-M. Gy, "La Responsabilité des évêques par rapport au Droit Liturgique," *La Maison-Dieu* 112 (1972) 13–19.

66. R. Kevin Seasoltz, *New Liturgy New Laws* (Collegeville: The Liturgical Press 1980) 86–90.

67. See for example Marion J. Hatchett, *Commentary on the American Prayer Book* (New York: The Seabury Press 1981) 289–422; Philip H. Pfatteicher and Carlos R. Messerli, *Manual on the Liturgy: Lutheran Book of Worship* (Minneapolis: Augsburg Publishing House 1979); Geoffrey Cuming, *The Godly Order: Text and Studies Relating to the Book of Common Prayer* (London: Alcuin Club/SPCK 1983).

68. Gelineau 12–19.

69. Kenneth Leech, *True God: An Exploration in Spiritual Theology* (London: Sheldon 1985) 285–294.

70. See E.C. Miller, "Presentation of the Gifts: Orthodox Insights for Western Liturgical Renewal," *Worship*, 66/1 (January 1986) 22–38.

PART III

The Ongoing Agenda

DAVID N. POWER, O.M.I.

14

The Eucharistic Prayer: Another Look

In a review of a Festschrift in honor of A. Couratin, Robert Taft remarked on the absence of any clear methodology in the study of early anaphoras. "Comparative anaphoral studies," he observed, "will yield no secure results until much more work has been done on the roots of our early sources, especially in those traditions that refuse to fit into the ever-so-neat Antiochene patterns favored by composers of contemporary eucharistic prayers. East Syria has already been visited. Egypt still awaits us."[1] In fact, as these places are visited, secure results seem to be ever wanting and hypotheses abound. Most of the contemporary compositions examined in this volume follow the Antiochene pattern, with greater or less rigidity, with the exception of the Presbyterian collection, which is more venturesome in developing other forms.

Methodologically, search for an Uranaphora seems mistaken, just as it seems mistaken to look for a clearly intended development from Jewish prayer to Christian prayer. On both the pattern of the anaphora and the influence of Jewish prayer, the sources suggest considerable variability and few clear conclusions result from attempts at historical reconstruction. Students of the eucharistic tradition are faced with questions similar to those facing students of the Hebrew and Christian Scriptures. How far is historical reconstruction possible? Is it necessary to be able to perform this task to get at the meaning of the tradition, or to establish historical continuity with our origins? What process is actually going on when contemporary scholars attempt historical reconstruction, or draw conclusions about the meaning of the eucharistic tradition and about the forms of eucharistic praying?

The supposition I propose is that historical reconstructions are at best tentative. The value of the attempt lies in what it reveals of the link between faith and culture, and in the questions which it puts to the contemporary churches about their own forms of eucharistic memorial. What is needed in current reflection is an orientation to practice, not only to liturgical practice, but to ethical practice and commitment.[2] Hence, in this essay I will first consider some of the major hypotheses about the historical anaphora. I will then ask what are the primary insights that these hypotheses offer, and third I will look at all of this in the light of present day ecclesial commitments. The result of all of this will be a further hypothesis, one about the forms which eucharistic prayers might well take in the future!

I. Hypotheses of Historical Reconstruction

This part of the essay will be a rather bald enumeration of hypotheses that appear to be of striking interest.

Now that anaphoral studies are prepared to start with Christian prayers and to relate these to Jewish traditions, rather than to start with the Jewish in an attempt to work forward to Christian prayers, there is some disagreement over the bipartite or tripartite structure of the Christian anaphora.[3] Some suggest that the pattern is a simple bipartite one, the prayer composed of an anamnetic and an epicletic section. To put it in every day terms, it is suggested that in the first part of the prayer the church keeps thankful memory of the saving deeds of God and in the second turns to God in supplication. Those who object to this hypothesis in favor of a tripartite structure argue that it passes too lightly over two points. It does not allow for the distinction between blessing or praising, on the one hand, and making thanksgiving on the other. This distinction is said to have its roots in the different verb usages of Hebrew, as these occur in the Jewish prayer tradition. While the blessing that precedes thanksgiving is eventually glossed over in Christian eucharistic prayers, it is argued that it was there originally and can be found in such a prayer as the anaphora of Addai and Mari. Moreover, this distinction is pertinent to the second point that the bipartite hypothesis passes over, namely, the inclusion of creation in the prayer. While blessing is made for creation, and thanksgiving for redemption, with the elimination of blessing much less focus is given to the works of creation in eucharistic prayer.

From this discussion, a number of points can be drawn. First of all, it would seem that some of our studies have been too prone to offer ready distinction between different Hebrew verbs and between different kinds of Hebrew prayer, so as to facilitate conclusions about Christian prayer.[4] In both Jewish and Christian prayer, when God's action in creation or in redemptive deeds is remembered, this can be probably expressed in a variety of forms of address, which mix blessing, praise, thanksgiving, doxology. It is not useless to examine and reflect upon these types of address to God, but it is prudent not to draw rigid rules about how memorial is to be kept. Second, it appears in the discussion that the address of supplication is one with the memorial praise or thanksgiving, that the two form an integral whole, the latter not being a mere adjunct to the former. This can be rather simply, and one hopes not simplistically, expressed in the formula: from remembering, we turn to ask God to remember.[5] Third, the elimination of the works of creation from eucharist is a great loss and is symptomatic of a kind of Christian spirituality which turns from material things and gives evidence of little harmony with the created universe.

The second hypothesis to be considered has to do with the study of East Syrian prayers.[6] From an examination of the *Didache*, Book VII of the *Apostolic Constitutions, Addai and Mari*, the *Sharar*, and the *Acts of Thomas*, a considerable emphasis on the sanctification of the gifts is noted. It is even surmised that in the *Acts of Thomas* the epicletic section of the prayer was cut loose from the anamnetic, so that the anaphora stands as an invocation of the divine Name over the bread. While such a separation of blessing as invocation from blessing as memorial seems unfortunate, the accent on the gifts in this tradition recalls the role which the communion plays in transmitting God's power to the church and in bringing to communicants both the forgiveness of sins and the hope of immortality. The solid imagery whereby a godly or spiritual power comes to reside in the elements and is transmitted corporeally to the participants thereof is not to be ignored in eucharistic prayer.

The third hypothesis has to do with the place of the supper narrative in the anaphora. In effect, we are here dealing not with a single hypothesis but with a set of hypotheses. Some have offered historical reconstructions which allow for the existence of prayers that do not include the narrative.[7] While the argument used to be largely over Addai and Mari, it has broadened to include the presence in the Egyptian and Antiochene traditions of much shorter thanksgiving prayers, which do not have this component. It has even been suggested by some that this might be a good model for weekday eucharists, and the Presbyterian collection of prayers examined in this book does have examples of prayers of this kind. It is also possible that this type of prayer could give validity to the Lutheran practice of separating the narrative from the prayer, as Martin Luther did.[8] This allows for a mode of joining proclamation with memorial thanksgiving in the celebration of the Lord's Supper different to that which occurs when the attempt is to include the proclamation in the prayer.

Other studies, of course, have concentrated on finding an explanation for the inclusion of the narrative in the prayer, since this is not immediately suggested by its general structure.[9] Louis Ligier was the first to examine this question in detail, and did so on the basis of a transition from the birkat hamazon to the Christian anaphora. He compared the appearance of the Supper narrative in the Christian prayer with the embolism for feasts found in Jewish sources for the birkat hamazon. Cesare Giraudo has more recently followed up the suggestion that a closer link needs to be sought between Christian prayer and a Jewish todah tradition which is larger than the practice of table prayers, even though it includes these. However, he also works on the hypothesis of an embolism. In both cases, the inclusion of the narrative as an embolism gives the foundation in a divine deed or ordinance for the entire act of memorial. The special prayer for the sabbath in Jewish forms is motivated by the recall of a divine ordinance, that relates to both creation and redemption. The special embolism for certain feasts, such as Pasch and Purim, includes both the memorial of what is kept in mind on that particular day and the command to keep memory. This appears to be the clue to the place of the institution narrative in the anaphora: the gift that Christ made at the Supper is remembered as the gift which he left in perpetuity to the disciples, and at the same time as the basis on which the church continues to keep memory of God's saving deeds in Christ. This is at times summarized in the notion of a "charter story."[10] In any case, these various hypotheses allow us to move firmly away from attaching a consecratory power to the words of Jesus in the eucharist, while at the same time grasping the import and importance of including the story and the memorial command in the anaphora.

The next area of hypothesis is that of offering. Though many prayers include offering in the anamnesis after the Supper narrative, there is enough evidence to indicate that earlier prayers made no mention of offering. On the other hand, in the Egyptian and Roman traditions offering is almost synonymous with eucharist.[11] Not only does it occur after the narrative, but it runs thematically right through the prayer. This does not mean that there is a focus on offering Christ, or the body and blood of Christ, to the Father. The image of offering or sacrifice is polysemic. The prayer itself is offered as a sacrifice of praise and thanksgiving. The bread and wine are offered with thanksgiving. The gifts that the people bring for the poor or for the church are offered in the prayer. Early eucharistic prayers themselves do not make explicit mention either of offering Christ or of self-offering on the part of the church's members, yet it is such themes that theology has singled out since medieval times and that scholars look for in early church writings. So much has this been taken as the agenda for eucharistic theology, that new compositions insert these themes explicitly into the prayer, as has been explained in the other essay that I have contributed to this volume. It is a question that many have tried to resolve ecumenically by use of the idea of anamnesis, supposedly derived from Jewish and early Christian tradition. The problem with this procedure is that sacrifice tends to become the dominant image or analogue for the salvific work of Christ which is commemorated and for the eucharist itself. However, it is more than the death of Christ which is remembered in the Lord's Supper, and of the work remembered sacrifice is only one of a number of images. Images of divine expiation, of covenant proclamation, of communion meal, or of the gift of the forgiveness of sins have to take equal place with sacrifice in describing the nature of eucharistic worship and action.[12]

Some have tried to incorporate the notion of sacrifice into Christian eucharist by elaborating on the connection between Jewish todah and Christian assembly.[13] To begin with, this allusion served to open up afresh the question of prayer forms, so that it is possible to take account of psalms and other biblical texts of historical remembrance as well as of table and synagogue prayer in looking for a Jewish background to Christian eucharist.[14] Apart from this, the connection between the prayer of remembrance and sin-offering has been cited as an analogue for the sacrificial meaning of the eucharist. The connection, however, seems quite hypothetical. In any case, if it does anything, it points up how much the idea of sacrifice has been spiritualized in its application, both to Christ's death and to Christian prayer. It also pinpoints the importance of historical remembrance and eschatological expectation as the very core of thanksgiving. Whether it serves to illustrate the analogue of sacrificial meal for the eucharist remains doubtful.

A fifth field for hypothesis in the study of the anaphora has to do with the epiclesis, or invocation for the descent of the Holy Spirit. The epiclesis in the anaphora has to be considered in conjunction with the epiclesis in other blessings, particularly those over the baptismal waters and over the myron for anointing.[15] The distinction between consecration and communion epiclesis, which a number of writers adopted some time ago as a way of dealing with the structure of the prayer, and which the Roman Sacramentary follows in its new compositions, no longer seems serviceable. It casts little light, either on prayer structure or on the meaning of this invocation, for it relates too much to the attribution of consecratory power to the repetition of the words of the Last Supper, and separates the presence of Christ in the community from the presence in the elements. The action of the Spirit is pervasive of the entire eucharistic celebration. Christ is present to the baptized people through the power of the Spirit, moves them to memorial through the Spirit, and gives himself in the gift of bread and wine in the power of this same Spirit. As far as the structure of the anaphora is concerned, it would seem that the prayer for the Spirit fits well into the supplication that follows memorial blessing. It can be suitably attached to the Supper narrative, inasmuch as this narrative includes the promise of that eschatological gift which is one with the gift of Christ's own body and blood. For those who, in recalling Christ's saving deeds, proceed to the celebration in his body and blood, there is the assurance of the eschatological gift of the Spirit.

In the sixth place, a number of studies have shown the existence from early Christian times of eucharistic prayers which are addressed to Christ, rather than to the Father.[16] There appears to be reasonable security to this historical discovery, but the hypotheses have to do with its meaning and with the place to be given to it as an authentic tradition. It lays to rest the opinion of Josef Jungmann that the address to Christ was the result of anti-Arian controversy.[17] Those who believe that the tradition is strong enough to warrant a continued usage of anaphoras addressed to Christ see in this a counter-balance to theologies which ignore other modes of Christ's presence in the assembly, in turning all their attention to the presence in the elements.[18]

Finally, as far as the field for hypothesis is concerned, the very proliferation of discoveries and ideas in the study of the early history of the anaphora makes it possible to give more serious attention to the liturgical contribution of the great Reformers. The rather acerbic dismissal of these liturgies by Louis Bouyer, together with the judgments of Gregory Dix,[19] seems to have set the accustomed approach in the revision of liturgical books in Reformation and post-Reformation churches. The effort has been to retrieve the Great Thanksgiving Prayer of early Christian tradition. This has done much to establish an ecumenical convergence in celebration.[20] However, because the Antiochene pattern seems to have set the stage for reform all too often, it has not been easy to see where some of the liturgical changes of the Reformers could offer possible alternatives. For example, celebrations of the Lord's Supper that set the Supper proclamation after the thanksgiving prayer, rather than within it, do not need to be seen as second best.[21] Nor are prayers that omit sacrificial imagery to be frowned upon. The rich variety of early traditions suggests the possibility of a richer variety in contemporary liturgical creativity, as well as the continued possibility of drawing on the creativity of the Reformation era.

II. Insights To Work With

If we are not to simply follow the Antiochene pattern in the composition of new eucharistic prayers, what harvest of guiding insights do all these studies and their hypotheses yield?

The first thing to consider is that when a Christian church engages in eucharist, it engages, not in repetition, but in remembering. Elements of rote are intrinsic to worship, but they are not what is its essential core. This is keeping memory, and keeping memory means telling the story. There is, in faith's perspective, a primordial act in history, but history is not reduced to it. Remembered in the course of ongoing history, it has a determining effect on the course of this history. However, since it is remembered by people caught up in very diverse historical and cultural circumstances, the way of remembering differs. The story is then retold in diverse manners, with diverse images and metaphors to reveal its power and the presence of the God who saves. The recollection of the Christ story is the foundation for the act of memorial prayer. Elements of story and proclamation are found in the prayer itself, but to grasp the orientation of each prayer known from the study of eucharistic traditions one has to work back, as it were, to the telling of the story that lies behind the act of thanksgiving. When this is done, attention is paid not only to the structure of the prayer, but also to the prayer's content, to the symbols, images, paradigms, or metaphors that represent the meaning for the church of the events of Christ's story.[22]

Attention to the remembrance in which a church engages is the way to an inclusion of the whole story of Jesus Christ in the eucharistic prayer. While the death and resurrection are at the heart of salvation, their meaning is lost if they are isolated from the rest of Christ's deeds, teaching and promises. It is then possible to note the variety of ways in which the recall of Jesus Christ is developed in eucharistic prayers.

In one case, the historical mode is that of an appeal to the Old Testament analogues of sacrifice, primarily those of Abel, Abraham and Melchisedech. In another case, it is the struggle of Jesus Christ with the powers of hell that is represented. In a third case, it is the crucifixion of the world in the flesh of God's only-begotten. In still another case, it is the expiation of the world's sin through the pouring out of Christ's blood. In yet another, it is the assumption of all humanity and all creation into the praise that the Word made flesh renders to God, the renewal of a world distorted by sin through the enfleshment of God's creative power.

The movement from narrative and remembrance to thanksgiving is quite acute in the early church's homiletic tradition. One finds it, for example, in the homilies of Leo the Great for the year's liturgical feasts, inclusive of that of the anniversary of his own ordination as bishop of Rome. In his homilies for the feast of the Ascension,[23] he takes the episode of the meeting of Christ with the two disciples on the road to Emmaus as a paradigm for the manner of Christ's continuing presence in the church. Christ continues to allay the fears and doubts of those who follow him. He continues to educate them in the faith and in a knowledge of mysteries. He draws them to a sacramental rather than to a fleshly communion with himself. Once the gospel reading serves to draw the congregation to an awareness of Christ's active presence in their midst, Leo invites it to praise and thanksgiving. Indeed, the homily itself closes with an eruption of praise, which is prelude to the thanksgiving prayer.

In his homilies for the paschal vigil, Augustine represents the entire celebration as a remembrance of the pasch of Christ and an expectation of what was promised in that pasch. He seeks to engage the congregation of believers in a paschal ethic, so that it may engage in the paschal celebration: "Ergo, si volumus agere Pascha salubriter, transeamus, patiamur, pascamus: transeamus a peccatis ad iustitiam, patiamur pro Christo, pascamus in pauperibus Christum."[24] This kind of recall of the past event in the actuality of present reality grounds the invitation to give thanksgiving and praise to God, for and in Jesus Christ.

These examples could be multiplied. They are quoted to make the point that the composition of eucharistic prayer is impossible without the effort that goes beyond the reading of the Scriptures to the active remembrance of a community. It draws the remembrance of Christ into its own story and submits its own story to the remembrance of Christ, in the confidence that this proclaims an abiding presence and an unfailing promise.

Another point for consideration that emerges from the study of eucharistic traditions is the importance of the creation motif.[25] It is not a constant in eucharistic prayers, but its very absence is a cause for reflection, given its importance in Hebrew literature. A study of the psalms of Israel shows the contrast between hymns addressed to God for the works of creation and the thanksgiving made for God's historical deliverance of the people.[26] However, while humanity is saved by God from a blind subservience to the forces of nature, the human bond with other works of creation needs to be kept. The accent on spirit and certain ascetical trends in Christian history appear to make it difficult to attain a harmony between praise for creation and thanksgiving for redemption. This is all the more reason why we need to be attentive to the creation motif in current compositions.

The link which Henri Cazelles suggested between Israel's todah and Christian eucharist had to do with the question of sacrifice.[27] However, in drawing attention to todah he also widened the scope of eucharistic studies, and allowed them to go beyond the berakah and table prayers to a fuller consideration of Israel's thanksgiving prayers. Todah is the noun that derives from the Hebrew word that is usually translated as "to give thanks." It is a prayer tradition of thankful remembrance, rooted in the historical recall of God's saving deeds. Some of the most powerful examples are found in the Book of Psalms, but there are many others.

As the various todah prayers are examined, one of the most important things that emerges is the way in which the Israelite people had to renew their remembrance of God's deliverance in historical circumstances that seemed to call God's promises into question. Far from being a tradition that remains untarnished, or that is set in its form once and for all, Israel's thanksgiving tradition needed to be constantly refurbished in the face of new situations, and in a way which could revive the hopes of the desolate in times of apparent abandonment, or of disorientation.

Giraudo points out that todah is both confession of faith and celebration of God's deeds. The most powerful prayer creations actually occur in times of emergency or disaster, where anguish and discomfort are as much a part of the people's feelings as is trust in God.[28] A classical situation that is taken up in the study of todah is that described in Nehemiah 9:6ff. The context is the proclamation and renewal of the covenant, after a period of exile. From their affliction, the people turn to God, looking for mercy and forgiveness and protection. The prayer raised up by Ezra proclaims God's works in creation and in redemption. The development of the theme of God's works is interrupted in vv. 16/17 to make mention of the sin of the people in worshiping the golden calf, a sin described as one of not remembering the wonderful works of Yahweh. After this, God's praises are resumed, lauding the divine mercy that did not abandon the people even in their sin. The flow of praise is again interrupted in vv. 26–31 to recall the further sin of the people and the disasters that flowed from it. In v. 32 the prayer passes on to supplication. God is asked to forgive all these sins and to look kindly on those who now renew the covenant and who ask to be taken out of the misery which has befallen them on account of their own sins and of the sins of their ancestors.

This example shows very clearly that the prayer of thankful remembrance is flexible enough to include the confession of fault. It has a narrative foundation that is motive for thanksgiving, for confession of sin, for hope, and for confident supplication. There is nothing abstract about the prayer, for it is comprehensible only in the actual situation of the people and in their effort to find new orientation, in virtue of God's deeds and promises.

While the insertion of the confession of sin into the prayer is quite dramatic, it is not nearly as dramatic as the insertion into a prayer of remembrance of a complaint against God or against one's enemies. There is, however, room for such insertions in Israel's todah tradition. Two clear examples of complaint against God are found in Job 29–31 and in Psalm 44. Indeed, lament is a very strong part of Israel's prayers of remembrance.[29] There is the lament of those who are oppressed, and the lament of the whole people in times of political and natural catastrophe. After 587 B.C., when there is no temple, only in lament can God be worshiped (cf. Is 40:27). Besides the suffering of catastrophe, there is the suffering of those who survive catastrophe, as exemplified in 4 Ezra. In the post-exilic period, as in the example from Nehemiah 9, lament can become repentance, but it should not be thought that all tragedy is attributable to the people's sin. At times, their suffering or abandonment simply appears incomprehensible in the light of Yahweh's past works, and so the complaint is addressed against Yahweh, even while the vow to continue to give thanksgiving and praise is not abandoned. Such language gives dignity to suffering, and allows the people to remain partners to Yahweh in covenant, even when reduced to impotency.

Claus Westermann remarks on the absence of lament or complaint in Christian prayer. Exhortations to patience and submission seem to have muted such a voice. But would it not be more true if a remembrance of Christ's suffering, of his engagement with sufferers, and of the promises made in his death were to allow Christian peoples to complain? He writes:

> Something must be amiss if praise of God has a place in Christian worship but lamentation does not. Praise can retain its authenticity and naturalness only in polarity with lamentation.[30]

All in all, then, an examination of Israel's todah tradition as an analogue for Christian eucharist opens up possibilities of creativity that far exceed the search for a formal structure or for a uranaphora that appears to be the risk involved in linking the anaphora too directly to the table prayers of the Jewish people. The prayer of thanksgiving derives from the activity of remembering, and this remembering takes on narrative form. The remembering, however, is done in an actual set of historical conditions and in face of the actual events of the living community's own existence. When there is a sharp contrast between God's deeds of old and any present calamity, thanksgiving is not enough to express the covenant relationship between God and people. Through the forms of remembrance and prayer, the people search out the meaning of such calamity. Hence, besides thanksgiving, room is made for lament, for complaint against God and against one's enemies, and in due season for the confession of sin. In the middle of all of this, the way in which the people relate to the land, which they acclaim as part of their covenant inheritance, has to be included, and this is broad enough to include the motif of creation within historical remembrance.

III. Eucharist and Commitment

It is the inclusion of lament, whether in the form of confession of sin, or in the form of complaint against God, in prayers of remembrance, that opens the way today for a link between eucharistic celebration and Christian commitment. With ritual ease, presiders daily repeat the invitation to give God thanks and praise. The clouds that darken the earth do not make it easy to respond from the heart. As did the Israelite people in times of yore, so Jewish and Christian assemblies today have to wrestle with the apparent failure of divine promises and the earth's abandonment by God.

No more than the Jewish people can Christian churches put aside the memory of the Nazi persecution of the Jews and of all the pogroms of Christian history when they remember God's salvation and the promises of God's rule. No one today can be oblivious of the threat of nuclear destruction hanging over the earth. It is not enough to invite people to the confession of sin in face of such evils, nor is it enough for Christians to lament their own complicity. In the proclamation of Christ, the church has proclaimed God's promise of peace and justice. It has rendered thanks for Christ's struggle with the powers of darkness and drawn hope and encouragement therefrom. But how can we see, in this time, the assurance of God's fidelity? Human sin, in face of the magnitude of grace and divine power that we proclaim, seems too weak an explanation for such vast evil.

It is not a matter of asking whether our generation is more perverse or more lost than previous generations. One could probably argue that point for a long time, but it can be put aside in this context. For Christians who gather together in the memory of Jesus Christ, there is a new consciousness today of evil which makes it difficult to name God, and so to make thanksgiving. This consciousness has to do with Christianity's own pathologies, pathologies which show that those who have engaged in the naming of God in Jesus Christ have been privy to the destructive forces that threaten not only humanity's but the earth's existence. The effect of this is not only to call us to the confession of sin but to make us ask whether the church has even named God aright. It is not easy to render thanks to an absent or to a badly named God.

Androcentrism, anti-semitism, and contempt for planet earth are the names for some of the more awful pathologies of Christian thought and Christian habit. This is not the place to demonstrate the existence of such pathologies. Suffice to say that many believers are growing more conscious of this part of Christian history, and that this consciousness renders eucharistic thanksgiving acutely problematic, just as it calls for new forms of ethical commitment and a new expression of the forms of hope. It is also important to note that the three named are pathologies that have marked the eucharistic tradition itself. Eucharistic structures have been male-dominated and unreceptive to women's ministry and women's voice. Eucharistic prayers have been exclusive in their God-language and selective in the choice of deeds and persons remembered. The history of the Jewish people is all too readily reduced to the form of being type of Christ and type of the church, an attitude which all too easily sees the assertion of an independent existence or a distinctive revelation among the followers of Yahweh as a threat to Christianity. The problem experienced in keeping the creation motif within Christian remembrance has already been mentioned in this essay, as well as its connection with certain forms of Christian spirituality.

The hearing of a divine voice, and the revelation of God in the memorial of Christ, will be given in our day to those who struggle with these issues, who live in the interests of a renewal of the joint story of humanity and the earth. Their paradigm for gathering is the call to a discipleship of equality in Christ and in Christ's Spirit. Their paradigm for space and action is reverence for bread, wine, oil and water, communion with the things of godly earth. Their paradigm for remembrance is God's solidarity with victims, a solidarity that is at the heart of the remembrance of Jesus Christ, and of the disciples of Christ. New paradigms do not take their place in human consciousness without considerable disorientation and dislodgment of the old. Disorientation cannot be suffered without lament. Without lament, it may well be camouflaged, and the old ways reinforced.

My concluding hypothesis, therefore, takes the form of a wager, of a deep conviction. Eucharistic memorial has to be renewed through lament. To give thanks, the community must weep, and the two may be strangely combined. Todah's inclusion of the confession of faith and hope, of the confession of sin, and of complaint against Yahweh, has much to teach us about assaulting God's ears in eucharistic memorial. To give the hypothesis more form, I offer this prayer by way of provocation.

Presider: God, promised of the ages, it is right and proper that as has been done of old, we too should give you thanks and praise.
Thus we are called by your word to do, thus we are prompted by all who have preceded us in the faith of your child, Jesus Christ. But when you are absent, O God, from our world, how can we praise and thank you?

Leader:[31] How, O God, can we sing your song in an alien land?

Congregation: How, O God, can we sing your song in an alien land?

Presider: We are surrounded by death all day long.
Our old leave this life without dignity, our sons and daughters have no dreams but those of destruction, our children have no future.
The world, which you claim as your creation, does not bear beholding, covered as it is by the dark shadows of the hungry, the bereaved, the war-torn, the oppressed and the feeble.

Leader: How, O God, can we sing your song in an alien land?

Congr.: How, O God, can we sing your song in an alien land?

Presider: Yet it is for this, giver and taker of life, that we praise you.

In our weakness, you have made yourself one with us.
You have embraced our struggle to sustain hope.
Our very death, you yourself have died.

Leader: Now is the Lord's coming.
Tomorrow we shall rise.

Congr.: Now is the Lord's coming.
Tomorrow we shall rise.

Presider: At the dawn of history, when after the first flush of happiness, our forebears came to know their fragility and their division, their boundedness and their destruction, you still walked with them across the barren face of the earth. When each laid claim to power against the other, you claimed the mark upon the foreheads of the hated as your mark.

Leader: Now is the Lord's coming.
Tomorrow we shall rise.

Congr.: Now is the Lord's coming.
Tomorrow we shall rise.

Presider: Calling to mind your love, it is a cross that we remember.
In the weak and humbled flesh of your child, Jesus, we acknowledge your presence upon this earth.
In his despisement, we see you lie down among the despised.
In his wounds, we see you afflicted with all our wounds.
In his unjust sentencing, we see you condemned with all those who have no power.
But in his death, we see you shattering death and its dominion.
For this, we praise you and give you thanks.

Leader: Now is the Lord's coming.
Tomorrow we shall rise.

Congr.: Now is the Lord's coming.
Tomorrow we shall rise.

Presider: Indeed, giver and taker of life, it is for this that we thank you: for your weakness and folly;
for the flesh in which you yourself longed for peace and for life;
for the Spirit that is your weakness in our hearts, and your strength in our weakness.
Therefore, we join with all those who from the dawn of time have searched for you and found you in humility and poverty, in the

exaltation of the lowly and the lifting-up of the bowed down;
with them, we give you thanks and praise, with them we sing a
hymn to your glory:

Congr.:   Holy, holy, holy . . .

Presider: You are indeed holy, giver and taker of life, and holy is your
child Jesus and holy your Spirit dwelling in our hearts.
Thrice holy are you,
in the holiness of death's struggle,
in the holiness of compassionate longing,
in the holiness of life reborn in weakness.
Standing before you as a people bound together in longing, we
remember your child, Jesus,
when opening his arms to death he took bread, blessed it, broke
it and gave it to his companions, saying:
Take and eat this, all of you, for this is my body which will be
given up for you.

Leader: Bread of affliction, bread of compassion, bread of life.

Congr.:   Bread of affliction, bread of compassion, bread of life.

Presider: We remember how at the end of the meal, before he went
out into the night, he took a cup, blessed it, gave it to his companions and said:
Take and drink this, all of you, for this is the covenant in my
blood, blood that is poured out for you and for many so that sins
may be redeemed.

Leader: Cup of affliction, cup of compassion, cup of life.

Congr.:   Cup of affliction, cup of compassion, cup of life.

Leader: Now is the Lord's coming.
Tomorrow we shall rise.

Congr.:   Now is the Lord's coming.
Tomorrow we shall rise.

Presider: Remembering, compassionate and loving God, we proclaim
the presence of your Word in our human flesh.
We proclaim the Spirit who settled upon him, drove him into the
wilderness to wrestle with profane hopes, and led him into the
company of the blind, the lame, the diseased, the imprisoned,
and the very dead.
We remember your Word bursting asunder the bonds of death,

and rising to your right hand, so that through the Spirit he might
continue to live amid the struggles of the torn world.

Taking this bread of tears and happiness, taking this cup of sorrow and inebriation, united with the blessings of Jesus over the
bread and over the cup, we offer you all that there ever has been
of human sorrow, struggle and hope, longing to be joined together where your folly holds sway in human hearts.

Leader: Bread of affliction, bread of compassion, bread of life.

Congr.:   Bread of affliction, bread of compassion, bread of life.

Leader: Cup of affliction, cup of compassion, cup of life.

Congr.:   Cup of affliction, cup of compassion, cup of life.

Presider: Gather us, giver and taker of life, into a communion of one
Spirit, a communion of faith, love and hope, a communion of
weakness, folly and strength.

Let your Spirit teach us how to sorrow, how to love, how to hope,
and how to praise.

Leader: Grant us, O God, your Spirit.

Congr.:   Grant us, O God, your Spirit.

Presider: Look with tenderness upon those who know their weakness and upon those who know it not.

Unite all who hear the name of Christ into the one communion
and the one hope.

Leader: Grant us, O God, your Spirit.

Congr.:   Grant us, O God, your Spirit.

Presider: Forgive us, O God, the affliction which, often in your name,
we have imposed upon those of our own community and those
of other faiths. Look upon them with healing compassion and
give them the power and strength which we have denied them.

Leader: Grant us, O God, your Spirit.

Congr.:   Grant us, O God, your Spirit.

Presider: Strengthen this community and the communion of communities that is your church. May the bonds of peace prevail.

Do not let the people whom you have loved be plundered and
divided, but let it be united in hope with all its ministers and bish-

ops, and with N. who presides in charity where the apostles and martyrs gave their lives in witness to your name.

Leader: Grant us, O God, your Spirit.

Congr.:   Grant us, O God, your Spirit.

Presider: Let us not forget the dead. Let their memory be strong in us. We mourn with them for what they had not and for what they suffered. We rejoice in their witness and in their present joy.
We beg to be united with them in the hope of a common resurrection.

Leader: Grant us, O God, your Spirit.

Congr.:   Grant us, O God, your Spirit.

Presider: Look with pity upon the earth laid waste.
Teach us to love the planet and to live in stronger communion with its energies.
Pardon us when we exploit it, lest we destroy the very dwelling place that you have given us, lest we exalt ourselves above the other works of your creation.

Leader: Grant us, O God, your Spirit.

Congr.:   Grant us, O God, your Spirit.

Presider: Grant to us, O God, who gather in faith, that in the name of Christ we may find the sign and assurance of your abiding presence, and that in this name we may, even in sorrow, give you thanks.

All: Through him, with him, in him,
in the unity of the Holy Spirit,
all glory and honor is yours, almighty God, for ever and ever.
Amen.

NOTES

1. Cf. R. Taft, *Worship* 56 (1982):178.

2. I am avoiding the word *praxis*, while still suggesting a necessary relation between action and the meaning which is formulated in symbol and theory.

3. See the works by Gerhards, Giraudo, and Talley, cited in my essay on Anamnesis.

4. Cf. R. J. Ledogar, *Acknowledgment: Praise Verbs in the Early Greek Ana-*

phora (Rome: Biblical Institute 1968); J. Heinemann, *Prayer in the Talmud: Form and Patterns* (Berlin & New York: de Gruyter 1977).

5. As noted in my essay on Anamnesis, Giraudo summarizes this in the formula: Memores–Memento.

6. Cf. G. Rouwhorst, "Bénédiction, actions de grâce, supplication: les oraisons de la table dans le judaisme et les célébrations eucharistiques des chrétiens syriaques," *Questions Liturgiques* 61 (1980):211–240; A. Verheul, "Les prières eucharistiques dans les Constitutiones Apostolorum," *Questions Liturgiques* 61 (1980):129–143.

7. Cf. G. Cuming, "The Anaphora of St. Mark: A Study in Development," *Le Muséon* 95(1982): 115–129; H. A. J. Wegman, "Pleidoor voor een Teskst de Anaphora van de Apostolen Addai en Mari," *Bijdragen* 40 (1979):15–43; H. Wegman, "Une anaphore incomplète?" in *Studies in Gnosticism and Hellenistic Religions*, edited by R. Van Den Broek and M. J. Vermaseren (Leiden: Brill 1981):432–450.

8. This is Option II in the *Lutheran Book of Worship*. On the compromises of the Swedish Lutheran Liturgy, cf. F. C. Senn, "Toward a Different Anaphoral Structure," *Worship* 58 (1984):346–358, and "Liturgia svecanae ecclesiae: An Attempt at Eucharistic Restoration during the Swedish Reformation," *Studia Liturgica* 14 (1980/81):20–36.

9. See the works of Giraudo, Ligier and Talley cited in the article on Anamnesis.

10. Kilpatrick, as cited in the article on Anamnesis.

11. Montminy and Stevenson, as cited in the article on Anamnesis. Cf. also L. Lies, "Ökumenische Erwagungen zu Abendmahl, Priesterwiehe und Messopfer," *Zeitschrift für katholische Theologie* 104 (1982):385–410, for another opinion on all this.

12. Cf. J. Reumann, *The Supper of the Lord: The New Testament, Ecumenical Dialogues, and Faith and Order on Eucharist* (Philadelphia: Fortress 1985):150–177.

13. Cazelles and Gese, as cited in the article on Anamnesis.

14. Giraudo, op. cit. Cf. also H. Guthrie, *Theology as Thanksgiving: From Israel's Psalms to the Church's Eucharist* (New York: Seabury 1981); X. Léon-Dufour, *Le Partage du Pain Eucharistique Selon le Nouveau Testament* (Paris: Seuil 1982):50–59.

15. Cf. Emmanuel-Pataq Siman, *L'Expérience de l'Esprit par L'Eglise d'après la Tradition Syrienne d'Antioche* (Paris: Beauchesne 1971):70–118.

16. Cf. A. Gerhards, *Die griechische Gregoriosanaphora: Ein Beitrag zur Geschichte des Eucharistischen Hochgebets* (Münster: Aschendorff 1984). See the review by G. Cuming in *Worship* 59 (1985):548f.

17. J. Jungmann, *The Place of Christ in Liturgical Prayer* (London: Chapman 1965).

18. Cuming, loc. cit.

19. L. Bouyer in *The Eucharist* and G. Dix in *The Shape of the Liturgy*.

20. See the collection of texts in M. Thurian and G. Wainwright, *Baptism and Eucharist: Ecumenical Convergence in Celebration* (Geneva: WCC 1983).

21. Cf. F. Schulz, "Luthers Liturgische Reformen: Kontinuität und Innovation," *Archiv für Liturgiewissenschaft* 25 (1983):249–275.

22. On "Re-Presentation," cf. C. Westermann, *Praise and Lament in the Psalms* (Atlanta: John Knox 1981):214–249.

23. See the sermons in Leo Magnus, *Sermons,* tome 3 (Paris: Sources Chrétiennes, Cerf):269–286. English translation in *Nicene and Anti-Nicene Fathers* XII:186–189.

24. Augustinus, Sermo Denis 7, 1 (ed. G. Morin, *Miscellanea Augustiniana* 1: Rome 1930):32–33.

25. Cf. J. Keenan, "The Importance of the Creation Motif in a Eucharistic Prayer," *Worship* 53 (1979):341–356.

26. Guthrie, op. cit. 1–30.

27. As cited in article on Anamnesis.

28. Op. cit. 163–166.

29. Besides Giraudo and Westermann, cf. also W. Brueggemann, *The Message of the Psalms: A Theological Commentary* (Minneapolis: Augsburg 1984).

30. Op. cit. 267.

31. The assumption is that at least the congregation's part of the prayer is sung, and hence that it may need a leader in its midst. As for the presider's part, gifts differ.

Index

A. DOCUMENTS AND SUBJECTS

This index contains no references to prayers, worship books, or parts of eucharistic prayers which are treated in whole chapters of this book. In Part I parts of eucharistic prayers (e.g. preface, institution narrative, anamnesis, epiclesis, intercessions, doxology) are treated in every chapter. In Part II all of the eucharistic prayers discussed in Part I are discussed in each chapter dealing with a part of the eucharistic prayer.

B. PERSONS